Yeats and the Heroic Ideal

YEATS
and the Heroic Ideal

By Alex Zwerdling

NEW YORK UNIVERSITY PRESS 1965

I AM GRATEFUL to The Macmillan Company for permission to quote from the following works by Yeats, originally copyright by the Company and renewed by Bertha Georgie Yeats: *Essays*, copyright 1924, renewed 1955; *Estrangement*, copyright 1935, renewed 1963; "The Words upon the Window Pane," from *Wheels and Butterflies*, copyright 1934, renewed 1962; "The Trembling of the Veil," from *Reveries over Childhood and Youth*, copyright 1916, renewed 1944; *Four Plays for Dancers*, copyright 1921, renewed 1949; also from the following poems in *The Collected Poems of W. B. Yeats*: "September 1913," "To a Wealthy Man Who Promised a Second Subscription to the Dublin Municipal Gallery If It Were Proved the People Wanted Pictures," "The Grey Rock," and "The Two Kings," copyright 1916, renewed 1944; "Nineteen Hundred and Nineteen" and "Sailing to Byzantium," copyright 1928, renewed 1956; "The People," copyright 1919, renewed 1946; "An Irish Airman Foresees His Death," copyright 1919, renewed 1934; "Coole Park and Ballylee" and "In Memory of Eva Gore-Booth and Con Markiewicz," copyright 1933, renewed 1961; "The Cold Heaven," copyright 1912, renewed 1940; "The Second Coming" and "Easter 1916," copyright 1924, renewed 1952; "To Ireland in the Coming Times" and "The Fisherman," copyright 1906, renewed 1934; "Ribh Denounces Patrick," copyright 1934, renewed 1963; "A Prayer for Old Age," copyright 1934, renewed 1962; "Meditations in Time of Civil War," copyright 1923 by The Dial Publishing Company, renewed 1951 by Bertha Georgie Yeats; "Beautiful Lofty Things," "Long-Legged Fly," "Under Ben Bulben," "A Crazed Girl," and "The Man and the Echo," copyright 1940 by Georgie Yeats; also from *Last Poems and Plays*, copyright 1940 by Georgie Yeats; and from *The Letters of* W. B. *Yeats*, copyright 1953, 1954 by Anne Butler Yeats.

I am also grateful to Mrs. Yeats and Messrs. Macmillan & Co., Ltd. for permission to quote from these works and from *On the Boiler*, copyright 1939. Part of the last chapter was published originally in the *University of Toronto Quarterly* and is reprinted here with the permission of the editor and the University of Toronto Press.

ACKNOWLEDGMENTS

A NUMBER of people have read all or part of this book in manuscript and made valuable suggestions. I am particularly grateful to Willard Thorp, John Unterecker, and Oscar Cargill, many of whose suggestions for revision I have adopted; also to Carlos Baker, Martin Meisel, Stephen Orgel, John Clive, and Norman O. Brown, who have helped with more particular problems along the way.

CONTENTS

*For Norbert and
Mary Zwerdling*

Yeats and the Heroic Ideal

1 · The Lost God

> Those who envy or calumniate great men hate God;
> for there is no other God.
>
> BLAKE

WE SEEM to have witnessed, in our own century, an extraordinary erosion of the unquestioning allegiance to the ideal of "heroic" human activity. The hero is subject to a kind of sceptical cross-examination to which he has seldom been forced to submit. We question the selflessness of his motives; we ask whether fame has not corrupted his integrity; we wonder whether history might not have been substantially the same without him; we may even feel that the idea of a class of "supermen" distinctly raised above the rules which their fellows must obey has had more harmful effects than healthy ones.

This study deals with a writer who was never tempted by such a sceptical vision of heroism, whose entire career can be seen as a continuous attempt to define and glorify the heroic man. Yeats seems to have used the forms of heroic literature as a vehicle for protesting against the religion, the social structure, the political principles, and the cultural standards of the country and the time in which he lived. The heroes of his plays and poems are dramatically conceived characters who have the sanction of their creator without exactly being his mouthpieces, who embody rather than preach the standards of a better society.

Yeats's world of heroes was, potentially, a world of ethical authority. For him literature is "the great teaching power of the world," [1] but it teaches in an indirect way. For the artist, by the mere process of selection, gives significance to certain things in life above others, and the transition from something of significance to something of value is relatively easy. Here literature

1

works hand in hand in the ideal society with the other "creators of value." Yeats realized that "No art can conquer the people alone," but he also knew that "the people are conquered by an ideal of life upheld by authority," [2] and that the good artist was one of the possible sources of such authority. If, in the modern world, the writer was often forced to undertake this task alone, to fight against rather than with the other sources of authority in a culture, it only meant that his function as creator of values had become more important than ever.

By presenting the heroic personality in action, a literary work can be moral without becoming blatantly didactic. The reader or spectator, when confronted with an authoritative heroic portrait, can for an instant see the noble life as in some way akin to his own. This method, Yeats says, is really one of unconscious persuasion, for "when the imaginary saint or lover or hero moves us most deeply, it is the moment when he awakens within us for an instant our own heroism, our own sanctity, our own desire." [3] This recognition of our own *potential* heroism, this momentary emotional identification of ourselves with the "something of value" in the literary work, is a more convincing and powerful form of persuasion than an abstract sermon, for the hero presents to the imagination of the audience a living example of human worth. Like the kings and queens of the old stories he shows them "life under the best conditions," and becomes for them "a type of the glory of the world." [4]

But what exactly is a hero? W. H. Auden in *The Enchafèd Flood*, says that he is simply the "exceptional individual . . . one who possesses authority over the average," [5] and this suggests that any theory of heroism implies the notion of inequality among men, the idea that a few men in any society are raised distinctly above the level of their fellows. It is only when we try to characterize the nature of their authority over the average that we become aware of how many possible kinds of heroism we acknowledge. Since the word will be used again and again in this study, it will be helpful to distinguish the way in which Yeats thought of heroism from the many ways in which the word has been used. The most basic distinction to be made is that between the historical and the literary hero. We think of the heroic individual in history as someone who profoundly altered the course of events. As Sidney Hook says, "The hero in history is the individual to whom we can justifiably attribute preponderant influence in determining an issue or event whose consequences would have been profoundly different if he had not acted as he did." [6] It is obvious that history is not always made by worthy men, which suggests that our judgment of such men is really amoral: "we must rule out as irrelevant the conception of the hero as a morally worthy man, not because ethical judgments are illegitimate in history, but because so much of it has been made by the wicked." [7] And yet in a sense we are making some kind of judgment even here, since we dismiss those who accidentally happen to be involved in crucial historical events as mere agents, rather than creators of, history. Hook finally feels obliged, then, to distinguish further between what he calls "eventful man" and "event-making man":

> The *eventful* man in history is any man whose actions influenced subsequent developments along a quite different course than would have been followed if these actions had not been taken. The *event-making* man is an eventful man whose actions are the consequences of outstanding capacities of intelligence, will, and character rather than of accidents of position. This distinction tries to do justice to the general belief that a hero is great not merely in virtue of what he does but in virtue of what he is.[8]

There seems to be a similar ambiguity in the way in which the word "hero" has been used in more strictly literary discussion. We often speak of the "hero" of a novel without implying any kind of moral judgment. When we say, for example, that Raskolnikov is the hero of *Crime and Punishment* or that Macbeth is the hero of Shakespeare's play we are probably bypassing rather than solving the extremely difficult problem of judging those characters. We are using the word amorally, simply to mean that these characters are the "eventful men" in those works. But the more normative use of the word is just as familiar. When Thackeray subtitled *Vanity Fair* "a novel without a hero," he presumably did not mean that it had a heroine instead, but rather that no character in it could be considered "heroic" in the evaluative sense of the word. Such a use of "heroism" implies a clear standard of judgment, since a hero in this sense must also deserve the prominent position he occupies or the authority he has. The normative hero in literature embodies the virtues endorsed by his creator.

It is also apparent that the conception of the hero in literature changes as a culture moves from primitive simplicity to its more sophisticated stages. Historians of the epic, for example, speak of a "heroic age," by which they refer not only to the world pictured in the epic but to the historical time which it might be said to reflect. Historically, our literature seems to have moved from a celebration of the mythological to the epic hero; then to the tragic hero, to the social hero, and finally to what has been called the anti-hero. Of course such a vast generalization is schematic and exaggerated, but it is useful for our purposes because it makes us aware of certain significant distinctions. The mythological or shamanistic hero is the subject of two important studies, Lord Raglan's *The Hero* and Joseph Campbell's *The Hero with a Thousand Faces*. Raglan argues that the heroes of primitive myth are religious rather than historical. He rejects the theory of euhemeristic mythographers that the characters of myth are merely deified human beings, the products of folk memory and poetic flattery. He finds that such heroes are constantly connected with ritual, and that the events of their lives follow a certain definite pattern, thus suggesting that their stories are the later stages of the enactments of primitive religious rituals. The mythological hero, he says, is not clearly distinguished from the gods: "the god is the hero as he appears in ritual, and the hero is the god as he appears in myth; in other words, the hero and the god are two different aspects of the same superhuman being." [9] Campbell similarly finds that the adventures of the mythological hero fall into a consistent pattern, usually involving a supernatural journey:

> A hero ventures forth from the world of common day into a region of supernatural wonder: fabulous forces are there encountered and a decisive victory is won: the hero comes back from this mysterious adventure with the power to bestow boons on his fellow man.[10]

"The power to bestow boons on his fellow man" is, however, already a social as well as a religious function, and in the primitive myth, the hero often refuses to perform that function:

The full round, the norm of the monomyth, requires that the hero shall now begin the labor of bringing the runes of wisdom, the Golden Fleece, or his sleeping princess, back into the kingdom of humanity, where the boon may redound to the renewing of the community, the nation, the planet, or the ten thousand worlds.

But the responsibility has been frequently refused. Even the Buddha, after his triumph, doubted whether the message of realization could be communicated, and saints are reported to have passed away while in the supernal ecstasy. Numerous indeed are the heroes fabled to have taken up residence forever in the blessed isle of the unaging Goddess of Immortal Being.[11]

The epic hero is not always easy to distinguish from the mythological one. Generally, however, he is much more clearly human; he distinguishes himself on the battlefield and his adventures have less of a supernatural aura; he pursues wordly glory and success. The heroic society, as it is pictured for example in *The Iliad*, still involves considerable communication between mortal and immortal worlds, but its heroes are mortal and constantly in danger: "They live always on the brink of death, while savouring beyond the rest the splendour of earthly existence, and their part in the after life is made unfruitful and meaningless to add poignancy to their courage and doom." [12] The epic hero is then not as clearly distinguished from his fellow men as the mythological one, but in one sense they are brothers: the hero of the primitive epic also usually ignores the rest of his society. His heroism is seldom social in intent; he frequently forgets to think of "the renewing of the community." As H. M. Chadwick points out, the hero of primitive epic desires personal glory, not the furtherance of a cause:

> It is essential to notice that the object so much prized is personal glory. . . . Occasionally we hear also of pride of family, but scarcely ever of any truly national feeling. Patroclos exhorts his men to bravery (II, XVI, 270 ff.) in order that they may win glory not for the Achaean nation but for their own personal lord; and he adds further that by so doing they will bring shame upon the national leader. Achilles himself retires from the conflict owing to a personal wrong, and only returns to it in order to avenge his friend.[13]

This heroic ideal reflects the organization of the society which it portrays. "In the Heroic Age," as Chadwick explains, "the state appears to have been regarded as little more than the property of an individual—or rather perhaps of a family." [14]

Historians of the epic, however, distinguish between the primary (or oral) and the secondary (or literary) kind.[15] *The Aeneid* is usually taken as an example of literary epic. In this later form, the pursuit of honor as a personal reward has been replaced by a more social ideal. As G. R. Levy explains:

> The hero, no longer solicitous only to maintain the freedom of intact honour, where personal prestige was the sole source of integration, henceforward owed his primary allegiance to a cause. He was the subject, even if also the creator, of a temporal or spiritual dominion with which he had become in some measure identified.[16]

This too seems to be moving toward the annihilation of the radical distinction between the hero and his society. In the primary epic, the hero's "poetic separation from the ordinary man is not social, not even occupational. It is a difference in kind." [17] But in accepting a social mission, for example the founding of Rome, the hero of secondary epic becomes much less distinguishable from his society; and he becomes the agent of a higher force.

The tragic hero is even less distinctly separated from his fellow man. The move from Greek epic to Greek tragedy is a move to a world of much more circumscribed human power. The "tragic hero" is often carefully distinguished from the "pathetic victim," but in worrying about such relatively fine distinctions we are tacitly admitting that confusion may occur. The possible victories of the tragic hero are internal rather than external; his defeat in the world of "events" seems assured from the first. The authority of the tragic hero, then, has little to do with physical prowess, with victory on the battlefield or with the more obvious forms of success. If it is anything, it is a moral victory; the distinction between the hero and his fellow man is no longer clear-cut. Despite his royal status, we begin to wonder in exactly what ways he is not "one of us."

The *normative* hero of tragedy (as distinguished from, say, a character like Richard III in Shakespeare's play) might still, however, be said to exemplify a kind of human quality which is simply not available to most human beings. Whether we think of that quality in strictly ethical terms or in more broadly psychological ones ("spiritual power" or "intensity," for example), we are still admitting that a radical distinction exists, and that the aim of such tragedy has little to do with an attempt to refashion us in the heroic mold. People do not "graduate" from membership in the Chorus to the role of tragic hero. This is by no means, however, the final literary conception of heroism. As literature becomes more realistic, as we move from poetic drama to prose fiction, for instance, we encounter a very different kind of hero. He is what Sean O'Faolain has called the "social hero," and he is "a purely social creation. He represents, that is to say, a socially approved norm, for representing which to the satisfaction of society he is decorated with a title. . . . The Hero was on the side of the long arm of the law, the Sûreté, the church, the kirk, the headmaster and the head of the family." [18] One can readily think of dozens of characters in English fiction who might be characterized in this way. Like the tragic hero, the authority of such characters is internal rather than external. But the significant distinction is that the code they may be said to embody is not radically different from the ideals (and possible conduct) of ordinary human beings. Mr. Knightley in Jane Austen's *Emma*, for example, should inspire emulation rather than awe.

The most recent stage in our conception of heroism seems to be reached when the term "social hero" begins to sound like an internal contradiction, when society is no longer thought to provide a place for the heroic man, or when the hero is pictured as struggling against a restrictive, alien world. "Non serviam" could be the motto of more heroic characters in our literature than one could easily discuss within the compass of a volume. In a sense, this idea, so familiar in the literature of the nineteenth and twentieth centuries, is the first break in the process of humanizing the hero, of making him seem more and more indistinguishable from common humanity. The rebellious hero (or the anti-hero, as O'Faolain calls him), like the hero of primary epic, is selfish. He often longs nostalgically for a simpler world; he seldom recognizes the state's supposed primacy over the individual; he scorns his "social duty" and he thinks himself different *in kind* from his fellow men. Twentieth century novelists, O'Faolain finds, dug out "private caves, or air-raid shelters, of their own, and there they started to compose private satires, laments, fantasies and myths in the effort to fill the vacuum left by the death of the social Hero with a-social rebels, martyrs, misfits, minor prophets, or, in short, with aberrants and anti-Heroes." [19] What makes these characters heroes? Merely that their creators insist on their authority over common humanity. The qualities of heroism in the twentieth century have become almost totally unpredictable because they depend on the individual, private code of the writer. This transition from social hero to anti-hero is particularly important for an understanding of Yeats's work, and will be more fully discussed below.

Yeats's form of heroic celebration must be seen, when examined against the pattern of this progression, as violently, as deliberately nostalgic and anachronistic. If the changes in the predominant conception of heroism have largely been responses direct or oblique to the growing complexity and democratization of modern society, Yeats's own transformation of the conception seems to be a desperate, eclectic attempt to rescue the very idea of heroism from oblivion. In that attempt, he reaches back to the more primitive stages of hero-worship, to the mythological hero in his visionary poems; to the epic and tragic hero in his use of the Irish heroic cycles. The most obvious fact about the Yeatsian hero is that he has not made his peace with the modern world. Industrialization, secularism, democracy, the state itself—all these perfectly familiar components of our civilization—strike him as alien, as the enemy. He not only longs for a simpler, more primitive world but frequently seems to be unaware of its disappearance. In this sense, many of Yeats's heroes are distinctly different from the anti-heroes of so much modern fiction. They seldom waste their time quarreling directly with the society they reject; they fashion for themselves an alternate, imaginary heroic world in which they do have a place. This is one of the reasons why so many of the characters in Yeats's poems and plays are connected with a dead civilization or a dying one: ancient Greece, Celtic Ireland, the eighteenth century, or the decadent modern aristocracy. We will see in chapter 4 that even the exceptions to this rule, Yeats's more modern and more "social" heroes, are nearly as anachronistically conceived.

The art which celebrates such heroism becomes, in Yeats's religious phrase, "an extension of the beatitudes." [20] Subsequent chapters of this study will clarify the major "types" of the Yeatsian hero and trace the important changes in the conception of each in some detail. But before entering upon distinctions, it is important to emphasize briefly that some things change little in Yeats's ideal hero. There are at least three heroic attributes which can be taken as constants: intensity, solitude, defeat. The hero's intensity is a product both of his absolute conviction and of the need to defend it against a hostile environment. In the ideal world of art, unlike the "real" and topsy-turvy world which Yeats pictures in "The Second Coming," passion and intensity are the attributes of the best and never of the worst human beings. The same general hostility also makes the hero's solitude inevitable, even if it is the solitude of fame, like that of the public man discussed in chapter 4. Finally, the hero, says Yeats, "makes his mask . . . in defeat." [21] The intensity and solitude of such a man are self-explanatory, but the idea of his defeat requires some clarification, for our ordinary conception of heroism is often coupled with success. The failure which Yeats's hero experiences is primarily external. His defeat in the world of circumstance prepares for his triumph in the internal world of the self. For Yeats, the word "heroic" referred neither to a man nor to a situation taken in isolation, but rather to a specific human reaction to the specific situation of defeat.

In attempting to discuss one of Yeats's central concerns in general terms, the temptation is usually to go to his philosophical prose work, *A Vision*, in the hope of finding the kind of coherent and synthetic statement which the more fragmentary and indirect poems and plays seldom provide. It is, however, a hope not frequently rewarded. *A Vision* is itself so often obscure and incoherent, its language is so seldom the language of abstract and logical thought, that the book often merely seems to confirm rather than resolve the contradictions and vacillations of the poetry. In addition, it is a mistake to think of *A Vision* as an encyclopedia of Yeats's most important ideas. Some of his most significant themes find only a very small place in it. Nevertheless, the work does provide some illumination of Yeats's conception of heroism, particularly in Book I, "The Great Wheel," in which he develops a psychological theory designed to classify "every possible movement of thought and of life." [22]

Since Yeats's twenty-eight categories (or "phases," as he calls them) are intended to provide a comprehensive system for classifying every type of human existence, it would be reasonable to expect to find the heroic man among them. In fact, we do find Yeats describing the twelfth phase as "before all else the phase of the hero, of the man who overcomes himself, and so no longer needs . . . the submission of others, or . . . conviction of others to prove his victory." [23] The idea is confirmed in the poem "The Phases of the Moon":

> Eleven pass, and then
> Athena takes Achilles by the hair,
> Hector is in the dust, Nietzsche is born,
> Because the hero's crescent is the twelfth.[24]

Certainly the kind of man he describes as belonging to the twelfth phase—the first of Yeats's types to trust his subjective nature, able to work in solitude though still too caught up in the world around him to be satisfied with monastic withdrawal —seems to be represented by many of the heroic characters we shall be examining in his work. Yet to restrict the idea of heroism to this one type does not do justice to Yeats's considerably more comprehensive vision of the possibilities of greatness and authority. In fact, the classification of men into the twenty-eight categories seems to have increased Yeats's tolerance and open-mindedness by suggesting the possibility of many kinds of human distinction. It has been argued, in a recent book, that the phase of complete subjectivity (Phase 15) is actually Yeats's "standard of perfection . . . with everything before Phase 15 leading up to that illumination, and everything after it declining from it," so that "Yeats's classification becomes nearly a new morality, with a sinless prototype and varying degrees of approach to that prototype." [25] Although it is certainly true that Yeats seems to lean naturally toward the ideal of subjective, imaginative "pure beauty" represented by the fifteenth phase, it is also apparent that he is ready (even anxious) to admire very different kinds of human existence. Phase 20, for example, is described as that of "The Concrete Man" and includes Shakespeare, "the greatest of modern poets," [26] and Phase 24, which is very far from subjectivity, corresponds very closely to Yeats's ideal of aristocratic life, discussed more fully in chapter 3; one of its examples is his close friend and patroness Lady Gregory. In addition, the section includes a chart called the "Four Perfections," [27] in which the virtues of "self-sacrifice" and "sanctity" are associated with the classifications opposite to the subjective life.

The psychological scheme of *A Vision*, then, seems to suggest a fundamental ambivalence in Yeats's own values. It is obvious that he feels himself constantly tempted to praise the man of imagination who cuts himself off from the objective world and pursues an ideal of pure beauty in independence and solitude. At the same time, the very determinism of the scheme seems to demand a less narrow view, since man can not choose such a way of life but is fated according to Yeats's cyclical theory to live through all twenty-eight incarnations at some time. This fact seems to force Yeats to recognize the existence of other kinds of human quality more closely associated with the values of those who can not choose to retreat from the world. Since each possible incarnation also provides the temptation of living "out of phase" rather than "true to phase" (thus rejecting the kind of quality which is provided for within its limits) the possibility of a "heroic" choice is included in any human existence. It is, however, possible to become too broad-minded, to feel with Sidney Hook, for example, that "a hero is any individual who does his work well and makes a unique contribution to the public good." [28] Commendable as such egalitarian sentiment may be, it does tend to make nonsense of the term "heroism," and Yeats was never tempted to be quite so democratic as that. It is important to realize, however, that he did allow for several different kinds of human heroism, and that he resisted the temptation to think of them in a hierarchical order.

Yeats's exaltation of the heroic ideal has significant connections with the forms of hero-worship in Victorian literature.

For the peculiarly Victorian celebration of heroic activity is closely connected with the growing sceptical attitude toward Christian belief. With the decay of a transcendental faith in God, the image of man becomes more and more exalted, until— as the epigraph from Blake suggests—the idealized human portrait is finally made to replace the lost God. As Eric Bentley has pointed out in A *Century of Hero-Worship*, the heroic ideal of the nineteenth and twentieth centuries "was intended by its champions to be to the centuries that lie ahead more than Catholicism ever was to the Middle Ages." [29]

It is therefore hardly surprising that the idea of hero-worship should take hold in earnest in a period of great religious doubt like the Victorian era. Walter Houghton's excellent study of the idea of hero-worship in *The Victorian Frame of Mind* deals with some of the writers most concerned with this problem: Carlyle, of course; Matthew Arnold, both in his attempt to define the "grand style" in *On Translating Homer* and in the well-known Preface to the 1853 edition of his poems; Disraeli in *Coningsby*; Tennyson in *The Idylls of the King*.[30] And one thinks also of the great popularity of the heroes in the works of Byron and Scott; of Emily Brontë's Heathcliff, a heroic character not because he is "moral," but because he is able to justify his actions by a coherent, powerful, private code; of George Eliot's *Middlemarch*, an attempt to redefine the idea of heroism and sainthood for a world without religious belief.

The idea of hero-worship, then, hardly begins with Yeats. Yet there is an important distinction to be made, for in general the Victorian hero is conceived as the savior of his society. He is the "social hero" discussed above. In Carlyle, in George Eliot, the heroic ideal is still an ideal of service, of "doing something" for society in general. Dorothea Brooke, for example, is obsessed with the idea of helping others, of involving herself in the world rather than retreating from it. Her "religious" instincts are turned from God towards man. The Yeatsian hero, however, has abandoned this ideal and is concerned only with self-fulfillment. His sole service to the world lies in a purely private exaltation which may function as an example to others.

How foreign such a conception of heroism is to Victorian thought can be suggested by the words of George Eliot's Daniel

Deronda: "Since I began to read and know, I have always longed for some ideal task, in which I might feel myself the heart and brain of a multitude—some social captainship, which would come to me as a duty, and not be striven for as a personal prize." [31] The same conception of heroism also helps to explain what seems at first Yeats's puzzling distrust of Carlyle. We might have expected him to find a model in the author of *On Heroes, Hero-Worship, and the Heroic in History.* Actually, the exact opposite is true. Yeats never refers to Carlyle with anything but contempt, condemning him for his "ill-breeding and theatricality," [32] his insincerity and rhetorical emptiness. The quarrel is more than stylistic. Carlyle ends his book with a chapter on "The Hero as King," but his king is different from Yeats's hero precisely because he is true to the needs of others before he is true to himself. Carlyle constantly stresses the *usefulness* of the hero to his fellow men. His accomplishments are usually examined from the point of view of the external judges who admire them. Carlyle reserves his greatest praise for the public man, the "Commander over Men." Yet his model is not the kind of lonely and aloof leader whom Yeats admired, but rather Oliver Cromwell, precisely the man who, Yeats felt, was responsible for the villainous egalitarian values of modern life. Carlyle confesses that he must "plead guilty to valuing such a man beyond all other sorts of men." [33] As we shall see, this could hardly have been more different from Yeats's "public" hero, who benefited mankind only by presenting an image of human value in action, and whose contempt for the masses was great.

In contrast to Yeats's ideal, we find the characteristic Victorian celebration of the hero who devotes himself to the public good. After the Queen herself, it is difficult to think of anyone more honored in Victorian society, for example, than Florence Nightingale. Lytton Strachey's famous biographical portrait of her in *Eminent Victorians* suggests how completely her life was devoted to reform, to the alleviation of human suffering. Her heroism, it would seem, was completely turned outward; she appeared to have no private needs, and all her battles were attempts to impose her will on the public world. It was this form of heroism which the Victorians chose to mythicize, in the picture of her as "the Lady with the Lamp." [34] And when Macaulay begins his peroration in the essay on Milton, we find him praising not simply the poet but the patriot, and "the zeal with which he laboured for the public good . . . the deadly hatred which he bore to bigots and tyrants, and the faith which he so sternly kept with his country and with his fame." [35] Such men "have been tried in the furnace and have proved pure." [36]

This is not to suggest that the Victorian writer was unaware of how restrictive and even degrading the ideal of social service could be in a world which had long since bypassed the simplicities of primitive society. Florence Nightingale's heroic task was only accomplished in very prosaic ways, "by strict method, by stern discipline, by rigid attention to detail, by ceaseless labour." [37] The complexity and indirectness of significant action in the modern world frequently frustrated a kind of vestigial romantic desire for solitary, independent heroic action. Contemporary society seemed to demand a heroic technician working patiently within its confines; but the old Faustian longing still remained, as is evident for example in Arthur Hugh Clough's *Dipsychus*.

Clough's poem crystallizes this divided loyalty by presenting it as an internal debate. Its hero, Dipsychus, begins as a Faustian rebel and ends as Lord Chief Justice, not without some regret, since he is drawn to both heroic ideals and finds it almost impossible to make the choice between them. In his agonized attempt to choose, Dipsychus becomes intensely aware of the difference between heroism in "the age of instinct" and in Victorian England:

> The age of instinct has, it seems, gone by,
> And will not be forced back. And to live now
> I must sluice out myself into canals,
> And lose all force in ducts. The modern Hotspur
> Shrills not his trumpet of 'To Horse, To Horse!'
> But consults columns in a railway guide;
> A demigod of figures; an Achilles
> Of computation;
> A verier Mercury, express come down
> To *do* the world with swift arithmetic.
> Well, one could bear with that; were the end ours,
> One's choice and the correlative of the soul,

> To drudge were then sweet service. But indeed
> The earth moves slowly, if it move at all,
> And by the general, not the single force.
> At the [huge] members of the vast machine,
> In all those crowded rooms of industry,
> No individual soul has loftier leave
> Than fiddling with a piston or a valve.
> Well, one could bear that also: one could drudge
> And do one's petty part, and be content
> In base manipulation, solaced still
> By thinking of the leagued fraternity,
> And of co-operation, and the effect
> Of the great engine. If indeed it work,
> And is not a mere treadmill! Which it may be;
> Who can confirm it is not? We ask Action,
> And dream of arms and conflict; and string up
> All self-devotion's muscles; and are set
> To fold up papers.[38]

And yet despite the doubt and despair of this passage, Clough's hero distrusts his romantic (and socially useless) quest for private fulfillment even more deeply, and finally gives it up in order to serve the public world.

We find an even greater distrust of "private" heroism in other Victorian writers.[39] Tennyson's Tiresias, Lucretius, and Tithonus, the "Soul" in his "Palace of Art," his self-indulgent Tristan and Iseult in "The Last Tournament," all are punished in one way or another because they seek and sometimes find a private fulfillment outside the needs and beyond the limits of the world in which they live. Arnold's Empedocles, torn between his social conscience and his need for solitude, commits suicide. Even the exceptions to this rule—Heathcliff, Tennyson's Ulysses—are examined within an ironic framework. Emily Brontë's sceptical narrators and Tennyson's dramatic monologue both suggest that the "hero" is kept at a distance from his creator. Of course the attempt to sum up the attitude of an age —even on a specific point—leads inevitably to distortion. But it is important to emphasize that a difference did exist and that Yeats, the "last Romantic," unlike most of his Victorian predecessors, felt no hesitation in resurrecting the romantic poet's praise of asocial and even *antisocial* heroism.

To trace the causes or the progress of this important shift

in the attitude toward heroism would require a separate book, but some notion of the change can be conveyed rather more briefly by looking at the relevant work of a writer who seems to have become involved with the question of the "heroism" of social action at what was probably a crucial moment in the growth of the disenchantment with it. In three novels written between 1885 and 1889—*The Bostonians, The Princess Casamassima,* and *The Tragic Muse*—Henry James dealt directly with political and social reform. In these works, James took on, respectively, the subjects of women's emancipation, social justice, and the political life. He was never, of course, infatuated with social reformers, but his treatment of the subject in these three novels seems to suggest a growing impatience with and contempt for their whole world.

In *The Bostonians,* this impatience is kept wholly beneath the surface of the novel. Even the attacks of James's hero Basil Ransom—who stands most firmly in opposition to the social reformers—are cryptic and elliptical. Ransom's distrust of generalization, which make him dislike the simplemindedness of the suffragettes, also makes him disdainful of saying, in so many words, what is wrong with them. And yet his attitude, and certainly James's, is not that of contempt. For *The Bostonians* presents, in the subtle portrait of Olive Chancellor, an ironic and yet sympathetic dissection of the social reformer whose cause may be public but whose need for believing in that cause is purely private—and has nothing to do with the cause itself. The novel in effect disposes of the heroism of the social reformer without, however, depriving him of his humanity.

The Princess Casamassima, a considerably more complicated novel, also deals with a social subject, the injustice of the class structure which permits desperate poverty to exist in a rich society. James's ironic picture of the reformers in this novel is not intended as a defense of the status quo. The poor *are* deprived; the rich *are* extravagantly, unnecessarily wealthy. But though James grants this, he seems anxious to present the illusions of the reformers as illusions, to mock the idea that any kind of social change—no matter what—will really bring Utopia any nearer. Life is imperfect because people are; and a redistribution of wealth will not make them any less so. As one of the characters in the novel says, when he places the idea of great social changes among "the dreams of his youth":

> For what was any possible change in the relations of men and women but a new combination of the same elements? If the elements could be made different the thing would be worth thinking of; but it was not only impossible to introduce any new ones—no means had yet been discovered for getting rid of the old. The figures on the chessboard were still the passions and jealousies and superstitions and stupidities of man, and their position with regard to each other, at any given moment, could be of interest only to the grim, invisible fates who played the game—who sat, through the ages, bow-backed over the table.[40]

And in this novel the illusions and self-deceptions of the reformers result indirectly in the perfectly meaningless and yet tragic death of the innocent hero of the book, Hyacinth Robinson. James's attitude seems to be moving away from detached observation.

In *The Tragic Muse*, the public "heroes" (and it is nearly mockery to call them that) are no longer idealistic reformers but politicians with a consuming passion for success. This fact in itself indicates how much less ambiguous James's treatment of the type will be, and the novel, we find, allows itself a directness of statement which we have not seen in *The Bostonians* or *The Princess Casamassima*. James's rejection of the political and social arena as a place unfit for the quintessentially human concerns comes as a shock after the delicate parrying of the previous books. It is a case of fighting fire with fire. The trouble with politics, says Gabriel Nash in the book, is that "it has simply nothing in life to do with shades! I can't say worse for it than that." [41] It is, in other words, a world of lies and overstatements, of gross simplifications. In an age of publicity and vulgarity, the corruption of the politician's integrity is inevitable. A passionate speech on the subject by Nick Dormer, the hero of the novel who resigns his parliamentary seat in order to devote himself to painting, suggests how complete is James's rejection of the possibility of idealistic social action. Politics, he says:

> has nothing to do with the truth or the search for it; nothing to do with intelligence, or candour, or honour. It's an

appeal to everything that for one's self one despises . . . to
stupidity, to ignorance, to density, to the love of names and
phrases, the love of hollow, idiotic words, of shutting the
eyes tight and making a noise. Do men who respect each
other or themselves talk to each other that way? They know
they would deserve kicking if they were to attempt it. A man
would blush to say to himself in the darkness of the night
the things he stands up on a platform in the garish light of
day to stuff into the ears of a multitude whose intelligence
he pretends that he esteems.[42]

In Nick's speech, as in his symbolic desertion of political life
for art, we can see that the rejection of the idea of social
heroism brings with it a sanction for a very different kind of
human quality, that of self-*fulfillment* rather than self-*sacrifice*.

It is important to ask exactly what inspired Yeats, like
James, to abandon an accepted ethos, although to answer this
question adequately we will have to deal with several significant
social, political, religious, and literary movements of Yeats's
time. This will be done, in detail, in the following chapters. In
brief, however, one might say that in all four of these spheres,
Yeats's Ireland, and often the world in general during his early
and middle years, was moving further and further away from
the climate of thought which makes a heroic ideal of any kind
generally acceptable. The traditional society had laid stress on
the existence of a *higher world*, whether social, political, religious, or national, and when the traditional society was destroyed
or replaced, the conception of a higher world was lost with it.
Once the modern Irish state had been successfully established,
the country was quick to forget her warrior heroes. Her ancient
aristocracy was rapidly being replaced by a commercial society
whose faith was in money and equality. Bureaucracy became
the final end of democratic government. Materialistic scepticism
or mere lip service to the traditional forms of religion replaced
the passionate faith of former times. All of these movements
may seen highly familiar to us now, since they are in fact only
extensions of certain currents of nineteenth-century thought.
Yet for Yeats, living in a country which was itself not yet part
of the modern world, they seemed the most living of realities.
Taken together, they impelled him to reject the new society,
and with it the ideal of heroic social service.

In addition, there were two other important forces at work in Yeats's transformation of the Victorian heroic ideal: the movement of realism in literature, and his reading of Nietzsche. The romantic movement, he said, "with its turbulent heroism, its self-assertion, is over, superseded by a new naturalism that leaves man helpless before the contents of his own mind." [43] Yeats felt that this new naturalism or realism, as he alternately called it, was the predominant literary movement of his time. In drama, in fiction, even in poetry, the realists had taken over. Yeats profoundly distrusted their choice of subject, their methods, and their style. To his mind, realism contradicted the first principle of all art. He writes of Antoine, the founder of the Théâtre Libre, "Art is art because it is not nature, and he tried to make it nature. A realist, he cared nothing for poetry, which is founded on convention." [44] As director of the Abbey Theatre, Yeats persistently fought against the demand for realistic drama, a drama that dealt with modern life and modern, familiar, "ordinary" people. It is not an exaggeration to say that all of his own plays were written in reaction to this dominant theatrical movement of his time, for he sincerely felt that the common man was not a fit subject for the highest art:

> Have we not been in error in demanding from our playwrights personages who do not transcend our common actions any more than our common speech. . . . We are, it may be, very stupid in thinking that the average man is a fit subject at all for the finest art. Art delights in the exception, for it delights in the soul expressing itself according to its own laws and arranging the world about it in its own pattern. . . . But the average man is average, because he has not attained to freedom. . . . At the first performance of *Ghosts*, I could not escape from an illusion unaccountable to me at the time. All the characters seemed to be less than life-size; the stage, though it was but the little Royalty stage, seemed larger than I had ever seen it. Little whimpering puppets moved here and there in the middle of that great abyss. . . . What is there left for us, that have seen the newly-discovered stability of things changed from an enthusiasm to a weariness, but to labour with a high heart, though it may be with weak hands, to rediscover an art of the theatre that shall be joyful, fantastic, extravagant, whimsical, beautiful, resonant, and altogether reckless? [45]

The movements in poetry and fiction paralleled the new realism of the drama. "I hate the pale victims of modern fiction," Yeats wrote to Olivia Shakespeare in 1934, "that suffer that they may have minds like photographic plates." [46] And at about the same time he refers with disapproval to "the realism of Eliot." [47] It seemed to him that the realists presented an image of man as the helpless victim of forces more powerful than himself and thereby succeeded in destroying the idea of man's potential or actual stature. In contrast, most of Yeats's literary production can be seen as a comprehensive attempt to reestablish the more traditional picture of man's heroic personality.

It is, however, important to keep in mind that the particular question of human stature is only one manifestation of a more far-reaching disagreement about the nature of art itself. For the ideal of the realist is mimesis: he attempts to present a faithful and recognizable picture of life as we know it. Yeats says that the entire movement is summed up in Stendhal's idea that art can be fruitfully compared to a mirror in the roadway which accurately records the spectacle of life.[48] His own ideal artist, on the other hand, is not simply a faithful reflector of what already exists or is ordinarily experienced. Rather he creates, out of his imagination or special perception, a deliberately elevated, extravagant, and exceptional picture of human life which an audience may not recognize but must respect. Yeats's ideal, in short, is "to chaunt a tongue men do not know" [49] but should learn.

The other highly important influence on Yeats's idea of the heroic personality was his reading of Nietzsche. In 1902, his friend John Quinn lent him Thomas Common's anthology of selections from Nietzsche's works. This copy still exists,[50] and Yeats's numerous underlinings and marginal notations in it testify to the seriousness of his interest and the care with which he read it. Nietzsche's influence on Yeats's thought is a complicated matter to assess. It is worth noting that three years after he read the German philosopher he still spoke of him with great enthusiasm. As Sir Herbert Grierson recalls, "I had not left the bedroom, to which I conducted him to change, before he had told me of his interest in Nietzsche *as a counteractive to the spread of democratic vulgarity*." [51]

The great similarity between Yeats's notion of heroism and that of Nietzsche at first suggests that the influence of the philosopher may have been overwhelming and decisive. In many ways, the Nietzschean "Uebermensch" compares with the Yeatsian hero. In Nietzsche too we find a theory of uncommon human stature which has little to do with the traditional view of the social savior. Both writers stress the hero's abandonment of the way of life and the common ideals of the world in which he lives. Both present the idea of a natural aristocracy among men, and both picture the ideal culture as one in which the noble personality is recognized and accepted as its unquestioned leader. The great evil, in the eyes of both men, is the spread of the democratic ideal. In addition, Nietzsche like Yeats believes in a cyclical theory of history which he calls the "eternal second coming," [52] and, again like Yeats, he insists that the response of the heroic personality to the knowledge of the inevitable historical cycle must be one of joy rather than of despair. This constitutes, in both writers, a theory of tragedy.

It therefore seems difficult to overestimate the effect on Yeats of his reading of Nietzsche. Yet at the same time we must remember that in almost every case the ideas which we might think were actually derived from the philosopher can in fact be seen in Yeats's own work before 1902. In the poem "Kanva on Himself," for example, the theory of eternal recurrence is used more than a decade before his reading of Nietzsche. What Yeats must have found, then, was a mind which worked in ways very similar to his own, the mind of a man who had already come to some of the conclusions which he had been struggling for years to formulate. As a result, Nietzsche's actual influence lay in providing authority and reassurance for Yeats's somewhat more hesitant and uncertain thinking. It must have been the example of the German philosopher, and particularly of his "outrageous" idea of the existence of two codes of morality, a "master morality" for the heroic individual and a "slave morality" for the rest of the world, which provided the final impetus for Yeats's abandonment of the Victorian ideal of the social savior. That he once took that ideal seriously is evident in the early plays *The Countess Kathleen* and *Cathleen Ni Houlihan*; but henceforth the only point of contact between the hero and the world in which he lives is that his exaltation crystallizes the highest human aspirations. Yet even this echo is almost accidental and certainly never considered the hero's "duty." As Yeats says in one of the annotations in the Nietzsche anthology, "A sacred book is a book written by a man whose self has been so exalted (not by denial but by an intensity like that of the vibrating, vanishing string) that it becomes one with the self of the race." [53]

All of this is not intended to suggest, however, that Yeats idealized the dissociation of the hero from his society. In fact, the exact opposite is true. His theory of history postulated the existence of certain periods in the life of any culture in which a unity of hero and society was possible. This is one of the reasons for Yeats's constant nostalgia for a "Romantic Ireland" in which heroism was still valued highly. But unfortunately for the present, "Romantic Ireland's dead and gone, / It's with O'Leary in the grave." Yeats had seen the more traditional aristocratic society in which there was no break between the noble figure and the rest of the world destroyed in his own lifetime. When such "unity of culture" existed, the hero was the accepted leader of his society in all possible spheres, political, social, and religious. But the modern world no longer demonstrated such unity, and the poem "September 1913" gives us a picture of a broken society where the ordinary man has dethroned and entirely forgotten the heroic individual:

> Yet could we turn the years again,
> And call those exiles as they were
> In all their loneliness and pain,
> You'd cry, 'Some woman's yellow hair
> Has maddened every mother's son':
> They weighed so lightly what they gave.
> But let them be, they're dead and gone,
> They're with O'Leary in the grave.[54]

One might say, in summing up this aspect of Yeats's literary career, that he took upon himself what he considered the all-important task of re-educating the world in the appreciation of the heroic individual, so that the broken circle could be closed once again. The poem "The Second Coming" suggests that in our own world the traditional hierarchy and the coherent culture which it had built has undergone a catastrophic reversal, for our topsy-turvy world is one in which "the best lack all conviction, while the worst / Are full of passionate intensity." Both classical tragedy and the medieval Irish epic, on the other hand, present a picture, Yeats thought, of the ideal unified society where the reverse of this is true, where the "worst" are hesitant and always follow the lead of the passionate, intensely alive heroic personality: compare Antigone and Ismene; Oedipus and the Chorus; Cuchulain and the lesser warriors. It is such a unified culture which Yeats worked at first to re-establish. He was no iconoclast; rather, his efforts were concentrated on restoring an icon now tarnished and all but forgotten: the icon of the hero.

Yeats thought that the fragmentation of Western civilization had occurred in the Renaissance: "Had not Europe shared one mind and heart, until both mind and heart began to break into fragments a little before Shakespeare's birth?" [55] The unity of the Middle Ages made all men "conscious of an all enfolding sympathy," whereas in the modern world "the distinction of classes had become their isolation." [56] The ultimate ideal was the culture of Chaucer's time, where "all, artist and poet, craftsman and day labourer would accept a common design." [57]

There was, however, a shift in Yeats's thought about the feasibility of artificially recreating such a unified culture for the modern world. He wrote in 1922, "this much at any rate is certain—the dream of my early manhood that a modern nation can return to Unity of Culture, is false." But an alternate, and more modest, ideal later suggested itself, for it was possible that such a unity might be achieved "for some small circle of men and women, and there leave it till the moon bring round its century." [58]

The great tragedy of modern civilization, in Yeats's eyes, was the fragmentation of society, for the specialization which it encouraged had a direct and devastating effect on the possible breadth and significance of the heroic achievement. To clarify his idea of the two societies, one unified and the other fragmented, Yeats once described two paintings in the Dublin National Gallery. The whole passage which leads up to this description is of great importance and must be quoted in full:

Somewhere about 1450, though later in some parts of Europe
by a hundred years or so, and in some earlier, men attained
to personality in great numbers, "Unity of Being," and became like a "perfectly proportioned human body," and as
men so fashioned held places of power, their nations had it
too, prince and ploughman sharing that thought and feeling. What afterwards showed for rifts and cracks were there
already, but imperious impulse held all together. Then the
scattering came, the seeding of the poppy, bursting of pea-
pod, and for a time personality seemed but the stronger for
it. Shakespeare's people make all things serve their passion,
and that passion is for the moment the whole energy of
their being—birds, beasts, men, women, landscape, society,
are but symbols and metaphors, nothing is studied in itself, the
mind is a dark well, no surface, depth only. The men that
Titian painted, the men that Jongsen painted, even the men
of Van Dyck, seemed at moments like great hawks at rest. In
the Dublin National Gallery there hung, perhaps there still
hangs, upon the same wall, a portrait of some Venetian
gentleman by Strozzi, and Mr. Sargent's painting of President Wilson. Whatever thought broods in the mind of that
Venetian gentleman, has drawn its life from his whole body;
it feeds upon it as the flame feeds upon the candle—and
should that thought be changed, his pose would change, his
very cloak would rustle for his whole body thinks. President
Wilson lives only in the eyes, which are steady and intent;
the flesh about the mouth is dead, and the hands are dead,
and the clothes suggest no movement of his body, nor any
movement but that of the valet, who has brushed and folded
in mechanical routine. There, all was an energy flowing outward from the nature itself; here, all is the anxious study and
slight deflection of external force; there man's mind and
body were predominantly subjective; here all is objective,
using those words not as philosophy uses them, but as we
use them in conversation.[59]

In this way, what we might call the internal unity of the
heroic personality is inevitably destroyed in the modern world.
The dissociation of mind and body is also a metaphor for the
fragmentation of society. Yeats admired the Irish and the
Homeric epics because he thought they presented a picture of
a world in which the noble individual was recognized as the
natural leader of society in all disciplines, a society in which he
is not forced to channel or limit his energies. Cuchulain, the
Irish hero Yeats used most frequently, combined the roles of

warrior, aristocrat, political leader, and visionary. For the modern heroic man, such a combination is no longer possible, in part because of the immense complexity of contemporary civilization. The modern hero is forced to become a specialist, either aristocrat or public leader or visionary, for he can no longer combine these ways of life. In this study, then, we will first investigate the unity of heroism and of culture which Yeats found in the world of the Irish epics and then trace the fragmentation of the hero of that world into the three kinds of modern "heroic specialists." The four following chapters will deal with the Irish hero, the aristocrat, the public hero, and the visionary, in that order.

It is true that Yeats thought such fragmentation had become inevitable in the modern world. Nevertheless, because of his cyclical view of history, he also believed that the true ideal society which neither has to restrict its "unity" to a small aristocratic class nor turn its great men into specialists would some day be restored. The re-establishment of such a world is not the work of the artist, but of Time. Yet in celebrating "the great race that is to come," the writer can at least recreate the idea, if not the reality, of a genuine heroic world. It is for this reason that the poet Seanchan's pupil in *The King's Threshold* triumphantly commands:

> O silver trumpets, be you lifted up
> And cry to the great race that is to come.
> Long-throated swans upon the waves of time,
> Sing loudly, for beyond the wall of the world
> That race may hear our music and awake.[60]

Notes

1. Yeats, *The Hour-Glass, Cathleen Ni Houlihan, The Golden Helmet, The Irish Dramatic Movement* (Stratford-on-Avon, 1908), p. 122.
2. Yeats, *Estrangement* (Dublin, 1926), p. 35.
3. Yeats, *Samhain*, No. 5 (Dublin, 1905), p. 11.
4. *The Letters of W. B. Yeats*, ed. Allan Wade (London, 1954), p. 219.
5. W. H. Auden, *The Enchaféd Flood* (London, 1951), p. 93.
6. Sidney Hook, *The Hero in History: A Study in Limitation and Possibility* (Boston, 1955), p. 153.
7. *Ibid.*
8. *Ibid.*, p. 154.

9. Lord Raglan, *The Hero: A Study in Tradition, Myth and Drama* (London, 1949), p. 207.

10. Joseph Campbell, *The Hero with a Thousand Faces* (New York, 1949), p. 30.

11. *Ibid.*, p. 193.

12. G. R. Levy, *The Sword from the Rock: An Investigation into the Origins of Epic Literature and the Development of the Hero* (New York, 1954), p. 94.

13. H. M. Chadwick, *The Heroic Age* (Cambridge, Eng., 1912), p. 329.

14. *Ibid.*, p. 336.

15. See, for example, C. M. Bowra, *From Virgil to Milton* (London, 1945), pp. 1–32, and C. S. Lewis, *A Preface to Paradise Lost* (London, 1942), pp. 12–50.

16. Levy, p. 215.

17. *Ibid.*, p. 89. Note also the interesting distinction between Hector and Achilles in C. M. Bowra's *Heroic Poetry* (London, 1961), p. 112: "Homer draws a contrast between him [i.e., Hector] and Achilles, between the human champion of hearth and home and the half-divine hero who has very few ties or loyalties. Perhaps in Hector we may see the emergence of a new ideal of manhood, of the conception that a man fulfills himself better in the service of his city than in the satisfaction of his own honour, and in that case Hector stands on the boundary between the heroic world and the city-state which replaced it."

18. Sean O'Faolain, *The Vanishing Hero: Studies in Novelists of the Twenties* (London, 1956), p. 14.

19. *Ibid.*, p. 18.

20. *The Letters of W. B. Yeats*, p. 832.

21. Yeats, *Essays* (New York, 1924), p. 500.

22. Yeats, *A Vision* (New York, 1956), p. 78.

23. *Ibid.*, p. 127.

24. *Ibid.*, p. 60.

25. Helen Hennessy Vendler, *Yeats's Vision and the Later Plays* (Cambridge, Mass., 1963), pp. 26–27.

26. Yeats, *A Vision*, p. 153.

27. *Ibid.*, p. 100.

28. Hook, p. 239.

29. Eric Bentley, *A Century of Hero-Worship* (Philadelphia and New York, 1944), p. 8.

30. See Walter E. Houghton, *The Victorian Frame of Mind 1830–1870* (New Haven, 1957), Ch. xii, pp. 305–40.

31. George Eliot, *Daniel Deronda* (New York, A. L. Burt, n.d.), p. 755.

32. Yeats, *Essays*, p. 291.

33. Thomas Carlyle, *Sartor Resartus; On Heroes and Hero-Worship* (London, 1956), pp. 434–35.

34. Lytton Strachey, *Eminent Victorians* (New York, 1918), p. 131.

35. Thomas Babington Macaulay, "Milton," *Critical and Miscellaneous Essays* (New York, 1880), I, 59.

36. *Ibid.*, I, 58.

37. Strachey, p. 151.

38. *The Poems of Arthur Hugh Clough*, ed. H. F. Lowry, A. L. P. Norrington, and F. L. Mulhauser (Oxford, 1951), pp. 272–73.

39. This idea is discussed in detail as it affects the work of Tennyson, Browning, and Arnold in E. D. H. Johnson's *The Alien Vision of Victorian Poetry* (Princeton, 1952). An even more radical distrust of romantic heroism is constantly evident in the Victorian novel, as Mario Praz has shown in his *The Hero in Eclipse in Victorian Fiction* (Oxford, 1956). The domestication of romantic titanism in the novels, however, presents such a complete contrast to Yeats's form of hero-worship that the distinction is too obvious to be useful here.

40. Henry James, *The Princess Casamassima* (London, 1886), p. 349.

41. Henry James, *The Tragic Muse* (London, 1948), p. 32.

42. *Ibid.*, p. 85.

43. Yeats, Introduction to J. M. Hone and M. M. Rossi, *Bishop Berkeley: His Life, Writings and Philosophy* (London, 1931), p. xxiii.

44. *The Letters of W. B. Yeats*, p. 440.

45. Yeats, *Samhain*, No. 4 (Dublin, 1904), pp. 26–27.

46. *The Letters of W. B. Yeats*, p. 827.

47. Yeats, *Essays 1931 to 1936* (Dublin, 1937), p. 26.

48. Yeats, Introduction to *The Oxford Book of Modern Verse* (Oxford, 1936), p. xxvii.

49. "To the Rose upon the Rood of Time," *The Variorum Edition of the Poems of W. B. Yeats*, ed. Peter Allt and Russell K. Alspach (New York, 1957), p. 101. Hereafter referred to as *Variorum*.

50. Thomas Common, *Nietzsche as Critic, Philosopher, Poet and Prophet* (London, 1901), T.R. 193 N 67 n in the Northwestern University Library. For a fuller discussion of Yeats's debt to Nietzsche, see Richard Ellmann, *The Identity of Yeats* (New York, 1954), pp. 91–98.

51. Sir Herbert Grierson, Preface to V. K. Narayana Menon, *The Development of W. B. Yeats* (Edinburgh, 1942), p. x. (Italics mine.)

52. From *Thus Spake Zarathustra* in Common, p. 251.

53. Common, p. 132.

54. *Variorum*, p. 290.

55. Yeats, *Four Years* (Churchtown, Dundrum, 1921), p. 86.

56. *Ibid.*, p. 87.

57. *Ibid.*, pp. 89–90.

58. Yeats, *The Trembling of the Veil* (London, 1922), p. 172.

59. *Ibid.*, pp. 168–70.

60. *The Collected Plays of W. B. Yeats* (New York, 1953), p. 94.

2 · The Irish Hero

We work to add dignity to Ireland.
LADY GREGORY

YEATS'S FORMULATION of the heroic ideal which was to become so important in his work may be said to begin with his interest in the movement for Irish independence. Few readers realize that Yeats never wanted to be a cosmopolitan writer. Although he came from an Anglo-Irish Protestant family and spent some of the most important years of his life in England, he thought of himself as a distinctly Irish writer dealing for the most part with peculiarly Irish problems. It is therefore not surprising that if we want to understand Yeats's early efforts to define and clarify the idea of the heroic personality we must go back to various attempts by several groups of Irishmen in the 1880s and 1890s to create a unified Irish culture. Without some knowledge of the more general problems involved, it is difficult, for example, to understand Yeats's participation in the movement to revive the Irish epics, from which many of his ideas on the hero are ultimately derived.

Many readers first faced with those of Yeats's plays and poems which depend on some familiarity with the events and personages of Irish myth are puzzled by what seems an almost perverse choice of obscure material. In a world where even the Greek legends are nearly forgotten, it seems extremely unlikely that a poet whose interests are to any degree universal would choose a body of legend so unfamiliar even to the restricted audience of modern poetry. Yet for Yeats, Irish heroic legend was no passing fancy. The very limits of his career are nearly established by the publication of two major works based on the ancient tales: *The Wanderings of Oisin* in 1889 and *The Death of Cuchulain* in 1939. To make things even more difficult, this interest was not, at first, a literary one, and so it becomes necessary to understand the whole history of the revival of interest in Irish legend in order to explain Yeats's first contact with it.

One of the basic problems facing Ireland in the eighteen eighties and nineties was the necessity of creating a national consciousness. During the latter part of the nineteenth century, the Irish found themselves in a situation common enough in a colonial country which has lived under a foreign yoke for so long that its people are no longer certain which part of the civilization is their own, which foreign. The first step in achieving Irish independence, then, was to restore to the Irish people a consciousness of their own culture. Various organizations to which Yeats belonged around the turn of the century felt the need to separate the native from the foreign, the Irish from the English, in a quite methodical and deliberate fashion. But Ireland was an old country, with its own language, literature, myths, and great historical figures—an embarrassment of riches, as a matter of fact—and the problem was which part of this complex cultural melange to emphasize. What was "quintessentially Irish," or what should be made to appear so? On this question Yeats and some of his associates were in sharp disagreement. His interest was always more directly focused on artistic endeavor; he despised the notion of art as a mere tool for political propaganda. As one critic has said, Yeats "was impelled to find a way of putting Ireland into some mental order, so that cultural symbols of dependable significance would be at the disposal of the artist." [1] But this does not mean that he dissociated himself at first from the more purely political or nationalistic organizations. Common necessity created strange bedfellows, and Yeats suddenly found himself in the same societies with people like John O'Leary, the Fenian, and Sir Charles Gavan Duffy, the former leader of the Young Ireland movement.

There was reason for this united front, for in a sense all the societies were fighting a common enemy, and one that was internal rather than external: the apathy and despair of the Irish people themselves. Ireland in the late nineteenth century had become a land without hope. The famine of 1847 and 1848 resulted in mass emigration, "the emigration of the young and the strong," in the words of the historian O'Hegarty. The effect, he says, was to create a new image of Ireland, the image of a dying country, in the minds of her own people:

> The Great Starvation was a turning point in our Nineteenth Century history. It enfeebled the national will, broke the spirit of the people, broke the revolutionary upsurge of national endeavour which had been gathering momentum for nearly a century, depopulated the country and established large-scale emigration as a habit.[2]

Emigration also had its political effects: a number of the societies and organizations which were working for Irish independence or political unity simply disbanded. When the young men left, Ireland lost many of her actual and potential leaders. Again in O'Hegarty's words:

> There set in, in addition to the Starvation emigration, a political emigration. Young Ireland, the Irish Confederation, the Repeal Clubs, all vanished. The blight of the Starvation was followed by a blight of the mind, and the men and women who were left in Ireland were left without hope and without spirit and without leaders.[3]

It is significant that Gavan Duffy, the important leader of the Young Ireland movement, left his native country for Australia in 1856 and did not return until 1891. He was appalled by the atmosphere of post-'48 Ireland, an atmosphere which seemed to make all heroic effort inconceivable: "Though the Irish people had exhibited a constancy of purpose which have few parallels in history, it was certain that they were now sunk in a torpor from which it was hopeless to lead them to heroic enterprises." [4]

Certainly there was little cause for hope in the fight for political independence. Irish insurrections had failed so often that they seemed only to emphasize the pointlessness of such perpetual sacrifice. The resultant political apathy lasted through the time of Yeats's youth and into his young manhood. He refers to Ireland as "a country demoralized by failure." [5] And even as late as 1898, P. H. Pearse, later the leader of the Easter Rebellion, was writing:

To-day, after a continuous fight lasting for eight long centuries, we are, Heaven knows, farther off than ever from the
goal towards which we have struggled. Who can look at our
political and national life at the present moment, and continue to hope? The men whom we call our leaders are engaged
in tearing out one another's vitals, and there is no prospect
that they will ever stop. The people are listlessly looking on
—for the first time in Irish history they seem to be sunk in
apathy.[6]

The various movements in the 1880s to revitalize Irish
culture were forced to begin, then, with the problem of restoring both a sense of national identity and a sense of national
purpose to this "demoralized" country. Many looked forward
with hope to a time in which Ireland would recapture the
freshness and vigor of former times. Lady Gregory, for example,
dedicates her book, *Gods and Fighting Men*, to the Irish
Literary Society of New York, to the exiles:

A few of you have already come to see us, and we begin to hope
that one day the steamers across the Atlantic will not go out
full, but come back full, until some of you find your real home
is here, and say as some of us say, like Finn to the woman of
enchantments. . . . "We would not give up our own country
—Ireland—if we were to get the whole world as an estate,
and the Country of the Young along with it." [7]

The dispute among various Irish leaders towards the close
of the century, then, was not concerned with ends, but rather
with means. We are interested here primarily in those groups
in Irish public life which emphasized cultural rather than
political phenomena, since Yeats eventually committed himself
to the work of this minority. Probably the most important
organization for our purposes was the Irish Literary Society,
founded by Yeats and others in 1891. Stopford Brooke's important inaugural address to this group suggests that the creation of a genuine and significant Irish literature would do more
for the final establishment of a true national community than
the exclusively political concerns of former times: "Irish Literature is not to Ireland what English Literature is to England.
The mass of the Irish people know nothing of it, and care little
about it. That they should know, and should care will do more

for the cause of a true Nationalism than all our political angers." [8]

Yeats was deeply committed, at the beginning of his career, to the creation of a truly national Irish literature. He was an Irish patriot if patriotism can also include the determination to take a significant part in the creation of a unified national image which gives to a people a legitimate pride in their country, a feeling for its distinctive qualities, a respect for its peculiar customs, traditions, and history. Many people agreed that Ireland must produce an independent literature, distinct and separate from the English literature on which it had so heavily relied in the past. Douglas Hyde, for example, in his influential essay on "The Necessity for De-Anglicizing Ireland" (1894), points out the irony of Ireland's policy of reflecting the culture of its enemy because it has none of its own, "imitating England and yet apparently hating it." [9]

The question of how exactly one was to "de-Anglicize" Irish literature and culture was the nucleus of much literary discussion around the turn of the century. In the chaos of conflicting opinions, it is possible to distinguish four distinct and important answers to this question. Certainly the brilliant literary critic John Eglinton represented a minority of Irish thought in his insistence that any truly great literature was inevitably and unconsciously "national." His is by far the most cosmopolitan and urbane argument in the literary discussion of the period, and his satiric attack on the catchword "de-Anglicization" suggests that he was aware of the dangers of a deliberate, self-imposed provincialism, the provincialism of patriotic writers like Thomas Davis [10]:

> One would like to live to see the day of what might be termed, without any disrespect to Davis, the de-Davisisation of Irish national literature, that is to say, the getting rid of the notion that in Ireland, a writer is to think, first and foremost, of interpreting the nationality of his country and not simply of the burden which he has to deliver. The expression of nationality, literature cannot fail to be; and the richer, more varied and unexpected that expression the better.[11]

But Ireland's—and Yeats's—solution to the problem was not that of Eglinton, at least during the nineties.

At the opposite pole were the political writers who used literature only as a particularly effective mode of propaganda to arouse the patriotic sentiments of an Irish audience. It was the method of the mid-century Young Ireland writers, now carried on by its last survivors. One of those most anxious to "use" literature in such a way was Maud Gonne, which meant that Yeats, constantly exposed to this point of view, was faced with a peculiarly personal difficulty in dissociating himself from it. Much as he disliked the idea of "a nation unified by political doctrine, a subservient art and letters aiding and abetting," [12] the argument kept coming up throughout his career. His attempts to answer the objection that writers of his sort were not patriots grew progressively more bitter. This is the subject of his "To Ireland in the Coming Times" (1892):

> Know, that I would accounted be
> True brother of a company
> That sang, to sweeten Ireland's wrong.[13]

More than three decades later, in his Nobel Prize speech, Yeats reflects with virulence on the damaging effects of so crude a conception of the function of literature:

> The danger to art and literature comes today from the tyranny and persuasions of revolutionary societies and forms of political and religious propaganda. The persuasion has corrupted much modern English literature; and during the twenty years that led up to our national revolution the tyranny wasted the greater part of the energy of Irish dramatists and poets.[14]

Between these two extremes, there were two other answers to the question of how to "de-Anglicize" Irish culture. The more radical involved the revival of Gaelic as the national language of Ireland. To many this seemed to be the obvious solution. If Irish literature were written once more in Gaelic, in the language of its old epics, in the speech of many of its peasants, there would be little difficulty in shaking off the English influence. With the formation of the Gaelic League in 1893, and the election of the Gaelic writer and scholar Douglas Hyde as its president, this idea rapidly attracted the enthusiastic attention of many people. Gaelic study groups were formed throughout Ireland. A language which had been formerly ridiculed for its crudeness and obvious provinciality suddenly became accepted as a powerful means of uniting Ireland.

But the enthusiasm was short-lived. Once the eager students began to cope with the immense difficulties of the language, once they grasped the fact that Gaelic was still the language of a nearly feudal society with no words or expressions for the complex institutions of a modern industrial culture, a more realistic view began to prevail. Certainly there was something comic in the spectacle of a nation of adults going to school to master its own "native" tongue, an aspect which the witty Eglinton delighted in exposing to ridicule:

> Dragged from obscurity in the hovels of the West, like the forgotten representative of some old dynasty restored by a sudden revolution, the ancient language of this country hears itself saluted as "Our own Tongue," "The *Irish* Language," even in the presence of that rival who has supplanted it, and who is now so securely established as the language of the country that it can afford to wink at these pretensions and even to extend municipal hospitalities to Gaelic in the decayed but still haughty capital of the Ascendancy. "Irish" Language is indeed only a title of courtesy: the ancient language of the Celt is no longer the language of Irish nationality. And in fact it never was.[15]

The fourth and final solution to the problem of how to de-Anglicize Irish culture was, for our purposes, the most important, since it was the policy of the Irish Literary Society as well as of the young Yeats. This was, in effect, a kind of compromise between the positions of the extremists, its aim being merely to encourage in a variety of ways the growth of a specific kind of national literature, a literature which dealt primarily with Irish life. Beyond that stipulation, however, the Irish Literary Society was not by policy more restrictive. Irish life was varied enough for many types of literary expression. As Yeats defines "nationality" the choice of subject matter remains wide, for he calls only for a literature which resolves "to celebrate in verse and prose all within the four seas of Ireland." [16] It is obvious that such a stipulation places no restriction on literary methods, aims, and forms. Even the subject matter, the raw material of literature, though it should be found "within the four seas of Ireland," still offered a wide choice.

The new literature could deal with Irish folk tales or with the people who had transmitted them from generation to generation; it could reach back into the far past of the Irish legends or into the near past of the heroic deeds of real men; it could deal with the present, it could deal with the future. The ultimate purpose of such literature, in Gavan Duffy's words, was "to tend the flame of national pride, which, with sincerity of purpose and fervour of soul, constitute the motive power of great enterprises." [17]

In the late eighties and the nineties, Yeats insisted more and more on the use of Irish subject matter by Irish writers. In this he may have been inspired by the principles of John O'Leary, with whom he was closely associated at this time, a man who "more clearly than any one, has seen that there is no fine nationality without literature, and seen the converse also, that there is no fine literature without nationality." [18] The choice of Irish subject matter became something like a touchstone, in Yeats's mind, for quality in literature. He continually denounced certain Irish writers because of their desire to be cosmopolitan. T. W. Rolleston, for example, "is a fine Greek scholar and quite the handsomest man in Ireland, but I wish he would devote his imagination to some national purpose. Cosmopolitan literature is, at best, but a poor bubble, though a big one. Creative work has always a fatherland." [19] In reviews, in essays, in letters, and in his conversation, Yeats came close to turning the issue into a kind of personal crusade. In a letter to his friend Katherine Tynan, for instance, he argues that Irish subjects are the only way to true originality and ultimate value in Irish literature: "Remember by being Irish as you can, you will be more original and true to yourself and in the long run more interesting, even to English readers." [20]

We must remember, however, that Yeats's vigorous defense of a national literature was primarily a product of the early nineties, and that his attitude towards the problem underwent significant change in later years. At this time, however, almost everything that Yeats wrote dealt with Irish subject matter. The exotic material of his earliest works, of *Mosada*, "Anashuya and Vijaya," or "The Indian upon God," is eliminated and replaced by a concentration on strictly Irish subjects in the years between 1888, the date of the *Fairy and Folk Tales of the Irish Peasantry*, and 1899, when the Irish Literary Theatre was founded. During these years Yeats wrote or edited *The Wanderings of Oisin, Stories from Carleton, Representative Irish Tales, The Countess Kathleen, The Land of Heart's Desire*, and *The Celtic Twilight*. The shorter poems tell the same story. Never again was Yeats so exclusively concerned with things Irish than in the collection of 1893, *The Rose*. And the variety of subjects dealt with in these books shows clearly that he was adopting his own principle that *all* within the "four seas of Ireland" was fit matter for literary endeavor.

If this situation had continued indefinitely, Yeats's interest in the hero might have had little to do with his concern for the revitalization of Ireland. But what actually happened was that he began to concentrate more and more on a single element of Irish culture, namely the ancient heroic legends and myths; it is here that his interest in the whole idea of heroism may properly be said to begin. We must, for this reason, try to understand exactly what appealed to Yeats in Irish myth. In part, this interest was stimulated by his gradual realization as a reader of plays submitted for production at the Abbey that there was suddenly an abundance of realistic dramas dealing with Irish society. It was only then that Yeats began to feel that his idea of a "national" literature had not been restrictive enough if it meant that English drawingroom comedy, for example, became acceptable as soon as some clever young writer with his eye on literary trends changed the "Trevors" to "Seans" and the "girls" to "colleens." Good literature, he said, must come "out of an imaginative recreation of national history or legend," not from the "life of the drawingroom, the life represented in most plays of the ordinary theatre of to-day" which "differs but little all over the world." [21] Yeats met this threat by limiting his interest to the particular aspects of Irish culture which seemed to him quintessential and unmatched. At this point, in the first years of this century, the idea of using the epics and epic heroes of ancient Ireland in the literature of today began to monopolize his thought.

In this way, what began as a very general interest in the nationalistic movements of late nineteenth century Ireland slowly became something more restrictive and more private. We can see the steps of this gradual process of specialization very clearly: the initial interest in the revival of Irish life in general replaced by a demand for a rebirth of Ireland's literary and cultural life, that in its turn giving way to a commitment towards one special province of Irish culture, the heroic legends and myths of the past. Yeats's part in the movement to restore this part of Ireland's heritage to her people is a significant one.

Most readers of Yeats's works know little if anything about how Irish heroic legend and myth was preserved, and indeed the whole subject is complicated enough even for the expert. Since there existed both an oral and a written tradition, and since the latter frequently consisted of many different Gaelic manuscript versions of the same tale written at different times by different bards or scribes, it is little wonder that *the* authoritative version of any particular heroic tale often simply does not exist. Although the surviving manuscript texts of the Irish sagas date from after the eighth century A.D., it is generally assumed that they are based on a long oral tradition and "probably reflect the social and political conditions of the time which they claim to describe, namely, the first century before Christ." [22] The oldest manuscripts are frequently merely collections, "miniature libraries," [23] of sagas along with many other unrelated works, lyric poems, saints' lives, and so on. In most cases, the author of any particular version is unknown, if indeed authorship is the right word for what Douglas Hyde sees as "the gradual growth of racial tribal and family history . . . stories which were ever being told and retold, and polished up, and added to, and which were—some of them—handed down for perhaps countless generations." [24]

To add to this confusion, most of these manuscripts had in fact never been published at the beginning of Yeats's career, or if they had been it was either in the original Gaelic (which Yeats did not read) or in scholarly translations designed and published for the specialist rather than the general reader. This situation, as we shall see, changed radically in the late nineteenth and early twentieth centuries. Gradually, through the work of many men, Ireland's rich literary heritage was made available to a much wider audience through the publication, translation, and adaptation of these old tales for the first time. The Irish epics, though they were nearly two thousand years old, were therefore practically new to the literary world of Yeats's time.

For Yeats, the revival of the ancient epics by translation, popularization, and adaptation was now to be the foundation of all Irish literary endeavor, including his own: "I had definite plans; I wanted to create an Irish Theatre . . . but before that there must be a popular imaginative literature." [25] He intended the myths and heroic legends to supply the basic subject matter for modern Irish literature, the stories and the characters, as the myths of Greece had done for the Greek dramatists. In the early part of his career his enthusiasm for this project matched his optimistic assurance of its eventual success. "I feel more and more," he writes as early as 1887, "that we shall have a school of Irish poetry—founded on Irish myth and history—a neo-romantic movement." [26] It would be difficult to exaggerate the importance which Yeats saw in a coherent and popular body of national myth, a single foundation which could give unity to the random special interests of a nation's individual artists. For this reason, he admired the civilization of ancient Greece even more than that of England, since the unity and simplicity of English myth had been destroyed by imports from many lands in the time of the Renaissance:

> Had there been no Renaissance and no Italian influence to bring in the stories of other lands, English history would, it may be, have become as important to the English imagination as the Greek Myths to the Greek imagination; and many plays by many poets would have woven it into a single story whose contours, vast as those of Greek myth, would have made living men and women seem like swallows building their nests under the architrave of some Temple of the Giants. English literature, because it would have grown out of itself, might have had the simplicity and unity of Greek literature, for I can never get out of my head that no man, even though he be Shakespeare, can write perfectly when his web is woven of threads that have been spun in many lands.[27]

Even more significant was the fact that Irish legend, unlike the myths of other European countries, had unusual value precisely because it was *not* well known. Here was a rare chance for freshness, for starting anew while employing elements which had the sanction of a long historical tradition. Yeats was enthralled by the idea of this untouched treasure awaiting the explorer: "In England I sometimes hear men complain that the old themes of verse and prose are used up. Here in Ireland the marble block is waiting for us almost untouched, and the statues will come as soon as we have learned to use the chisel." [28]

The enthusiasm for Irish legend recalls the Yeats who extolled the virtues of Irish subjects in general. Here again we find an insistence on the great *variety* found in what may at first strike one as excessively limited material: "There is humour and fantasy as well as miraculous poetry in our old legends, and one can find in them all kinds of meanings. . . . They are the greatest treasure the Past has handed down to us Irish people, and the most plentiful treasure of legends in Europe." [29] And this time, it is the choice of legendary subject matter which becomes the touchstone in the judgment of the literary works of one's contemporaries: "When I was first moved by Lord Dunsany's work I thought that he would more help this change if he could bring his imagination into the old Irish legendary world instead of those magic lands of his with their vague Eastern air." [30] Once again, then, what in other poets might remain a mere personal conviction with limited applicability becomes for Yeats the single proper way for the modern Irish poet to work.

Yeats's interest in Irish myth was of course only part of a much more comprehensive movement to revive the old epics. Standish O'Grady, for example, the most widely read of the early popularizers of these heroic tales, also felt that they must become part of Irish culture. He sought "to make this heroic period once again a portion of the imagination of the country, and its chief characters as familiar in the minds of our people as they once were." [31] Stephen Gwynn, an Irish literary critic of Yeats's generation, reflected on the increasing popularity of the material of the epics in the literature of the day, and understood that this demanded a new audience, equipped with the kind of knowledge of Irish mythology which the average reader of the mid-nineteenth century could not possibly have had:

The essential point about the revival is that writers of Celtic race turn increasingly for subjects to the Celtic mythology and to the history, past or present, of their own people, addressing themselves more and more to an audience presumably Celtic in sympathy, and equipped with some knowledge of Celtic history and tradition.[32]

In addition, Yeats and others insist that although Irish poets might begin with something of merely national significance, they would eventually produce a literature meaningful to the entire world. "If we can but put those tumultuous centuries into tale or drama," Yeats writes, "the whole world will listen to us and sit at our feet like children who hear a new story." [33] One also senses a kind of nostalgia, common enough among writers and critics in our own time, for a culture in which the subject matter of poetry is familiar to the people, in which the gap between writer and society is never even felt to exist. Yeats says that he "delighted in every age where poet and artist confined themselves gladly to some inherited subject matter known to the whole people." [34]

We must not lose sight of the fact that the revival of Irish legend was usually thought to be a means to more significant ends. O'Grady, for example, felt that the mighty examples of heroic action in the epics could spur patriotic achievement by establishing an ideal of national courage and a history of great deeds which might act as an antidote to the despair so prevalent in the Ireland of his time:

The Greek race performed mightier achievements than the fabled labours of Heracles or of the mountain-rending Titans. The gigantic conceptions of heroism and strength, with which the forefront of Irish history is thronged, prove the great future of this race and land, of which the mere contemplation of the actual results of time might cause even the patriot to despair.[35]

The dichotomy suggested in these words, between "the conceptions of heroism and strength" and "the actual results of time," is important for both O'Grady and Yeats. It introduces a different—and for our purposes most significant—kind of nostalgia into the literary discussion of the period, one founded on a contrast between ideal and actual. The ideal is an ideal of conduct, "heroic" in the sense that it suggests a way of life which exploits all the finest potentialities of human nature and affords a standard or gauge by which to measure the present. For both Yeats and O'Grady, the acceptance of the heroic ideal of the past went hand in hand with the rejection of the sordid vulgarity of the present. Thus the heroic world of the epic tales becomes an imaginary land of escape from the modern world. O'Grady contrasts the two worlds: "A nation's history is made for it by circumstances, and the irresistible progress of events; but their legends, they make for themselves. In that dim twilight region, where day meets night, the intellect of man, tired by contact with the vulgarity of actual things, goes back for rest and recuperation." [36] It is no wonder that Yeats still spoke of O'Grady even towards the end of his career, after they had parted company, with great respect, "his mind full of Homer," retelling the "story of Cuchulain that he might bring back an heroic ideal." [37] The ultimate goal of all of Yeats's work is not very different, and in *The King's Threshold* he suggests that it is actually the goal of all poetry:

> I said the poets hung
> Images of the life that was in Eden
> About the childbed of the world, that it,
> Looking upon those images, might bear
> Triumphant children.[38]

More specifically, the revival of Irish myth and legend might restore a sense of the dignity of heroic sacrifice to an Ireland which seemed to recognize only despair. It might recreate, as Yeats says, "the ancient simplicity and amplitude of imagination." [39]

Yeats also took the religious element of Celtic myth seriously. These are "myths," after all, only from the point of view of the sceptic; originally, they had the same kind of religious authority as the Greek "myths" had for many Greeks. That is, they were thought to express ultimate truth. Was it possible to restore this religious significance to them? Jeremiah Curtin, for example, in a book on Irish myth published in 1890, looks back to a time when belief in mythology "sanctified" the real world: "A mythology in the time of its greatest vigor puts its imprint on the whole region to which it belongs; the hills, rivers, mountains, plains, villages, trees, rocks, springs, and

plants are all made sacred. The country of the mythology becomes, in the fullest sense of the word, a 'holy land.' " [40] It
will come as no surprise to readers familiar with Yeats's life-long
search for some form of spiritual authority that he uses almost
the same words as Curtin does, not about the past, but about
the future:

> To us Irish these personages should be more important than all
> others, for they lived in the places where we ride and go
> marketing, and sometimes they have met one another on the
> hills that cast their shadows upon our doors at evening. If we
> will but tell these stories to our children the Land will begin
> again to be a Holy Land, as it was before men gave their hearts
> to Greece and Rome and Judea. [41]

How were these ancient Gaelic works to be made available
to the general reader? The first step, clearly, was to translate
them into modern English and publish them in popular editions. There was some controversy, however, on what the next
step should be, how the material could be used once it had
been made generally available. Stopford Brooke's influential
essay on the subject gives an orderly, almost methodical, plan
for the future. As soon as the modern, accurate translations
become generally known, the stories would have to be retold
in modern versions by Irish authors so that they might have
the kind of unity which the old epics, because of the confusion
of the manuscripts, simply did not have:

> Irishmen of formative genius should take, one by one, the various
> cycles of Irish tales, and grouping each of them round one
> central figure, such as Manannàn or Cuculainn or Finn, supply
> to each a dominant human interest to which every event in the
> whole should converge. . . . I want, in fact, the writers to
> recreate each cycle in his own mind into a clearly constructed
> whole, having an end to which the beginning looks forward, and
> to promote which every episode is used. [42]

After this was accomplished, complete liberty could be granted
to the lyric poet to recreate for his own purposes and without
concern for historical accuracy, selected episodes or characters
from the epics. This last step, of course, presupposes the general
availability of the legends in their expanded form, since such a

use of mythological subject matter is essentially a kind of shorthand.

Brooke's view is comprehensive and permits the greatest variety of treatment. It was not the view of all writers, however. Ironically enough, O'Grady, perhaps the man most responsible for the popularity of the modern translations and adaptations, deserted the fold at the crucial moment. He was appalled that works essentially designed for an élite had already filtered down as far as they had by 1900, and he advised Irish dramatists that the material of the legends could not be put on the stage without "banishing the soul of the land." It was the attitude of a man who has created an ideal world only to see the grubby world of reality encroach upon it. He advised Irish writers to "leave heroic cycles alone, and not to bring them down to the crowd." [43]

Despite O'Grady, however, the Irish epics quickly became a literary fashion. In 1888, the publisher Kegan Paul writes Yeats about the unpopularity of the Celtic legends and suggests that the books of John Todhunter "may help each other by drawing attention to the subject of old Celtic Romance." [44] Only two years later, Yeats can already recommend a considerable list of books to readers interested in the subject: O'Grady's *History of Ireland: The Heroic Period*, Lady Ferguson's *Ireland Before the Conquest*, and Mrs. Bryant's *Celtic Ireland*.[45] He speaks with enthusiasm of Douglas Hyde's plan, in 1892, to translate the old epics in eight or nine volumes, for when completed it would "make the old stories accessible for the first time to everybody." [46]

Naturally, the fact that such books existed did not mean that a writer could expect his readers to know the stories in them, but the eventual goal was to be able to write for "one's own people, who come to the playhouse with a knowledge of one's subjects." [47] In his first years as playwright for the Abbey, Yeats felt compelled to supply program notes to educate those still ignorant about Celtic myth. After explaining in *Beltaine*, the organ of the Irish Literary Theatre, the many references in *The Countess Kathleen* to the cycle of Oisin and Finn, to the Shee, to Cuchulain and Conchobar, Yeats apologizes by saying that it "is necessary to explain these things, as the old Irish mythology is still imperfectly known in modern Ireland." [48] And in the edition of his *Poems* published in 1895, he supplies a glossary giving the same kind of information.[49] By the end of his career, however, Yeats was not so tolerant of those who did not come equipped with knowledge of the Irish legends, since by that time they had been made easily available to all who were interested. The late play *The Death of Cuchulain* begins with a speech by the Old Man who demands that the audience of "fifty or a hundred" must "know the old epics and Mr. Yeats' plays about them; such people however poor have libraries of their own." [50] But that is only because the process of popularization had been completed long before 1939. Even by 1895, Yeats could add several important works to his list of books dealing with Irish mythology: three more books by O'Grady, P. W. Joyce's *Old Celtic Romances*, and the *Mythologie Irlandaise* by D'Arbois de Jubainville.[51]

Finally, in the first few years of the twentieth century, came the books Yeats had really wanted, Lady Gregory's version of the two basic heroic cycles of Irish legend, *Cuchulain of Muirthemne* (1902), a translation of the stories of the Red Branch Cycle, and *Gods and Fighting Men* (1904), which retold the deeds of Finn. Yeats wrote prefaces to both of these works and praised them ecstatically. Of the Cuchulain book he writes:

> I think this book is the best that has come out of Ireland in my time. Perhaps I should say that it is the best book that has ever come out of Ireland; for the stories which it tells are a chief part of Ireland's gift to the imagination of the world—and it tells them perfectly for the first time. . . . Lady Gregory has done her work of compression and selection at once so firmly and so reverently that I cannot believe that anybody, except now and then for a scientific purpose, will need another text than this.[52]

These books, "done in consultation with Mr. Yeats," [53] were to some extent tailor-made to suit Yeats's needs, so that his enthusiasm comes as no surprise. Now, instead of preparing elaborate notes to the poems and plays in their printed version, Yeats simply sends his readers to Lady Gregory:

The greater number of the stories I have used, and persons I have spoken of, are in Lady Gregory's *Gods and Fighting Men* and *Cuchulain of Muirthemne.* If my small Dublin audience for poetical drama grows to any size, whether now or at some future time, I shall owe it to these two books, masterpieces of prose. . . . I wrote for the most part before they were written, but all, or all but all, is there.[54]

Before we try to see exactly what appealed to Yeats in the ancient epic tales, a very brief summary of the main characteristics of Irish mythology will be helpful. It is first of all necessary to understand the difference between the heroic mortals and the immortals in this "system," if it can be called that, since elements of both eventually form part of Yeats's heroic ideal. As in Greek myth, there is here a race of immortals, known variously as the Shee or Sidhe, the Faery People, or the Tuatha De Danann, who live forever in Tir-na-n-Og, or the Country of the Young. Like the Greek gods, these immortals possess many of what we might call distinctly human attributes and often engage in "human" activities. As a result, the descriptions of the faery world are not vague and "mythical." "There was nothing illusive," Brooke assures us, "nothing merely imaginary, in these faery worlds for the Irish hero or the Irish people. They believed the lands to be as real as their own, and the indwellers of fairyland to have like passions with themselves." [55]

In fact, the Country of the Young was very much like the mortal world in every respect except that it was relieved of the *sorrows* of a worldly existence. Douglas Hyde has suggested that Heraclitus' summary of Greek mythology, that men were "mortal gods" and gods "immortal men" applies just as well to Irish myth.[56] Since sorrow was connected most particularly with death and growing old in Irish legend, the Shee were eternally young, and eternally joyous. In this land no puritanical restrictions on conduct exist; it is a land of freedom. "Our lives have known no law nor rule," as Yeats's Oisin puts it; the joys of Tir-na-n-Og, he tells us, are hunting, fishing, "wassails" and love.[57] The Shee were never really thought of as gods, however, for they were neither worshiped nor served by sacrifice.[58] Nevertheless, they do have supernatural powers and often take pleasure in interfering in human affairs, sometimes by transporting mortals to their own world, as in Yeats's play *The Land of Heart's Desire*. They are not above a good practical joke, but neither are they always playful, since they take their jobs as patrons of great warriors rather seriously, again like their Greek counterparts.

Yeats was attracted to Irish myth because of the connection between poetic material and popular belief, but it is possible that he exaggerated the popularity of such belief even among the peasants. There were enough people in Ireland who examined the Celtic revival with a sceptical eye. An anonymous correspondent to the *All Ireland Review*, for example, writes sarcastically in 1900:

> I notice your reference to your contemplated or quasi-contemplated intention to ride on the Fairy Wave of sentiment that seems to you to have come over our Irish writers. Good poetry may of course find Fairyism a fitting material to work on, but I fear much of the so-called Fairy Poetry, Celtic glamour, and the rest, is the merest affectation. . . . Strange that when the peasant has ceased to believe in Fairies public writers should pretend to believe in them.[59]

And Synge, in a poem called "The Passing of the Shee," joyfully renounces the Faery kingdom for the no-nonsense energy of the modern flesh and blood Irishman:

> Adieu sweet Angus, Maeve and Fand,
> Ye plumed yet skinny Shee
> That poets played with hand in hand
> To learn their ecstasy.
>
> We'll stretch in Red Dan Sally's ditch
> And drink in Tubber Fair
> Or poach with Red Dan Philly's bitch
> The badger and the hare.[60]

But such sceptical attacks did not seem to diminish Yeats's enthusiasm.

The country of the Shee, then, is the true paradise where all wishes are fulfilled, where "there is neither sickness nor age nor death; where happiness lasts forever and there is no satiety; where food and drink do not diminish when consumed; where to wish for something is to possess it; where a hundred years

are as one day." [61] Their country does not know evil, for they
are, as Jubainville writes, "the most exalted representatives of
one of the two principles that divide the world . . . day, life,
knowledge, goodness." [62] The other principle, "Death, night,
ignorance, evil," is the mortal realm. This is a significant point
for Yeats's conception of heroic tragedy. His tragedies do not
deal, like those written within a predominantly Christian framework, with the conflict between good and evil. Rather they substitute for the Christian idea of transcendental evil in the
universe the worldly "evil" of death, which is not transcen-
dentally conceived. It is interesting that old age and death are
also the equivalent of evil in Yeatsian tragedy, which ends in a
kind of victory if the hero triumphs over the "evil" of death
and the despair which it brings. When the hero is successful,
he approaches the condition of this "land of perpetual youth,
where they live a life of joy and beauty," [63] the Country of the
Young. His emotion will be what Yeats's Oisin tells us is the
central emotion of Tir-na-n-Og, that of joy and exultation.[64]

There is, however, a sharp distinction between the human
heroic figures of the epics and the immortal Shee, despite the
important relationship which exists between them. Since Yeats
was more interested in the achievements and personality of
the mortal hero, some understanding of this relationship, and
of the character of the hero, is desirable. According to one story,
Cuchulain himself was descended from a god, Lug of the Long
Arm, who still interfered in his behalf at difficult moments in
battle. Again as in the Greek epics, the heroic mortals are often
the favorites of certain gods and receive supernatural aid from
them in time of great need. The famous battle between
Cuchulain and Ferdiad in the *Táin* is a case in point, since
Cuchulain could never have won it without divine help.[65]
Nevertheless, it is indicative of the extremely tenuous relationship between man and god in Irish legend that Cuchulain's birth
is really a matter of controversy, one legend affirming the descent
from Lug the sun-god, the other suggesting that he was the
son of King Sualtam, a mortal. In *On Baile's Strand*, Yeats permits his Cuchulain to affirm the former lineage: "For he that's
in the sun begot this body / Upon a mortal woman." [66]

Such high descent reinforces the godlike qualities of the

hero. But those qualities achieve significance only when it is understood that the hero is basically human, and that his achievements match those of the gods *despite* his mere humanity. Whoever Cuchulain's father was, his mother remains a mortal, and so does he. Otherwise his strength, his courage, his feats, would not be extraordinary. It is only because he is ultimately vulnerable, capable of fatigue and despair, and subject to death that his actions achieve epic proportions. Yeats is anxious to preserve this human quality; he explains that in the Red Branch cycle which is the ultimate source of his plays and poems about Cuchulain, "the supernatural world sinks farther away. Although the gods come to Cuchulain, and although he is the son of one of the greatest of them, their country and his are far apart and they come to him as god to mortal." [67]

The inevitable comparison between the Irish and the Greek epic helps to answer the question of just how human the Irish hero is. Certainly when compared to Achilles, Cuchulain seems less human, closer to his divine father. As Alfred Nutt says:

> It may confidently be urged that Cuchulainn belongs to an earlier, more primitive stage of saga evolution than does Achilles. In the *Iliad*, despite the prominence of the supernatural element, the original myth has been heroicised, suited to human conditions, set within the limits of a historic framework, and thereby compressed, modified, run into new forms, more than is the case with the Cuchulainn stories.[68]

It is true that the heroes of Greek legend are in general more recognizable as human beings. Their capacities are more clearly simple exaggerations of the powers of ordinary men. The difference is one of degree rather than of kind. Most important, perhaps, is that they are subject to all the human weaknesses: rage, jealousy, despair, stubbornness, love. It is important to remember, however, that part of the difference between Greek and Irish myth is accounted for by the fact that the latter survives primarily in the form of heroic epics, while the popular conception of the Greek heroes, with the exception of the Homeric ones, comes to us from the drama, where the exigencies of stage representation necessarily bring things down to a more strictly human level. At the same time, the use made of the Irish legends in the twentieth century is not radically different from the methods used by the dramatists of Periclean Athens. Yeats, Synge, and others also made use of the old heroic stories in their plays and were forced to present a more recognizably human picture than their sources provided. In addition, half of their work had already been done by such popularizers as Lady Gregory, who removed a number of grotesque and exaggerated details from the originals in rewriting for an Irish audience trained in the techniques of realistic fiction and drama. It is reasonable to suggest, therefore, that modern Irish writers concerned with the epic heroes were completing a process which John Eglinton claimed never reached fruition in earlier times:

> It is plain . . . to any one who has read such a creation as the Tain bo Cuailgne, that this race was on the verge of a great poetic literature; that the Irish bards came very near to setting up in Cuchullin a commanding type of the universal world-hero. As yet he is in process of formation from the mythological stage; sun, air, and earth are in a whirl to produce him; and he does not stand finally incarnated on the soil of Ireland as a human personality, taking upon himself the common lot of man . . . . A great inheritance surely awaited some Irish Vyasa or Homeros, who should have pruned this luxuriance of marvels and shown "the one favourite of Erinn's poets" in all the sweet humanity which appears in his combat with Ferdia or at his last battle of Muirthemne.[69]

Yeats was certainly interested in retaining an essentially human status for his heroes. Particularly in plays like *On Baile's Strand* and *Deirdre*, there is a deliberate attempt to recreate the effect of Greek tragedy by depicting the fall of great human beings capable of sorrow, suffering, and remorse. Nevertheless, it would be inaccurate to suggest that this humanizing process ever went as far in Yeats's poetry or drama as it could go, or even as far as it had gone in the drama of Greece. Yeats was too interested in emphasizing the distinction between his heroic mortals and the common run of humanity to risk going too far in the direction of the merely human. As a result, his plays do not create a situation in which the audience identifies with the hero, but one in which he is to be regarded with admiration, in which the relationship between audience and hero, if it is successfully established at all, becomes one of awe rather than sympathy. The loss as well as the gain in making such a choice is obvious enough. It was a conscious one, however, and it seems unlikely that Yeats regretted his decision.

What distinctive qualities of the Irish epics particularly appealed to Yeats? In the first place, they presented a picture of a hierarchical society ruled by kings, a world whose simplicity of organization emphasized both the sharp distinction between noble, freeman, and slave and the unity created by their mutual interdependence. It is difficult to say whether Yeats admired the epics because they gave a picture of this ideal world, or whether he eventually formed the ideal from what began as a more strictly literary appreciation of the cycles. No doubt the process worked both ways and one taste reinforced the other, but it would be hard to overemphasize the importance of his interest in Irish myth for the ideal of heroism which was beginning to take shape in his mind. In the epics, a sharp distinction between nobility and ordinary humanity is firmly maintained, although there are a number of ways to be "noble." One rightly thinks first of the warrior, isolated in the tradition of single combat, and certainly prowess in battle was the most common of the noble qualities. But there were others: wealth, distinguished ancestry, and learning all separated the great men from the "churls." In addition, it is not difficult to understand why a poet of the twentieth century should admire a society in which the bard was "in the place of honour higher than the warrior," [70] respected by all around him and accepted as a vital, indispensable part of the culture to which he belonged.

For Yeats, the most appealing quality of this world was its emphasis on the power of the solitary individual, its concentratration on the uniqueness possible in a society, unlike that of the modern city, in which people, events, and institutions are recognized as unique. The artist concerned with great men naturally longs for such a world. J. B. Yeats once wrote to his son that "In these days social man is well represented. He has invaded us and occupies all the positions and captured the poets. In this congested city we sleep, as it were, fifteen in a bed. Art is solitary man." [71] And no doubt his son would have agreed with him, for, like O'Grady, he saw modern times as a falling off, a shabby substitute for the heroic world that he connected with Eden and the Golden Age of Hesiod.

In Yeats's later life, two other aspects of Irish legend began to appeal to him more and more. There was, first of all, a kind of powerful barbarism in these tales. Readers familiar with Yeats's later poetry will easily see the connection with the constant praise one finds there of violence, primitive energy, and conflict. Yeats was interested not in violence for its own sake, but rather in the fruits of violence, since he believed that the great man is tested and purified by the barbarism which he encounters and in part creates. The old epics constantly supplied the opportunity for such heroic tests; in them the hero is put on trial at every battle and his glory is always new. This gives him something akin to perpetual youth in a world where youth is the greatest good. As Stopford Brooke has put it:

> This mingling of the beauty of youth and the honour of ancientry runs through all the Irish tales. Youth and the love of it, of its beauty and strength, adorn and vitalize their grey antiquity. But where, in their narrative, the hero's youth is over and the sword weak in his hand, and the passion less in his and his sweetheart's blood, life is represented as scarcely worth the living. The famed men and women die young—the sons of Turenn, Cuchulain, Conall, Dermot, Emer, Deirdre, Naisi, Oscar. Oisín has three hundred years of youth in that far land in the invention of which the Irish embodied their admiration of love and youth. His old age, when sudden feebleness overwhelms him, is made by the bardic clan as miserable, as desolate as his youth was joyous.[72]

One of the most important appeals of Irish myth for Yeats was purely literary. He fought all his life for the kind of writing which could employ excess and exaggeration, and was in fact expected to do so as a matter of course. He tried to create a literature with the freedom for imaginative invention which he felt was denied to the realist by the necessities which his subject matter imposed. Here, in the Irish epics, was an art which was not controlled by an ideal of verisimilitude, in which the artist was not reflector but creator. The warriors in these tales constantly perform feats which no ordinary mortal could perform; events and persons are not treated realistically: Cuchulain, in the *Táin Bó Cúalnge*, for example, is described as having several pupils in each eye. Such exaggeration, often approaching the grotesque, appealed particularly to the Yeats who delighted in sounding a kind of perpetual death knell for the realists, and who welcomed a literature "so heightened as to transcend any form of real life." [73]

The "heightening of reality" which Yeats found in the epic world is carried over into his own work when he appropriates the Irish heroes. But where the exaggeration of the epics is frequently physical, his concentrates on internal qualities. There is an interesting contrast here between Yeats and Standish O'Grady, for O'Grady's treatment of these stories often reflects his nostalgia for a world of physical perfection and leads him to write passages of rapturous description which almost invite parody, if indeed they require it:

> As in some bright young dawn, over the dewy grass, and in the light of the rising sun, superhuman in size and beauty, their long, yellow hair curling on their shoulders, bound around the temples with torcs of gold, clad in white linen tunics, and loose brattas of crimson silk fastened on the breast with huge wheel brooches of gold, their long spears musical with running rings; with naked knees and bare crown, they cluster around their kings, the chieftains and knights of the heroic age of Ireland.[74]

Yeats occasionally comes close to such rhapsodic evocation of heroic beauty. He tells the story of an old peasant woman who saw a vision of Queen Maeve and comments, "This old woman, who can neither read nor write, has come face to face with heroic beauty, that 'highest beauty,' which Blake says, 'changes least from youth to age,' a beauty that has been fading out of the arts, since that decadence, we call progress, set voluptuous beauty in its place." [75] And sometimes Yeats like O'Grady uses the idea of this heroic physical perfection to stress the contrast with the world of the present, as in the poem "The Grey Rock":

> We should be dazed and terror-struck,
> If we but saw in dreams that room,
> Those wine-drenched eyes, and curse our luck
> That emptied all our days to come.
> I knew a woman none could please,
> Because she dreamed when but a child
> Of men and women made like these.[76]

In general, however, Yeats had little interest in the physical characteristics of the epic heroes, and concentrated on the qualities of mind and spirit which make a hero. There are few important distinctions between the heroic virtues as Yeats saw them and the heroic virtues in the Irish epics. The question of how much the reading of the epics influenced his thought is difficult to establish, since so many of the writers he was interested in between 1890 and 1910—Blake, Nietzsche, Castiglione, and others—wrote in praise of some of the same qualities of the human personality. However, the parallels do exist and are important, for both the epics and Yeats's plays and poems stress certain central aspects of the heroic ideal: generosity and courtesy, courage and leadership, worldliness and vision.

1. *The aristocratic virtues: generosity and courtesy.* Generosity and courtesy are the traits of the aristocratic hero. The truly great man is bountiful and gives to all who are deserving. In the Irish myths, there is almost a kind of competition in giving, related, of course, to the feudal organization of society which makes the vassal dependent on the generosity of his lord for survival. Cuchulain, for example, boasts "I have never yet been reviled because of my niggardliness or my churlishness." [77] And Maeve, in the *Táin Bó Cúalnge*, is horrified at the prospect of an avaricious husband, for "we were ill-matched together, inasmuch as I am great in largess and gift-giving." [78] Caeilte tells the King of Ulidia of the overwhelming generosity of Finn's men:

> "For knowest thou . . . the four that of all such as in Ireland and in Scotland lived at the one time and in the same epoch with them excelled in generosity: Finn mac Cumall and Ossian his son, and Dubh son of Treon of the Ulidians here, with his son Fial mac Dubh? In which two latter was even a degree of bountifulness in excess of the others; for though all that was in Ireland and in Scotland had been bestowed on them yet, had they but found one to crave it of them, they would have given away the whole of it." [79]

Yeats translates this virtue into a kind of modern noblesse oblige by insisting that the hero be generous toward his inferiors, not only in giving them worldly goods, but in treating them with charity and respect,[80] as his Countess Kathleen does, for example. In the epics, this virtue remains more a form of generosity to equals, like Cuchulain's bounteous gifts to Fergus.[81]

The aristocratic courtesy of the Irish heroes especially

pleased Yeats. The scenes of combat in the epics are full of a
ceremonial ritual common in a society which makes fighting
the duty of the highest class. The first rule restricted combat to
armed equals. "Fear nothing; I will not slay thee at all, boy,"
says Cuchulain; "for I slay nor charioteers nor horseboys nor
persons unarmed." [82] The Irish warriors usually swear an oath
never to attack weaker men.[83] Yeats, in defending the virtue of
courtesy, suggests something more akin to courtliness as a quality
of the epic world: "If we understand by courtesy not merely
the gentleness the story-tellers have celebrated, but a delight
in courtly things, in beautiful clothing and in beautiful verse,
one understands that it was no formal succession of trials that
bound the Fianna to one another." [84] The story of Finn and his
men, he says, "is full of fellowship . . . made noble by a
courtesy that has gone perhaps out of the world." [85]

2. *The public virtues: courage and leadership.* Courage and
leadership are, of course, the most traditional heroic virtues
in any civilization. In Irish mythology they are exaggerated,
Cuchulain defending Ulster, for example, against an entire army
single-handed. In the epics, such mass slaughter often suggests
that there is a basic savagery at the root of the hero's valor,
which gives him much of his passion and fierceness. There is
also a kind of stubbornness in his brand of courage. Maeve, for
example, accepts but pays little attention to the prophecy of
her defeat in the cattle-raid. Fear, she says, will never affect her
resolution.[86] The hero of the epics often seems to squander the
gift of life carelessly. He expects and welcomes death and prepares himself for it in a ritualistic way. In "Cuchulainn's
Death," for instance, the hero "drank his drink, and washed
himself, and came forth to die, calling to his foes to come to
meet him." [87] Yeats gives us a more familiar picture of the
virtue of courage, which differentiates it from the fearlessness in
the epics that makes a man throw himself into battle, alone
against several hundred enemies. His play *Deirdre*, for example,
presents a deliberate contrast between the reckless courage of
the royal characters and the more prudential, commonsense, but
nevertheless cowardly morality of the common people, it is true.
But the courage is of a quiet kind, for as Deirdre and Naoise
await their inevitable death, they abandon all passion, all frenzy,

all fear and sit down to a game of chess. In the Irish epics, the warrior-hero is also generally the leader of his people in times of peace, and this too appealed to Yeats, for he had little sympathy with the modern separation of leadership into military and bureaucratic spheres.

3. *The spiritual virtues: worldliness and vision.* The heroes of the Irish epics are not ascetics. They enjoy eating, drinking, and making love; "for there never was a time," as Maeve says, "that I had not my paramour." [88] They fight not for heavenly rewards but for earthly immortality and worldly renown: "Little it recks me, though I should be but one day and one night in the world," cries Cuchulain, "if only the fame of me and of my deeds live after me!" [89] In Yeats's modern versions of these tales, the worldly quality is retained: "that amorous, violent man" [90] one of his characters calls Cuchulain, whose list of mistresses is long. But the Irish hero was not worldly at the expense of a spiritual life, and it is precisely his combination of worldliness with the capacity for visionary experience which must have pleased Yeats. For although these men and women are not ascetics, he says, "they are more visionary than any ascetic." This is possible because they are so close to the gods themselves that "their invisible life is but the life about them made more perfect and more lasting, and the invisible people are their own images in the water." [91] In the Ulster cycle particularly, according to Myles Dillon, "Magic is still potent, and gods interfere in the affairs of men." [92] Christianity, which stresses the Augustinian separation between worldliness and vision, could not provide Yeats with the kind of world view for which he longed, one which held both of these seemingly opposite attributes in a harmonious balance. In Yeats's works, as in the Irish myths on which he drew, Cuchulain could seek both worldly renown and the kind of spiritual insight which he strives for in Yeats's play *At the Hawk's Well* without apparent contradiction.

These three sets of heroic attributes, it will be seen, are really the qualities of personality which Yeats emphasized in his three heroic specialists, aristocrat, public hero, and visionary, and they will be discussed in detail in the next three chapters. At this point, however, it is important to emphasize once again that what appealed most to Yeats in the Irish epics was simply that all of these qualities of mind and spirit could be found together in the typical epic hero. There is no need in that world to sacrifice one kind of nobility for another nor to specialize in one kind of heroic action. In "The Second Battle of Moytura," for instance, Lugh announces himself as (among other things) a wright, a smith, a champion, a harper, a hero, a poet and historian, and a sorcerer, and the doorkeeper presents him to the King as "the man of each and every art." [93] In the world of the Irish epics, the aristocrat, the public hero, and the visionary are one.

Yeats never abandoned his vision of the perfection of this world, but as he grew older, his doubts about the efficacy of the attempt to recreate it in the literature of the present seemed more and more difficult to ignore. These doubts did not seriously affect him before the First World War, however. At the beginning of his career, he was anxious to write a modern version of the heroic tales in the form of a cycle which would eventually be unified by its common subject matter. In 1897 he already speaks of his "long-cherished project—a poetical version of the great Celtic epic tale, Deirdre, Cuchullin at the Ford, and Cuchullin's death, and Dermot and Grainne." [94] Four years later he writes to Sturge Moore that his new play on Cuchulain "is part of a greater scheme," that he is "doing all the chief stories of the first heroic age in Ireland in a series of poems." [95] And after a period of discouragement, Yeats writes to Quinn as late as 1915 that "All my mythological people have come alive again and I want to complete my heroic cycle." [96]

In a sense, of course, this cycle was completed with the publication in 1939 of *The Death of Cuchulain*. By that time, Yeats had used the incidents which interested him in the life of Cuchulain and added to them the stories of Deirdre, Oisin, Maeve and others. He had spent a major portion of his literary career in fulfilling the promise to "Sing of old Eire and the ancient ways." [97] The Celtic tales were now almost universally available in good and accurate translations, partly through his own efforts.[98] Yet Yeats must somehow have felt, in surveying the literary scene which he had helped to create, that his deeper hopes had not really been fulfilled. It is true that the legends were now at last being used in modern literary works. But like most things which suddenly become fashionable, the vogue had lost the freshness and promise which Yeats had hoped to retain. Even more important, the popularity of Irish legend had not fulfilled the ambitious dreams of its initiators: it had not created the unified Irish culture envisioned by Yeats in his early years. If there had indeed been a renaissance of Irish myth, it was really only a fashion, a movement which concentrated on surfaces. In 1914, Yeats attacked this superficial debasement of the material of the epics in the scornful poem from *Responsibilities*, "A Coat":

> I made my song a coat
> Covered with embroideries
> Out of old mythologies
> From heel to throat;
> But the fools caught it,
> Wore it in the world's eyes
> As though they'd wrought it.
> Song, let them take it,
> For there's more enterprise
> In walking naked.[99]

This poem records a disillusionment not so much with the epics as the specific subject matter of modern Irish poetry, but with the whole idea of specifying the subject matter of any literature. Great plays and poems are written—even in Ireland— by great artists, and their choice of subject matter, of plot and characters, is in a sense the most superficial choice they make. At the same time, Yeats became disillusioned with the possibility of synthetically creating a national culture unified by an ideal borrowed from its past. How differently the new state had in fact turned out! As the Irish historian Mansergh says,

> Yeats's romantic conception of Irish nationality left him in mind and in sympathy divorced from the makers of the new Ireland. His ideal of an aristocratic intellectual liberal state was indeed repellent to and repelled by the new conception of a Gaelic-Catholic country with its Puritan outlook and its Censorship Act.[100]

In his later poetry Yeats often ridicules his former optimistic hopes for the future glory of Ireland:

> We pieced our thoughts into philosophy,
> And planned to bring the world under a rule,
> Who are but weasels fighting in a hole.[101]

The time had indeed come to learn "that we were crack-pated
when we dreamed." [102] But this lesson did not force Yeats to
abandon the use of Irish mythology in his own work. Rather, it
at last made him aware that the real importance of his Irish
heroes was what they had come to mean to him. He continued
to write plays and poems based on Irish myth after World
War I, but they were not essentially different from those which
used the "myths" of other cultures, Hellenic, or Christian, or
Eastern. Consequently, Yeats's heroic cycle is a cycle only in
the most superficial sense of the word. Its unity can be seen
only when viewed as part of Yeats's whole production. If we
examine the works based only on the Cuchulain legend, for
example, the result seems to be fragmentary and episodic.
Everything in these poems and plays does not point to one
simple and unified conception of Cuchulain. Nor is it surprising
that this is so, since these works display a variety of styles
representing many periods and interests in Yeats's own long life.
The more important unity of Yeats's heroic works is one of
theme rather than source, and the themes which interested him in
his later life were no longer restricted to what might be found
within "the four seas of Ireland." The gradual universalization
of what may be called Yeats's parochial interest in Irish mythology is best revealed in a casual footnote which he adds to
his essay "The Celtic Element in Literature" when it is reprinted in 1924. The passage in the original 1903 edition reads,
"I will put this differently and say that literature dwindles to
a mere chronicle of circumstance, or passionless phantasies, and
passionless meditations, unless it is constantly flooded with the
passions and beliefs of ancient times." But in the note written
in 1924, Yeats re-examines this premise: "I should have added
as an alternative that the supernatural may at any moment
create new myths, but I was timid." [103]

Such new myths had as much validity as their more traditional counterparts in Yeats's new scheme. Gradually his vision
expanded until it included not only the myths of other civilizations, but the "myths" which the great writer could himself

create, for he saw now that mythopoeia could accomplish the ultimate goals of the poet or dramatist as effectively as the exploitation of accepted myth. The test of the true writer was his ability to give to the personages he invented as much significance, universality, and moment as the more familiar figures possessed. What Yeats saw earlier in the heroes of Irish mythology, he now understood, was available not only in the legends of other cultures, but in those characters which began only with the personal significance which the poet attached to them. Crazy Jane, Robert Gregory, Parnell—all could eventually achieve the same kind of literary and even cultural importance, could exemplify the same ideals of conduct, as those with a more traditional mythological sanction.

It thus becomes more and more difficult, in Yeats's later work, to isolate the Irish hero from the many heroic characters derived from other sources. Once the world of the Irish epics was fully absorbed in Yeats's mind, it was not surprising that its limits were no longer quite so rigidly defined, nor that its heroic personages began to seem similar in important ways to figures from very different worlds. The society and the heroes of the Irish epics were of the greatest importance for the development of Yeats's idea of the heroic personality, most particularly because he saw in this world a unity which seemed to be missing from his own. Yet the noble qualities which these Irish heroes demonstrated—their generosity and courtesy, their courage and leadership, their worldliness and vision—were after all only human qualities, however rarely encountered in ordinary life. That is, they could easily be revealed in the actions of men of any country and of any age. The heroic ideal which began so distinctly in Yeats's mind as an answer to the problem of creating an Irish national culture which was, in a sense, at first only a by-product of this larger purpose, soon expanded to become more important than the original purpose itself. Heroism, in short, became a universal rather than a national set of ideals. It therefore seems more accurate to examine Yeats's heroic ethic as a series of separate though related qualities of mind, without dividing the representatives of these attributes into "Irish" and "non-Irish." For Yeats's poetic and dramatic personages can be understood best as examples of certain characteristic "heroic specialists" who demonstrate relatively fixed heroic virtues. The remainder of this study will concentrate, then, on the three most important of these exemplary types— the aristocrat, the public hero, and the visionary—in an attempt to clarify the qualities of mind which together make up the Yeatsian heroic ideal.

Notes

1. David Daiches, *Poetry and the Modern World* (Chicago, 1948), p. 134.
2. P. S. O'Hegarty, *A History of Ireland under the Union, 1801 to 1922* (London, 1952), p. 326.
3. *Ibid.*, p. 376.
4. Quoted in *ibid.*, p. 406.
5. Yeats, *The Arrow*, No. I, p. 2.
6. P. H. Pearse, *Three Lectures on Gaelic Topics* (Dublin, 1898), pp. 48–49.
7. Lady Gregory, *Gods and Fighting Men* (London, 1905), dedication page.
8. Stopford A. Brooke, *The Need and Use of Getting Irish Literature into the English Tongue* (London, 1893), pp. 19–20.
9. *The Revival of Irish Literature*, ed. Sir Charles Gavan Duffy et al. (London, 1894), p. 121.
10. Thomas Davis founded the organ of the Young Ireland group, *The Nation*, and contributed patriotic lyrics to it.
11. John Eglinton, *Bards and Saints* (Dublin, 1906), p. 43.
12. Yeats, *The Trembling of the Veil*, p. 87.
13. *Variorum*, p. 137.
14. Yeats, "The Irish Dramatic Movement," *Les Prix Nobel en 1923* (Stockholm, 1924), pp. 10–11.
15. Eglinton, *Bards and Saints*, p. 7.
16. Yeats, *Representative Irish Tales* (New York, 1891), p. 16.
17. *The Revival of Irish Literature*, p. 59.
18. Yeats, *Letters to the New Island*, ed. Horace Reynolds (Cambridge, Mass., 1934), pp. 75–76.
19. *Ibid.*, p. 74.
20. W. B. *Yeats Letters to Katharine Tynan*, ed. Roger McHugh (Dublin and London, 1953), p. 38.
21. Yeats, *The Arrow*, No. I, p. 1.
22. Myles Dillon, *Early Irish Literature* (Chicago, 1948), p. xii.
23. *Ibid.*, p. xvii.
24. Douglas Hyde, *The Story of Early Gaelic Literature* (London, 1895), p. 58.
25. Yeats, *The Trembling of the Veil*, p. 84.
26. W. B. *Yeats Letters to Katharine Tynan*, p. 26.
27. Yeats, *Essays*, pp. 133–34.
28. Yeats, *Letters to the New Island*, pp. 158–59.
29. *The Letters of W. B. Yeats*, p. 308.

30. *Selections from the Writings of Lord Dunsany*, ed. W. B. Yeats (Churchtown, Dundrum, 1912), Introduction, Sec. iii.

31. Standish O'Grady, *Early Bardic Literature, Ireland* (London, 1879), p. 17.

32. Stephen Gwynn, *Today and Tomorrow in Ireland* (Dublin and London, 1903), p. 37.

33. Yeats, *Letters to the New Island*, p. 159.

34. Yeats, *Four Years*, p. 84.

35. Standish O'Grady, *Selected Essays and Passages* (Dublin, Cork, and Belfast, n.d.), p. 43.

36. *Ibid.*, p. 27.

37. Yeats, *Wheels and Butterflies* (London, 1934), p. 70.

38. Yeats, *The King's Threshold* (Dublin, 1905), p. 20.

39. Yeats, *The Celtic Twilight* (New York, 1894), p. 6.

40. Jeremiah Curtin, *Myths and Folk-Lore of Ireland* (Boston, 1890), p. 12.

41. Yeats, Preface to Lady Gregory, *Cuchulain of Muirthemne* (London, 1902), p. xvii.

42. Brooke, *The Need and Use of Getting Irish Literature into the English Tongue*, pp. 30–32.

43. Quoted in *Samhain*, No. 2 (Dublin, 1902), p. 5.

44. *W. B. Yeats Letters to Katharine Tynan*, p. 48.

45. Yeats, *Letters to the New Island*, p. 107.

46. *Some Letters from W. B. Yeats to John O'Leary and His Sister*, ed. Allan Wade (New York, 1953), p. 12.

47. *The Letters of W. B. Yeats*, p. 406.

48. *First Annual Volume of Beltaine*, ed. W. B. Yeats, No. 1 (London, 1899–1900), p. 9.

49. Yeats, *Poems* (London, 1895), pp. 281–86.

50. Yeats, *Last Poems and Two Plays* (Dublin, 1939), p. 32.

51. *The Letters of W. B. Yeats*, p. 247.

52. Gregory, *Cuchulain of Muirthemne*, pp. vii–viii.

53. Gwynn, *Today and Tomorrow in Ireland*, p. 47.

54. Yeats, *The King's Threshold. On Baile's Strand. Deirdre. Shadowy Waters.* (Stratford-on-Avon, 1908), p. 254.

55. Stopford A. Brooke, Introduction to T. W. Rolleston, *The High Deeds of Finn* (London, 1910), p. xxxix.

56. Douglas Hyde, *A Literary History of Ireland* (London, 1906), p. 79.

57. Yeats, *The Wanderings of Oisin* (London, 1889), pp. 15–16.

58. Dillon, p. 52.

59. *All Ireland Review*, I, 3 (No. 42, October 20, 1900).

60. *The Works of John M. Synge* (Dublin, 1910), II, 215.

61. Dillon, p. 101.

62. H. D'Arbois de Jubainville, *The Irish Mythological Cycle* (Dublin, 1903), p. 79.

63. Lady Wilde, *Ancient Legends, Mystic Charms, and Superstitions of Ireland* (Boston, 1888), p. 256.

64. Yeats, *The Wanderings of Oisin*, p. 13.

65. Joseph Dunn, *The Ancient Irish Epic Tale Táin Bó Cúalnge* (London, 1914), pp. 255 and 264.

66. Yeats, *In the Seven Woods* (Dundrum, 1903), p. 47.

67. Yeats, Introduction to Gregory, *Gods and Fighting Men*, p. xii.

The mortality of the heroes of Irish legend is emphasized in Irving D. Suss's "Yeatsian Drama and the Dying Hero," *South Atlantic Quarterly,* LIV (1955), 369–80.

68. Alfred Nutt, *Cuchulainn, The Irish Achilles* (London, 1900), p. 38.
69. John Eglinton, *Pebbles from a Brook* (Dublin, 1901), p. 26.
70. Sophie Bryant, *Celtic Ireland* (London, 1889), pp. x–xi.
71. J. B. Yeats, *Letters to His Son W. B. Yeats and Others* (London, 1944), p. 194.
72. Brooke, Introduction to *The High Deeds of Finn,* p. liii.
73. Yeats, *The Arrow,* No. I, p. 1.
74. O'Grady, *Selected Essays and Passages,* p. 26.
75. *First Annual Volume of Beltaine,* No. 2, p. 17.
76. *Variorum,* p. 272.
77. Whitley Stokes, trans., "Cuchulainn's Death," *Revue Celtique,* III (1876–1878), 178.
78. Dunn, pp. 2–3.
79. O'Grady, *Silva Gadelica,* II, pp. 185–86.
80. One of Yeats's marginal comments in his edition of Nietzsche (discussed in chapter 1) is particularly revealing. Nietzsche says "one has only obligations to one's equals." Yeats underlines part of this statement and then writes in the margin: "Yes but the necessity of giving remains. When the old heroes praise one another they say 'he never refused any man.' "
81. Dunn, p. 118.
82. *Ibid.,* p. 83.
83. Whitley Stokes, trans., "The Training of Cuchulain," *Revue Celtique,* XXIX (1908), 141.
84. Yeats, Introduction to Gregory, *Gods and Fighting Men,* p. xvi.
85. *Ibid.,* p. xvii.
86. Dunn, p. 17.
87. Stokes, "Cuchulainn's Death," p. 181.
88. Dunn, p. 2.
89. *Ibid.,* p. 62.
90. Yeats, "The Only Jealousy of Emer," *Two Plays for Dancers* (Dublin, 1919), p. 19.
91. Yeats, Introduction to Gregory, *Gods and Fighting Men,* p. xviii.
92. Dillon, p. 3.
93. Whitley Stokes, trans., "The Second Battle of Moytura," *Revue Celtique,* XII (1891), 79.
94. *The Letters of W. B. Yeats,* p. 280.
95. *W. B. Yeats and T. Sturge Moore: Their Correspondence 1901–1937,* ed. Ursula Bridge (London, 1953), p. 2.
96. *The Letters of W. B. Yeats,* p. 595.
97. "To the Rose upon the Rood of Time," *Variorum,* p. 101.
98. Brooke, Introduction to *The High Deeds of Finn,* p. xvii.
99. *Variorum,* p. 320.
100. Nicholas Mansergh, *Ireland in the Age of Reform and Revolution* (London, 1940), p. 221.
101. "Nineteen Hundred and Nineteen," *Variorum,* p. 429.
102. *Ibid.,* p. 431.
103. Yeats, *Essays,* p. 228 n.

3 · The Aristocrat

If we would create a great community—and what
other game is so worth the labour—we must recreate the old foundations of life.

W. B. YEATS

FEW WORDS came as readily to Yeats's mind as the word "aristocracy." If we are to understand the ideal of heroism in his work,
we must first try to clarify both the meaning of this word as he
used it and the particular importance which he gave to the
whole idea of aristocratic society. The Greek roots of "aristocracy" deceive us by suggesting a false simplicity. Etymologically,
the word means "the rule of the best," but if we are interested
in Yeats's use of it, we must try to see who "the best" are in his
eyes, and in what sense they may be said to "rule." The question
is further complicated by the various and often contradictory
ways in which the word is ordinarily used: in political, social, and
cultural contexts; to suggest certain kinds of breeding, education, power, leisure, and ancestry; to stand for wealth or (these
days) the lack of it. Yet despite all these sources of confusion,
Yeats's aristocrat, the first man in his heroic triumvirate, is
clearly and consistently delineated in his own work.

Yeats differentiated the aristocrat from the other "exceptional individuals" in his gallery by suggesting first that he is
always part of a small group, a group of his own kind. He is not
the solitary heroic man, independent, aloof, working out a private salvation without the need to consider other people. Like
the other heroes, he lives by a kind of code; but the aristocrat's
code is primarily a social one, outlining the way of life of a small,
nearly discrete community and suggesting the desirable relationship between that group and the rest of the world. In general,
the distinction between the *one* and the many (the heroic code)

is clearer and less ambiguous than that between the *few* and the many (the aristocratic code) which tends to be a good deal more elaborate and confusing. Nevertheless, the sense of being exceptional, of being separate from the mass of humanity, gives the aristocrat a feeling of kinship with the heroic man and establishes a kind of *entente cordiale* between them against "the masses."

Yeats was neither a political writer nor a social critic. His interests, however, were significantly political and social as well as literary; so much so, in fact, that the distinction is sometimes lost in his writings. Would one be right, for instance, to call *On the Boiler* and essays like it purely or even primarily literary? Despite his distrust of polemics and his frequently reiterated, emphatic rejection of the whole world of "opinion," Yeats was in fact often a polemical writer who held to his beliefs tenaciously and tried to make them the beliefs of other men. This means that an attempt to understand what Yeats meant by aristocracy will involve us significantly in social theory and political discussion in addition to our more limited cultural and aesthetic concerns.

Yeats's aristocrat is something of an amalgam of several kinds of "best": the most cultured, most polished, most powerful (in an ideal society), most urbane, the product of the oldest and best families in the land. As with the epic hero, Yeats looks back nostalgically to the kind of world in which such people were the natural leaders of society in all significant areas. But this time he is recalling neither a fictional world nor one so very far removed from his own time. His ideal society is the Renaissance, and the villain who destroyed it Cromwell, a symbol in Yeats's eyes, of modern egalitarianism and its annihilation of significant distinctions among people:

> You ask what I have found, and far and wide I go:
> Nothing but Cromwell's house and Cromwell's
>   murderous crew,
> The lovers and the dancers are beaten into the clay,
> And the tall men and the swordsmen and the horsemen,
>   where are they? [1]

Yeats's real villain, however, is named Legion; for in the modern world he is everywhere to be met, nowhere to be avoided. "Cromwell's house" is the world of trade and the city; his "crew" the merchants, businessmen, and shopkeepers who create the commercial community and substitute the lust for money and the taste for mediocrity for the standards of a former time.

Because of this attack on the very fabric of modern life, Yeats's interest in the aristocrat is often looked at as another of his attempts to escape from the realities of the modern world. There is a certain justice to this point of view. In his early works particularly, Yeats was content to lament the passing of the old order while divorcing himself completely from the new. No doubt such an attitude is "unrealistic," for it is futile to wish that the Industrial Revolution had simply never happened and to dream of escape to one of the numerous island Utopias which fill Yeats's early poetry, islands in which all the problems of existence seem to be solved with some wattles and a little clay. But Yeats is "unrealistic" about commercial society in his later poetry too, and this fact helps us to understand that the whole notion of the evils of "escape" is a justifiable objection only from the point of view of the social and not the literary critic. The rejection of the real world for an ideal one has provided material for so much good literature that the question of its "escapism" becomes, for our immediate concerns, meaningless. Only the clarity and intensity of Yeats's vision of both real and ideal change significantly in his work; the distinction between the real commercial society and the ideal aristocratic one remains constant. The fact is that Yeats wrote some of his best works in the service of an aristocratic ideal, as part of an attempt to "make, or to help some man some day to make, a feeling of exclusiveness, a bond among chosen spirits, a mystery almost for leisured and lettered people" in an Ireland which had "suffered more than England from democracy." [2] His passionate belief in this project is responsible for the intensity, extravagance, and imaginative power of many of his finest poems.

Yeats's preoccupation with the aristocracy is in part the product of his recognition of the impossibility of the ideal, unified Irish society which has been discussed in the previous chapter. From a sceptical point of view, we might say that one disillusionment only led to another illusion, for an aristocratic society was not much closer to the realm of possibility in the modern world than the heroic one had been. But the two ideas are not quite parallel. Yeats's aristocratic ideal was less ambitious: its "perfect community" was conceivable because it was exclusive and could coexist with the ordinary commercial world. In 1897 Yeats first visited Lady Gregory at Coole Park, and there he was exposed to a way of life which combined all the finest qualities of the Protestant Irish Ascendancy, a life clearly intended only for a small and select group of men and women. At about the same time, Yeats began to suspect and fear that, as he was to put it some years later, "the dream of my early manhood, that a modern nation can return to Unity of Culture, is false." Yet this realization, because of the aristocratic way of life which he saw embodied at Coole, made him think that the situation was perhaps not hopeless after all, that something like the Unity of Culture of the Renaissance could at any rate be achieved "for some small circle of men and women." [3] We shall see that his hope for such unity within this "small circle" sustained Yeats through the greater part of his career until it ended, like the more ambitious hope, in a kind of disillusionment too.

Such an elite body of men must "rule," Yeats felt, by assuming leadership of the significant institutions of modern culture. In this way, it could control "the great instinctive movements that come out of the multitude," [4] by imposing its own values in a direct or an indirect way upon the society which it controlled. This, at any rate, was Yeats's early view. Later, in the last dozen years of his life, he began to think of the aristocracy as a more self-sufficient body, living a nearly hermetic existence apart from the corruptions of the general life, successful only if it remained outside the great social forces which were changing the world around it, defending the aristocratic way of life by practicing it in near-seclusion. At the same time, the opposing world seems less and less controllable and more and more of a threat. As a result, Yeats's conception of the aristocracy changes, in his later years, from a group whose primary importance is social to one which only preserves a heroic code in private in the hope that it may some day be of social significance once more. Nor is this a surprising change for a writer who has helped to shift the field of literature, as Edmund Wilson once said, "from an experience shared with society to an experience savored in solitude." [5]

How large is an aristocratic society? "They are a small body," Yeats says, "not more than one in five thousand anywhere, but they are many enough to be a priesthood." [6] Nor is there any need for large numbers, for "a hundred men, their creative power wrought to the highest pitch, their will trained but not broken, can do more for the welfare of a people, whether in war or peace, than a million of any lesser sort no matter how expensive their education." [7] The exact number, of course, does not matter. The important point is that the aristocrats are rare enough that their life may be distinguished from the all but communal life of "the masses," and that their small number permits them a kind of compromise between complete isolation and complete commitment to the public world. The beauty of this life remains the model for the whole world, no matter how aloof the aristocrat chooses to be:

> the courtly life,
> Being the first comely child of the world,
> Is the world's model.[8]

Before attempting to describe Yeats's picture of the aristocrat fully, we should deal briefly with the question of influences. One of the unusual things about Yeats's ideas on this subject is the relative ease with which one can name writers whom he read in the first decade of the century (when he was formulating these ideas) who are likely to have had an important effect. The most significant of these writers is Nietzsche, who has already been briefly discussed in the introductory chapter. There were, however, three other writers who may be said to have had some influence, or who, at any rate, confirmed ideas of his own: John Eglinton, Castiglione, and Ezra Pound. Each of these writers suggests one or two elements which go into the composition of Yeats's completed portrait of the aristocrat.

John Eglinton was an Anglo-Irish essayist, literary critic, and editor, generally perhaps more brilliant than influential in Irish letters, but nevertheless a man of unusual insight whom Yeats respected. There is no doubt that he was familiar with his work, since he prepared an edition of selections from several volumes of Eglinton's essays for his sister's press in 1905. Yeats called him "our one philosophical critic." [9] What seemed to attract him most about Eglinton's "philosophy" was the insistence on the overwhelming importance of the Anglo-Irish Protestant Ascendancy in all of Ireland's significant cultural achievements. Eglinton was always conscious of being a Protestant in a Catholic country and seems to have felt a certain isolation in this position. One of his books, for example, is called *Anglo-Irish Essays*, and in another he writes, "No man calls himself an Irishman without some attribution of nationality to the Irish people as a whole; but it is idle to deny that the nationality which most of us have in our mind is one which has its nucleus in the Anglo-Irish population rather than in the peasant hinterland." [10] As soon as Yeats began to feel the absurdity of the attempt to create a truly unified Irish culture, his respect for the achievements of the Protestant Ascendancy in Ireland became more marked. Eventually, as will be seen later, this respect for the existing aristocracy of Ireland influenced his vision of the ideal one which he sought to create.

Castiglione's *The Courtier*, which Yeats read in 1907 in the Opdycke translation at the instigation of Lady Gregory,[11] provided him among other things with a useful word which was to form one of the most important characteristics of the ideal aristocratic hero. The word, *sprezzatura*, has been variously translated as "nonchalance" or "recklessness." Castiglione insists that the courtier must avoid affectation in all his actions, must do things with an ease, a naturalness, a nonchalance which will give the impression that "what is done and said is done without effort and almost without thought." Grace, which is so important a part of the courtier's equipment, is derived from this quality, "because everyone knows the difficulty of those things that are rare and well done, and therefore facility in them excites the highest admiration; while on the other hand, to strive and as the saying is to drag by the hair, is extremely ungraceful, and makes us esteem everything slightly, however great it be." [12] All the courtier's actions must be unstudied, seemingly artless and effortless "because it impresses upon the minds of the bystanders the idea that he who does well so easily, knows much more than he does, and that if he were to use care and effort in what he did, he could do it far better." [13]

This quality of *sprezzatura*, the casual air of the courtier, is particularly important because it separates the older and true aristocracy from the *arrivistes*, the pretenders, the self-made men who are, as Yeats says in *Purgatory*, "educating themselves out of the book societies." [14] Yeats valued this quality so highly that he once suggested that "we lose life by losing that recklessness Castiglione thought necessary even in good manners." [15] The aristocrat, unlike the man of trade, shows this grace in all he does, "and if a man has it not," Yeats says with characteristic snobbishness, "he will be gloomy, and had better to his marketing again." [16]

Castiglione's perfect man, however, has more than superficial polish; his external charm and grace reflect his inner wisdom and worth, and *The Courtier* ends with a picture of the most perfect courtier of all, the ideal prince, a picture which forms part of Castiglione's argument for the value of traditional aristocracy and monarchal rule:

> And to be good and wise ought to be deemed possible for a king of noble race, inclined to worthiness by his natural instinct and by the illustrious memory of his predecessors, and practised in good behaviour; and if he be not of another species more than human . . . being aided by the teachings and by the education and skill of so prudent and excellent a Courtier as these gentlemen have described, he will be very just, continent, temperate, strong and wise, full of liberality, magnificence. In short, he will be very glorious, and very dear to men and to God (by whose grace he will attain that heroic worth which will make him exceed the limits of humanity), and may be called a demigod rather than a mortal man.[17]

This implied praise of monarchy and the near-apotheosis of the aristocratic ruler of men is echoed in Yeats's own political views. The courtier's determination to shun the crowd ("it pleases me well that we should avoid the crowd, and especially the ignoble crowd" [18]) clearly reinforced Yeats's growing contempt for the mass of men. Looking back on his early life in a poem called "The People," he mourns the time he has wasted in trying to compromise with the "people" and reflects on his longing to live a life like that of the Duchess's court described in Castiglione's book:

I might have lived,
And you know well how great the longing has been,
Where every day my footfall should have lit
In the green shadow of Ferrara wall;
Or climbed among the images of the past—
The unperturbed and courtly images—
Evening and morning, the steep street of Urbino
To where the Duchess and her people talked
The stately midnight through until they stood
In their great window looking at the dawn;
I might have had no friend that could not mix
Courtesy and passion into one like those
That saw the wicks grow yellow in the dawn.[19]

But at this stage of his career, around 1916, there is still a voice arguing the other side of the case. The other speaker in this poem (it is the voice of Maud Gonne) nearly convinces him that the people cannot really corrupt a person of stature and gives herself as an example. In later years, however, this other voice is silenced and Yeats's stand agianst the people becomes less ambiguous.

Two other things about *The Courtier* must have made a deep impression, since they also form part of Yeats's finished aristocratic ideal. The first is the picture of the mutual dependence of artist and well-born patron delineated in the book, an informal union of people in the pursuit not of "culture," which they already possess, but of wisdom. This will be more fully discussed below. The second is Yeats's identification of the time in which Castiglione wrote with his own. This is a new and more sympathetic view of the late Renaissance for Yeats. In some of his early writings he thought of it only as a time in which chaos descended upon the cultural unity of the Middle Ages and early Renaissance. The courtiers of Castiglione's book interested him particularly because of their acceptance of a situation like the one which Yeats had just come to see was inevitable in his own time. Castiglione seemed to realize that a unified culture was impossible to recreate artificially once it was gone and that the only proper reaction to this loss lay in the attempt to recreate the finest qualities of the disappearing culture in a small, select group of people detached from the problems of the world. The "steep street of Urbino" leads to a kind of tower-retreat where the remnants of a lost culture can be guarded against the encroaching town below. Yeats admired these people because he felt they understood so clearly what was to be done:

> Our present civilisation began about the first Crusade, reached its midpoint in the Italian Renaissance; just when that point was passing Castiglione recorded in his "Courtier" what was said in the court of Urbino somewhere about the first decade of the sixteenth century. These admirable conversationalists knew that the old spontaneous life had gone, and what a man must do to retain unity of being, mother-wit expressed in its perfection.[20]

The last important influence on Yeats's picture of the aristocrat was his friendship with Ezra Pound. Yeats met Pound in 1909, and soon spent a great deal of time with him, Pound acting, for a number of years, as his secretary. Under the circumstances, it is likely that Pound's conversation influenced Yeats more than his writings, especially since he admired the brashness and outspokenness of the young American. Perhaps Pound did not actually teach him anything new, but the violence and uncompromising quality of his belief in an intellectual and political aristocracy must have affected Yeats, for here was a man who was saying without the least touch of hesitation some of the things which Yeats had come to feel only after the greatest disillusionment, and about which he still had his doubts and misgivings. Pound attacked the notion of popular culture in characteristically vitriolic fashion: "As for the 'eyes of too ruthless public': damn their eyes. No art ever yet grew by looking into the eyes of the public, ruthless or otherwise." [21] Pound also attacked the existence of a popular culture in the past as a historical fallacy, and in this he went much further than Yeats, who usually thought of the past nostalgically, as a foil; for him it is a time in which the wrongs of the present do not exist. For Pound, on the other hand, there is no such ideal past:

> Nothing but ignorance can refer to the "troubadours" as having produced popular art. If ever an art was made for a few highly cultivated people it was the troubadour poetry of Provence. The Greek populace was PAID to attend the great Greek tragedies, and it damn well wouldn't have gone otherwise, or if there had been a cinema. Shakespeare was "Lord Somebody's players," and the Elizabethan drama, as distinct

from the long defunct religious plays, was a court affair. Greek
art is about as fine an example of UNINTERRUPTED decadence as one could want, and its decay keeps pace with the
advance of popular power.[22]

It is not difficult to imagine how such an uncompromising
stand against "the populace" might have affected someone who
was hesitating—as Yeats was—between the idea of a "social
aristocracy," one which concerned itself with the people and
the good of society, and a "private aristocracy" which simply
ignored such problems.

Pound, like Yeats, was concerned also with the problem of
creating a form of aristocratic patronage of the arts, and he
writes to potential subscribers:

> There is no organized or coordinated civilization left, only in-
> dividual scattered survivors. Aristocracy is gone, its function
> was to select. Only those of us who know what civilization is,
> only those of us who want better literature, not more literature,
> better art, not more art, can be expected to pay for it. No use
> waiting for masses to develop a finer taste, they aren't moving
> that way.[23]

Most important of all, perhaps, is Pound's complete faith in the
artist as the only creator of values in a civilization: "All values
ultimately come from our judicial sentences. . . . Humanity is
malleable mud, and the arts set the moulds it is later cast
into." [24] And like Yeats, Pound saw the aristocracy of intellect
as a small elite group, and he did not hesitate to suggest precise
figures: "There were 16 millions that did *not* elect Hoover. It
takes about 600 people to make a civilization. There were ump-
teen billions of unbreached barbarians in the north woods when
Athens etc. . . ." [25]

The relationship between art and aristocratic patronage
also concerned Yeats, and he would most probably have agreed
with Pound's insistence that the difference between individual
artistic creation and a true general renaissance of art is precisely that of patronage. As Pound puts it, "Great art does not
depend upon comfort, it does not depend upon the support of
riches. But a great age is brought about only with the aid
of wealth, because a great age means the deliberate fostering of
genius, the gathering-in and grouping and encouragement of

artists." [26] Anyone familiar with Yeats's life will know that he worked constantly for this "deliberate fostering of genius," by using the organizations and societies which already existed, by establishing new ones of his own, and by dealing individually with people of means and culture, that the renaissance of Irish literature might truly come.

We can guess, then, that the influence of Eglinton, Castiglione, and Pound might have been considerable in the formulation of Yeats's aristocratic ideal. Ultimately, however, it is just as difficult to discuss the problem of influence here as with most other artists. Although the parallels in thought and even in expression are often striking, Yeats was learning much of the same thing from personal experience as well as from books. The continuing apathy of most people to his ambitious plans for Irish cultural unification, the persistent stupidity of the audiences at the Abbey despite Yeats's various attempts to bludgeon them into liking the "right" things, the riots over Synge's *The Playboy of the Western World*—all these and many other experiences like them made Yeats see the futility of anything other than an aristocratic culture for the things he was most anxious to accomplish. The fact that in Eglinton, in Castiglione, and in Pound he found his own ideas amplified or clarified with significant variations was no doubt of great importance to him. These people provided authority; they sometimes provided the right words; but they probably did not radically change his ideas. It seems likely that he read their works with such enthusiasm because they confirmed the things he had himself been thinking.

To understand what Yeats looked for in his ideal aristocratic culture we must examine some of the major problems which especially concerned him: the relationship between the classes of society, the connection between art and the culture which supports it, the political ramifications of aristocratic leadership, and, finally, the problem posed by the decay of the aristocracy in contemporary society.

There were three classes for Yeats: peasant, aristocrat, and merchant; and this fact emphasizes the difference between his view of society and that of our own time. Today, at least in Europe and America, the "merchant" class has become so important that it is no longer possible to place all "merchants" —as Yeats did—in one category. There is a significant distinction, in most modern minds, between workman and shopkeeper, or between shopkeeper and great industrialist. Yeats deemphasizes this distinction, first because the "newness" of the whole idea of industrialization in the predominantly agricultural Ireland of the turn of the century permitted writers to see the whole commercial revolution as a single definite entity, and second because Yeats insists on stressing for polemical reasons the essential fraternity among all people involved in any way with the commercial world. Shopkeeper, factory owner, workman—they were all identified in his mind precisely because they were doing something *new*, which lacked the "traditional sanctity" which he saw and praised in the lives of both peasant and aristocrat. But these traditional classes were rapidly disappearing from Ireland as more and more farms and old estates were sold or abandoned. The great new "middle class"—which is the most innocuous of the many terms by which Yeats refers to the industrial society—was almost entirely independent of the two other classes. In Yeats's eyes the merchants were dispossessed and deracinated and were therefore forced to make everything new, their speech, their values, their tastes, their ideas. And as with the products which they manufactured, they made these things as cheaply, and therefore as uniformly, as possible.

Yeats despised this middle class with such intensity for several reasons. First they were the antithesis, in his eyes, of everything noble, heroic, and unusual. They could not understand anything beyond themselves and their own way of life and hence, as Yeats says contemptuously in his poem "The Leaders of the Crowd," they "accuse / All that are different of a base intent." [27] As a result, the middle-class Irishman was a perpetual threat to the life of the great man, and the situation reminded Yeats of a remark of Goethe's which seemed to illuminate the situation: "Those who accuse Synge of some base motive are the great-grandchildren of those Dublin men who accused Smith O'Brien of being paid by the Government to fail. It is of such as these Goethe thought when he said, 'The Irish always seem to me like a pack of hounds dragging down some noble stag.' " [28] Like Hamilton in his famous description of the people as "a great beast," Yeats sees them as essentially irrational and destructive, annihilating the work of civilization in order to substitute the law of the jungle for culture. The true ideal of middle-class life, uniformity, represents the greatest threat to the whole idea of human distinction—and distinctions:

> Instead of individual men and women and living virtues differing as one star differeth from another in glory, the public imagination is full of personified averages, partisan fictions, rules of life that would drill everybody into the one posture, habits that are like the pinafores of charity-school children.[29]

Public morality is a leveller, an efficient system which can eventually destroy the great man. Yeats "explains" this middle-class anxiety to dismiss the idea of exceptional quality satirically in his poem on the *Playboy* riots, with the picture of an impotent rabble staring with self-consuming envy and hatred at the great man:

> Once, when midnight smote the air,
> Eunuchs ran through Hell and met
> On every crowded street to stare
> Upon great Juan riding by:
> Even like these to rail and sweat
> Staring upon his sinewy thigh.[30]

The great middle class is uncreative because it is gelded, and nowhere does Yeats's contempt for these people come out as clearly as when he "translates" this poem into prose:

> The root of it all is that the political class in Ireland—the lower-middle class from whom the patriotic associations have drawn their journalists and their leaders for the last ten years— have suffered through the cultivation of hatred as the one energy of their movement, a deprivation which is the intellectual equivalent of a certain surgical operation. Hence the shrillness of their voices. They contemplate all creative power as the eunuchs contemplate Don Juan as he passes through Hell on the white horse.[31]

This middle-class envy and hatred of greatness is perfectly brought out in *The Countess Kathleen*. In that play, the devils' real goal is the soul and therefore the life of Kathleen. They bargain for the lives of the peasants, it is true; but they are not really interested until they have forced Kathleen to surrender herself to them. It is no accident that Yeats pictures these devils quite clearly as merchants, bargainers, men of business. They come with bags of gold; their negotiations are thoroughly commercial; they set a price for everyone, and their highest price is for Kathleen. It is difficult to miss the obvious barb in one of the speeches of the First Merchant: "We travel for the Master of all merchants," [32] in which the Devil becomes the God of the new class, and his disciples on earth his commercial travelers. Kathleen, on the other hand, demonstrates the characteristic aristocratic contempt for the methods of the merchants in her reckless generosity in helping the starving people:

> I still have bags of money, and can buy
> Meal from the merchants who have stored it up,
> To prosper on the hunger of the poor.[33]

She tells her servants to sell all she has and "give out gold to all who come." [34] Kathleen's impulsive generosity is thus intended to contrast completely with the bargaining spirit of the merchants.

This brings us to the second serious objection which Yeats had to the Irish middle classes: they translated all experience into financial terms. This was true even of the richer members of the middle class who "put everything into a money measure": "When anyone among them begins to write or paint they ask him 'How much money have you made?' 'Will it pay?' Or they say 'If you do this or that you will make more money.' " [35] But it is no different with the small shopkeepers whose standards are at least as mercenary, if not more so. Yeats addresses them with savage irony in "September 1913":

> What need you, being come to sense,
> But fumble in a greasy till
> And add the halfpence to the pence
> And prayer to shivering prayer, until
> You have dried the marrow from the bone?
> For men were born to pray and save.[36]

And in the same poem he sets against these people the great men of the Irish past who are ignored and forgotten in the modern pursuit of profit because the value of their sacrifice cannot be measured in shillings and pence.

Finally, Yeats's contempt for the middle classes was a reaction against what and how they thought. Their ideas were never independently arrived at; rather, they simply appropriated the ideas of others without examination. In fact, it was even inaccurate to call these thoughts "ideas," for they were in reality nothing but half-formed attitudes and prejudices, spread uniformly throughout the length and breadth of the commercial world. Yeats called this "mechanical thinking" and described a typical product of the machines which produced it:

> I have been talking to a man typical of a class common elsewhere but new in Ireland: often not ill-bred in manner and therefore the more manifestly with the ill-breeding of the mind, every thought made in some manufactory and with the mark upon it of its wholesale origin—thoughts never really thought out in their current form in any individual mind, but the creation of impersonal mechanism—of schools, of textbooks, of newspapers, these above all. He had that confidence which the first thinker of anything never has, for all thinkers are alike in that they approach the truth full of hesitation and doubt. Confidence comes from repetition, from the breath of many mouths. This ill-breeding of the mind is a far worse thing than the mere bad manners that spit on the floor. Is not all charm inherited? Whether of the intellect, of the manners, of the character, or of literature.[37]

The intellectual vulgarity of the middle classes was a product of the mass education which the whole commercial movement suddenly made necessary. As the city grew, this education had to be made uniform and new, and consequently all the traditional knowledge and culture of this new "displaced class" was thoughtlessly abandoned. Yeats speaks of their "unremembering hearts and heads," [38] and suggests by this that the traditional ideas and values transmitted from generation to generation among the peasantry of Ireland and therefore "remembered" were quickly abandoned in exchange for the hasty, half-formed, only partially understood prejudices of the new society. Yeats held to this opinion throughout his life. By 1939, when he could permit himself the fierce and unrestrained polemics of the essays in *On the Boiler*, he called these people not only semi-educated but semi-educable:

It seems probable that many men in Irish public life should not have been taught to read and write, and would not have been in any country before the middle of the nineteenth century. . . . Forcing reading and writing on those who wanted neither was a worst part of the violence which for two centuries has been creating that hell wherein we suffer.[39]

The middle classes, in short, were responsible for the mediocrity which Yeats saw enthroned in modern Ireland. Their contempt for the great man, their mercenary standards, their intellectual vulgarity, and their lack of traditional values seemed to him pernicious and frightening. Unlike American mediocrity, which Yeats saw (at a distance) as "so potent because it is so magnificent, with Whitman for its bard & Roosevelt for its man of action—Ireland or a least Dublin is in the grasp of another kind of mediocrity—for it is sordid & repulsive and issues from the cynicism of the slums." [40]

The peasant and the aristocrat, on the other hand, create a bond of mutual dependence which eliminates the commercial middle classes entirely, since it forms the working agreement on which the more traditional agricultural-aristocratic society is based. Once again, this bond is best represented in *The Countess Kathleen* where the country people worship their great lady, and the great lady reciprocates by respecting and appreciating them enough to sacrifice her own life and property for their welfare. The peasant's life has several connections with the general aristocratic ideal which Yeats was working out in his own mind: it is simple, it is traditional, and it is imaginative. It is simple because of the small round of activities in rural life, as contrasted with the proliferating complexities of the town. This simplicity along with the pride in their own work give Yeats's peasants a heroic quality which he seldom saw in more complicated ways of life. That is why he told Synge that the Aran Islands, for all their starkness, were ultimately more fruitful for the purposes of art than the sophisticated Paris where he was living. In these islands Synge might be free of the distortions and complications which occur only when life becomes so elaborate that its most primitive and basic needs are forgotten or ignored.

Peasant life was traditional because of the permanence

of its needs and methods. Since the land was inherited, it was unnecessary to move constantly to other districts and to assume new fashions and persuasions. Here there was neither any deliberate search for change nor the unthinking adoption of the half-digested which makes for vulgarity in any class. Everything that happened in such a life was tested against traditional standards.

Finally, Yeats's nearly idyllic picture of country life was made complete by the imaginative gifts of the peasant. A basic part of his traditional way of life was the passing on from generation to generation of stories, superstitions, and beliefs. Yeats compared the beauty of these tales to the manners of the aristocracy and the creative work of the artist:

> Three types of men have made all beautiful things. Aristocracies have made beautiful manners, because their place in the world puts them above the fear of life, and the countrymen have made beautiful stories and beliefs, because they have nothing to lose and so do not fear, and the artists have made all the rest, because Providence has filled them with recklessness.[41]

The implication, of course, is that beauty is created only when motives of prudence can be completely ignored.

Yeats learned much about the "peasant imagination" when he spent his summers in Sligo with his uncle, George Pollexfen, and collected material for his book *Fairy and Folk Tales of the Irish Peasantry* (1888); and later when he and Lady Gregory went from cottage to cottage for many years beginning in 1898 and worked together on her *Visions and Beliefs in the West of Ireland* (1920). It is not so strange, then, that in Yeats's picture of the ideal audience for his own work the countryman forms a significant part. His poem "The Fisherman" (1919) describes such a man:

> All day I'd looked in the face
> What I had hoped 'twould be
> To write for my own race
> And the reality.[42]

Clearly, however, the most important class in any society for Yeats was the aristocracy. What was his ideal aristocrat really like? Yeats saw him, first of all, as similar in many ways to the old heroes of Irish legend discussed in the previous chapter, a fact which emphasizes once again the essential identification in his mind of the various seemingly different personalities which together made up his heroic ideal. For one thing, the aristocrat has warrior roots; the Irish aristocracy, Yeats said, is founded "like all aristocracies upon conquest." Irishmen must therefore boast "in the words of a medieval Gaelic poet 'We are a sword people and we go with the sword.' " [43] To Yeats, the fact that Lady Gregory, who represented in his mind the best qualities of the traditional aristocracy in modern Ireland, should have been instrumental in the revival of the Irish epic tales seemed altogether appropriate, because the greatness of the epic heroes was inseparable in his mind from the greatness of the aristocrat:

> Looking back, *Cuchulain of Muirthemne* and *Gods and Fighting Men* at my side, I can see that they were made possible by her past; semi-feudal Roxborough, her inherited sense of caste, her knowledge of that top of the world where men and women are valued for their manhood and their charm not for their opinions.[44]

Kathleen too lives in a world which provides constant reminders of the great epic feats. Kevin (or Aleel in the later versions), the bard who is always by her side, sings songs of Fergus, and like the bards of the early epics,

> His mind ran all on sheogues, and on tales
> Of Finian labours and the Red-branch kings,
> And he cared nothing for the life of man.[45]

And Kathleen's generosity and reckless courage echo the virtues of the old warrior-kings. Yeats was also anxious to approach the identification from the other direction, to suggest that the time of Cuchulain and the Red Branch warriors was far from barbaric or truly primitive, that it was actually almost as civilized as the life of the modern aristocrat:

> One never hears of Cuchulain delighting in the hunt or in woodland things; and one imagines that the storyteller would have thought it unworthy in so great a man, who lived a well-ordered, elaborate life, and had his chariot and his chariot-driver and his barley-fed horses to delight in. If he is in the woods before dawn one is not told that he cannot know the

leaves of the hazel from the leaves of the oak; and when Emer laments him no wild creature comes into her thoughts but the cuckoo that cries over cultivated fields. His story must have come out of a time when the wild wood was giving way to pasture and tillage, and men had no longer a reason to consider every cry of the birds or change of the night.[46]

More precisely, the modern Irish aristocracy at its best, even though it was relatively powerless, seemed to Yeats to retain the virtues of the days in which it really ruled the land. For the lives of these people combined several characteristics which seemed to Yeats the very essence of an ideal aristocracy: a sense of feudal responsibility, a feeling for custom and ceremony, an emotional reticence, an active intellectual life, and even a kind of physical perfection. In Lady Gregory in particular he saw and admired the "sense of feudal responsibility, not of duty as the word is generally understood, but of burdens laid upon her by her station and her character, a choice constantly renewed in solitude." [47] This gladly accepted sense of responsibility emphasized the privileges of the privileged class while it underscored, at the same time, its obligations. The result was a kind of beautiful balance of power and duty which did not seem possible in a commercial society, where Yeats saw only the exploited and the exploiters.

Yeats also delighted in the obvious artificiality of aristocratic life, in the elaborate customs and ceremonious behavior which were substituted for the crude display of feeling and passion common in lives less restrained. Such emotional reticence represented a kind of triumph over man's cruder necessities, though there is some loss as well as gain. Only the common people become "gushing and sentimental. Educated and well-bred people do not wear their hearts upon their sleeves, and they have no artistic and charming language except light persiflage and no powerful language at all, and when they are deeply moved they look silently into the fireplace." [48] This reticence, the shunning of all forms of emotional display, was close to the stoical acceptance of adversity which Yeats pictured on the stage in Deirdre's preparation for death. But he finds it as well in Robert Gregory, Lady Gregory's son, in the poem

"An Irish Airman Foresees His Death"; for here is a man who
accepts the death which is about to come to him without a trace
of hysteria:

> I know that I shall meet my fate
> Somewhere among the clouds above. . . .
> I balanced all, brought all to mind,
> The years to come seemed waste of breath,
> A waste of breath the years behind
> In balance with this life, this death.[49]

And Lady Gregory, when she hears the news of her son's death,
accepts all as calmly as he did, in Yeats's pastoral elegy "Shep-
herd and Goatherd":

> She goes about her house erect and calm
> Between the pantry and the linen-chest,
> Or else at meadow or at grazing overlooks
> Her labouring men, as though her darling lived,
> But for her grandson now; there is no change
> But such as I have seen upon her face
> Watching our shepherd sports at harvest-time
> When her son's turn was over.[50]

Along with such aristocratic self-possession, which is a
silent form of heroism, goes the other important manifestation
of custom and ceremony: the ritual of courtesy. Both are a
product of a powerful will creating order out of chaos. Yeats
compared this activity to that of the artist:

> In life courtesy and self-possession, and in the arts style, are
> the sensible impressions of the free mind, for both arise out
> of a deliberate shaping of all things, and from never being
> swept away, whatever the emotion, into confusion or dullness.
> The Japanese have numbered with heroic things courtesy at
> all times.[51]

Courtesy is perfectly consonant with both inner passion and
manhood. Its antithesis is merely the *display* of passion. The
"highest life," Yeats says, "unites as in one fire, the greatest
passion and the greatest courtesy." [52] And "Manhood is all, and
the root of manhood is courage and courtesy." [53]

The mind of the aristocrat turns naturally to the emblems
of culture, which he collects not because they bring prestige,
but simply because he loves them. Looking about at Coole

House, one can see "Beloved books that famous hands have bound, / Old marble heads, old pictures everywhere." [54] Even the people themselves seem to have a kind of physical beauty; the classes of society form a hierarchy of intelligence and physical perfection as well as of wealth and social position "if you arrange an ascending scale from the unemployed to skilled labour, from skilled labour to shopkeepers and clerks, from shopkeepers and clerks to professional men. There is not only an increase of mother-wit but of the size of the body and its freedom from constitutional defects." [55] This was Yeats's most uncompromising stand on the natural perfection of the higher classes of society, typical of the excesses of the essay, *On the Boiler*, in which it appeared.

The aristocratic virtues are the subject of two of Yeats's most important poems: "In Memory of Major Robert Gregory," [56] and "A Prayer for My Daughter." [57] Gregory is pictured as a kind of Sidney, a perfect and complete Renaissance man, as much at home in one pursuit as another; in the words of the refrain, "Soldier, scholar, horseman, he." But the man's particular personality is only slightly more important than Edward King's was for "Lycidas," and the idea that the poem is excessive praise for an obscure man is a total misunderstanding of Yeats's actual subject. Although Robert Gregory is clearly individualized, he is also meant to represent the class of society from which he comes. He combines the various virtues of the aristocratic way of life and epitomizes the ideal society in which the man of thought is also the man of action. Gregory was a soldier and a sportsman:

> At Mooneen he had leaped a place
> So perilous that half the astonished meet
> Had shut their eyes.

And yet, Yeats is careful to point out, "his mind outran the horses' feet." He was a painter himself and he loved Coole because he understood "All work in metal or in wood, / In moulded plaster or in carven stone." Yeats also reminds us of the ideal of effortlessness, of *sprezzatura*, from Castiglione's *Courtier* in the lines "And all he did done perfectly / As though he had but that one trade alone." Yeats's portrait of Gregory,

then, "Our Sidney and our perfect man," was precisely that, a
picture of his ideal or perfect man rather than a primarily
realistic portrait of the son of his close friend, for his life, like
his death, was meant to be symbolic of the group to which Yeats
had in effect pledged his sympathy.

, In "A Prayer for My Daughter" Yeats can concentrate
even more on an idealized picture of the aristocratic life, since
the daughter he speaks of is only an infant. This leaves Yeats's
imagination free to create an image of her as a perfected young
woman, an image which can be seen as the feminine counterpart
to the picture of Robert Gregory. Here too we find the aristocratic values which Yeats discusses more fully in his prose. "In
courtesy I'd have her chiefly learned," he says, for courtesy is
part of the "custom" and "ceremony" which he admires so
much in the poem. So is the great house to which he prays her
bridegroom will take her, "Where all's accustomed, ceremonious." He hopes that she, like the landed gentry of Ireland,
will not move from place to place, constantly changing her
way of life, but asks that she may "live like some green laurel /
Rooted in one dear perpetual place." Most important, perhaps,
is that in this poem Yeats's ideas on the subject are so effort-
lessly established and sustained that he can begin to speak more
metaphorically about them and allow himself greater poetic
leeway than he does in poems with a more obvious polemic
cast. Here the laurel tree and the cornucopia are used symbolically to represent the virtues of custom and ceremony
throughout the poem, the more abstract identification being
made only in the last two lines. Yeats also prays that his
daughter will be able to avoid the disease which infects a commercial world that has abandoned all traditional beliefs, a
world full of argument, opinion, and controversy. He contrasts
her with Maud Gonne:

> An intellectual hatred is the worst,
> So let her think opinions are accursed.
> Have I not seen the loveliest woman born
> Out of the mouth of Plenty's horn,
> Because of her opinionated mind
> Barter that horn and every good
> By quiet natures understood
> For an old bellows full of angry wind?

The word "barter" in these lines is a significant choice, since Yeats identifies all the base values with the huckster's mercantile world: "For arrogance and hatred are the wares / Peddled in the thoroughfares."

One last attribute of the Irish aristocrat was added later to Yeats's picture, for only after his disillusionment with the ideal unified society was complete did he venture to talk about a highly controversial and delicate issue—the Protestantism of the Irish gentry. Although Ireland was and is an overwhelmingly Catholic country, the greater part of the upper class was Anglo-Irish and Protestant. This situation obviously presented great difficulties for a writer like Yeats who was trying to create an ideal of aristocratic culture outside the bounds of religious controversy. He realized soon enough that this was hardly possible, and we can trace the growth of Yeats's distrust of the Catholic Church and his growing identification of himself with the group to which he belonged, the Protestant Anglo-Irish. It is true that in some of the early plays and poems, *The Land of Heart's Desire*, for example, the Church represents the antithesis of all heroic action. But Church and priest in this play seem to represent all organized religion rather than any specific sect. Their philosophy, ironically enough, is one of worldly common sense and prudence rather than of vision. But there are other early works in which the religious life is treated more kindly, *The Countess Kathleen*, for example. Yeats's distrust of the Catholic Church really began in earnest in 1890 when it condemned Parnell. The civil war also raised the religious question in an acute form. The retaliations of Collins for the Black and Tans raids were directed specifically against the Protestant Irish gentry.[58] Yeats slowly began to feel that any institution which represented the mass of men, as the Irish Catholic Church did, was likely to reflect their mediocrity.

It is difficult to say exactly when Yeats became so anti-Catholic and pro-Anglo-Irish. In the mid-1920s he grew quite outspoken about his preferences, particularly in his speech to the Irish Senate on the divorce bill (1925), a subject on which of course the Church took a strong stand. Here he praises the Protestant Ascendancy with passionate conviction and self-identification:

I think it is tragic that within three years of this country gaining its independence we should be discussing a measure which
a minority of this nation considers to be grossly oppressive.
I am proud to consider myself a typical man of that minority.
We against whom you have done this thing are no petty
people. We are one of the great stocks of Europe. We are
the people of Burke; we are the people of Grattan; we are
the people of Swift, the people of Emmet, the people of
Parnell. We have created the most of the modern literature of
this country. We have created the best of its political intelligence.[59]

To these names, Yeats later adds Berkeley and Goldsmith, and
together they become a kind of roll call of the great men of
Ireland which he continually repeats during the twenties and
thirties. He gradually identifies his own life with those of the
Anglo-Irish intellectual gentry:

> I declare
> This winding, gyring, spiring treadmill of a stair
>   is my ancestral stair;
> That Goldsmith and the Dean, Berkeley and Burke
>   have travelled there.[60]

Berkeley's idealism, Burke's conservatism, Swift's contempt for
democracy, his passion and his rage, his dissatisfaction with
ordinary human life, all these come to represent for him the
achievement of a specific aristocratic class. He thinks of all of
them, justly or unjustly, as foes of the democratic levellers:

> Whether they knew it or not,
> Goldsmith and Burke, Swift and the Bishop of Cloyne
> All hated Whiggery; but what is Whiggery?
> A levelling, rancorous, rational sort of mind
> That never looked out of the eye of a saint
> Or out of drunkard's eye.[61]

Gradually, this interest focused more and more sharply on
Swift, a writer for whom Yeats had little respect in his early
years. Eventually, however, he came to consider Swift a hero
of the aristocratic tradition because of his "mind so con-
temptuous of average men" [62] and because Yeats felt he had
argued the case against democratic government so persuasively
in his *Discourse of the Contests and Dissensions Between the
Nobles and Commons in Athens and Rome*.[63] Yeats's admira-

tion is evident in his play, *The Words upon the Window Pane,* in the poem "Swift's Epitaph," and in numerous other works.

Yeats's final picture of the aristocrat, then, was a good deal more precise and limited than his earlier versions of the same heroic personality. But his view of the basic distinction between the privileged class and the middle classes did not change significantly from about 1900 to the end of his life, despite the greater insistence on the Anglo-Irish background in the later works. Yeats emphasized this distinction by inventing or using an entire cast of familiar characters in his work, the Gregorys and the Gore-Booths, the Anglo-Irish writers and statesmen, the members of his own family in Sligo. But he also crystallized the difference between the aristocratic and mercantile way of life by suggesting the sense of place, by using the City and the Great House symbolically in his works. These two places were the shrines of merchant and aristocrat, embodying as they did in visible form the values and customs of the people whose homes they were. Because of this identification, Yeats could translate his abstract ideas and opinions on the subject of aristocracy into visual and concrete terms.

Yeats hated the City for many reasons, but perhaps most strongly because its size and complexity tended to dwarf man, to make him seem insignificant. Ironically enough, the institutions and inventions which had come from the human brain eventually made man seem physically negligible in the maze of streets and tall buildings with which he had surrounded himself. In Yeats's selections from John Eglinton's essays, there is a passage which describes this phenomenon and echoes Yeats's own ideas: "Set a man anywhere under the sun and he will adorn any landscape, and at night the empyrean will light his face; but in the midst of his own ingenious contrivances, in a library, or as a social unit in one of his large towns, he does look small." [64] When Yeats was in his twenties, he spent most of his time in London, doing various kinds of hackwork for English publishers. Later, when he reflected on this period of his life, he said that in London he "saw nothing good, and constantly remembered that Ruskin had said to some friend of my father's— 'As I go to my work at the British Museum I see the faces of people become daily more corrupt.' I convinced myself for a time, that on the same journey I saw but what he saw." [65]

Yeats's most deliberate attack on the City is found in his long prose tale, *John Sherman* (1891), the story of a young man who moves to London from a small village in western Ireland. In his role of naive observer, John Sherman examines the City with a fresh eye, and what he complains of most consistently is that London forces people to be specialists in living, simply because they can be familiar with only a small part of the complicated machinery which makes the City possible. In the country, on the other hand, life is not so overwhelmingly difficult that one can not see its true variety, for the different classes are interdependent and see much of each other: "In your big towns a man finds his minority and knows nothing outside its border. He knows only the people like himself. But here one chats with the whole world in a day's walk, for every man one meets is a class." [66] *John Sherman* is interesting partly because it is so thoroughly uncharacteristic of Yeats's work. It is a deliberately anti-heroic tale, a realistic yet compassionate story of people with limited vision and restricted capacities. This rare attempt to write realistic narrative examines contemporary urban culture in detail and without rancor, as it contrasts Ballah, the small, sleepy Irish town which John Sherman leaves, with the bustle and false busyness of London. The hero's decision to return to Ballah is of course a rejection of town life and thus hardly unusual as a Yeatsian theme; but the interesting and uncharacteristic thing here is that this rejection, unlike similar ones in his other works, is done with great moderation and temperance, without a trace of the violence with which Yeats later treats the same kind of situation.

In *Where There Is Nothing*, Yeats's early version of *The Unicorn from the Stars*, Paul Morel's speeches as he encourages the people to destroy the cities suggest this kind of violence: "We must put out the towns as I put out this candle." [67] The destruction of the towns would bring back the kind of pre-urban world which Yeats so much preferred: "We could march on the towns, and we could break up all settled order; we could bring back the old joyful, dangerous, individual life." [68] This healthy, individual life has been lost or extinguished in the impersonal machinery of urban living.

The Great House, on the other hand, epitomizes the virtues of the aristocratic way of life, since it generally forms a kind of miniature but almost totally self-sufficient unit, a small community providing for its own necessities and uniting a small group of people into a mutually dependent, hierarchical organism. The house itself constantly brings to mind the previous generations of the family who own it. A walk through its rooms is a kind of voyage into the past, which is evoked by every portrait and every book, by the furniture and the blackened fireplace, by the view of lawns and trees from the great windows. That, at least, was what Yeats saw at Coole, a way of life which he tried to recreate for his own family when he purchased Ballylee and its ancient tower and made it his summer house. In "A Prayer on Going into My House" (1919) he asks that the sense of historical presence grace his own newly-acquired, though hardly new, property:

> and grant
> That I myself for portions of the year
> May handle nothing and set eyes on nothing
> But what the great and passionate have used
> Throughout so many varying centuries
> We take it for the norm.[69]

Coole and Lissadell, the home of the Gore-Booth family, are the two Great Houses which Yeats most frequently mentions in his poetry. Both seem to him to combine the sense of history with the feeling of leisure and serenity which comes of permanence and imperviousness to change. Yeats's mind worked naturally in dichotomies, so that these qualities contrast perfectly with the life of the City, in which there is constant change, respect for the new rather than the old, and the perpetual bustle of people just getting settled.

Yeats's concern with the aristocracy was also closely connected with two more general interests, one aesthetic, the other political. The aesthetic question was one which he tried to answer during his whole career: that of the ideal audience. A special kind of art clearly required a special kind of audience, and as Yeats's art changed, as it became more difficult and required greater and more subtle equipment to be properly appreciated, his ideal audience changed with it. His work with the Abbey Theatre had given him an accurate picture of what people wanted, of which qualities satisfied and pleased them. Generally they were, to his mind, always the wrong things. His own play, *Cathleen Ni Houlihan*, for example, was very popular; but Yeats felt that it was popular for the wrong reasons. People would regularly cheer the so-called patriotic sections and remain apathetic to some of the most poignant scenes and speeches. The Irish theatrical audiences essentially taught Yeats the same lesson as his life in London had, that mass appeal could only be achieved by the sacrifice of quality. After the surrender of his plans for a unified Irish culture, he became less and less willing to make sacrifices of this sort for any reason. Here Pound's influence must have been most significant, for Yeats started to attack the whole notion of the popular appeal of art in language almost as bitter as Pound's. Like Stephen in Joyce's *Ulysses* he began to see "the cracked looking-glass of a servant" as the proper symbol for popular Irish literature, and he feared that the commonness which must result from an attempt to appeal to all was affecting his own work. One of the standard objections to Yeats's later work, of course, is that he overcompensated and produced an art so obscure that it was incomprehensible to master and servant alike. There would be little point in rehearsing this argument here, but it is important to remember that Yeats's choice was deliberate, and that it was connected with his growing appreciation of the virtues of the aristocratic life.

His contempt for a mass audience is found in the poem "Against Unworthy Praise," first published in 1910, in which Yeats refers to the applause he gets from his audience as the praise of "dolt and knave." [70] But the most direct attack on the whole idea of mass culture and a reliance upon the taste of the people is found in the poem addressed "To a Wealthy Man Who Promised a Second Subscription to the Dublin Municipal Gallery If It Were Proved the People Wanted Pictures" (1913). This bitter, satirical poem, addressed to the potential patron Lord Ardilaun during the controversy over Hugh Lane's gift of paintings to Dublin, contrasts the notion of popular

culture with Yeats's own cultural ideal of Renaissance en-
lightened patronage:

> You gave, but will not give again
> Until enough of Paudeen's pence
> By Biddy's halfpennies have lain
> To be 'some sort of evidence',
> Before you'll put your guineas down,
> That things it were a pride to give
> Are what the blind and ignorant town
> Imagines best to make it thrive.
> What cared Duke Ercole, that bid
> His mummers to the market-place,
> What th' onion-sellers thought or did
> So that his Plautus set the pace
> For the Italian comedies? [71]

Yeats's later plays move in the same direction, particularly
when he abandons the whole concept of the popular theater and
substitutes for it the audience for which the Japanese Noh play,
to which Ezra Pound introduced him, was intended. Yeats's
so-called "dance plays" are to be presented in a room no bigger
than a good-sized drawing room, for an audience of fewer than
a hundred people. They thus become, in fact, part of the ritual
of the Great House by simply moving inside it. With more than
a hundred people in the audience, says the Old Man in *The
Death of Cuchulain*, "I wont be able to escape people who are
educating themselves out of the book societies and the like,
sciolists all, pickpockets and opinionated bitches." [72]

The Noh play form seemed to solve the problem of a
theatrical elite, since in Japan these plays were intended for an
aristocratic audience trained to catch their allusions and sub-
tleties. Yeats attempted to create a similar kind of audience in
his own country. In his later years, he constantly stressed the
connection between great art and a fit audience, and suggested
that it was impossible to have one without the other. Here
again, the example of the audience of the epics came to mind;
for as he had written in the first decade of the century, "When
one reads of the Fianna, or of Cuchulain, or of some great hero,
one remembers that the fine life is always a part played finely
before fine spectators. There also one notices the hot cup and
the cold cup of intoxication; and when the fine spectators

have ended, surely the fine players grow weary, and aristocratic
life is ended." [73] As a result, Yeats's ideal audience after 1915
or so became a more and more select circle of men and women,
the patrons of a deliberately unpopular theater which had been
created "for ourselves and our friends." [74] The dance plays were
meant to be a new form of drama, "distinguished, indirect, and
symbolic, and having no need of mob or press to pay its way—
an aristocratic form." [75]

Yeats really tried to approximate the old form of aristocratic patronage, in which the artist was attached to the court of
a great nobleman and was respected and encouraged and had his
audience at all times around him. He believed that the bond
between aristocrat and artist had been the most fruitful combination of talents in the history of culture, and Coole House
was a memorial to the things it had produced:

> Great works constructed there in nature's spite
> For scholars and for poets after us,
> Thoughts long knitted into a single thought,
> A dance-like glory that those walls begot.[76]

In the poem "Coole Park and Ballylee, 1931," Yeats represents
this natural connection between artist and patron concretely
and pictorially rather than abstractly by tracing the path of
the river that races past his house and the home of Raftery,
the blind Irish poet, until it runs into the lake on Lady
Gregory's land. By using experience metaphorically in this way,
Yeats's poetry moves further and further away from the realm
of opinionated, abstract argument:

> Under my window-ledge the waters race,
> Otters below and moor-hens on the top,
> Run for a mile undimmed in Heaven's face
> Then darkening through 'dark' Raftery's 'cellar' drop,
> Run underground, rise in a rocky place
> In Coole demesne, and there to finish up
> Spread to a lake and drop into a hole.[77]

But to make his metaphoric meaning perfectly clear, Yeats
quickly adds "What's water but the generated soul?"

The union of artist and well-born patron is fruitful ultimately because there is a kind of kinship between them:

Every day I notice some new analogy between the long established life of the well-born and the artists' life. We come
from the permanent things and create them, and instead of
old blood we have old emotions and we carry in our heads
always that form of society aristocracies create now and again
for some brief moment at Urbino or Versailles. We too despise
the mob and suffer at its hands, and when we are happiest we
have some little post in the house of Duke Frederick where
we watch the proud dreamless world with humility, knowing
that our knowledge is invisible and that at the first breath of
ambition our dreams vanish.[78]

In writing for a small, select audience, in choosing material
and using techniques which would appeal to them, the artist
could take advantage of this natural affinity and produce in the
twentieth century an approximation of the Renaissance alliance
between patron and artist.

We turn now to the last general problem, that of the
political ramifications of Yeats's theory of aristocracy, a subject
on which he was extremely outspoken and uncompromising.
This subject will be more fully discussed in the next chapter,
but some aspects of it are relevant here. Like many great writers
of the twentieth century—Eliot, Pound, Joyce, Mann come to
mind—he distrusted both the theory and the practice of democracy.[79] In the Ireland of his own time, he wrote in 1926, power
had passed "to men who lack the training which requires a
certain amount of wealth to ensure continuity from generation
to generation, and to free the mind in part from other tasks." [80]
In these half-educated men, political wisdom had degenerated
into factionalism and controversy. Members of warring parties
spent their time fighting each other and forgot the real needs
of the country. The inevitable proliferation of opinions and
prejudices, when power passed into the hands of the many,
accounted for the unnecessary complexity of the bureaucratic
state.

In contrast, Yeats's own theory of government presents a
different kind of balance of "the One, the Few, and the Many"
from that which exists in modern Ireland:

All States depend for their health upon a right balance between the One, the Few and the Many. The One is the
executive . . . the Few are those who through the posses-

sion of hereditary wealth, or great personal gifts, have come to identify their lives with the life of the State, whereas the lives and ambitions of the Many are private. The Many do their day's work well and so far from copying even the wisest of their neighbours affect 'a singularity' in action and in thought; but set them to the work of the state, and every man's Jack is 'listed to a party' becomes the fanatical follower of men of whose characters he knows next to nothing, and from that day on puts nothing into his mouth that some other man has not already chewed and digested. And furthermore, from the moment of enlistment thinks himself above other men and struggles for power until all is in confusion.[81]

This confusion comes about only when "the best lack all conviction" and "the worst are full of passionate intensity," an accurate description, Yeats must have felt, of the chaos of modern Irish political life as well as of Western culture in general. In his dealings with members of the Government on matters of business for the Abbey Theatre, Yeats said that he often felt that such public officials were on his side but were powerless to act because "the mob reigned." And he predicted that if this reign were not broken, "our public life will move from violence to violence, or from violence to apathy, our Parliament disgrace and debauch those that enter it; our men of letters live like outlaws in their own country." [82]

Yeats's public utterances on this subject came late in his career, primarily after 1925. We can only speculate that he eventually began to feel something like a sense of mission in becoming the spokesman for a highly unpopular position. In 1933 he wrote to Olivia Shakespeare that he found himself "constantly urging the despotic rule of the educated classes as the only end to our troubles." [83] As with so many of his opinions, Yeats's statements on the virtues of aristocratic government are found in their most violent form in the essays in *On the Boiler* (1939). There he complains that the "representative system has given Ireland to the incompetent." [84] And he outlines what he considers the right attitude of Few towards Many:

> The whole State should be so constructed that the people should think it their duty to grow popular with King and Lord Mayor instead of King and Lord Mayor growing popular

with them; yet, as it is even, I have known some two or three men and women who never, apart from the day's natural kindness, gave the people a thought, or who despised them with that old Shakespearean contempt and were worshipped after their death or even while they lived. Try to be popular and you think another man's thought, sink into that slow, slothful, inanimate, semi-hypocritical thinking Dante symbolised by hoods and cloaks of lead.[85]

In the very excess and passion of such statements, Yeats places himself outside the realm of practical political argument. But of course by this time he felt himself to be well out of the business of politics, which he had experienced at first hand in his years as Senator (1922–1928); he was more free to say what he liked. In his eyes, the greatest weakness of a democratic state was the inability of the electorate to tell a true philosopher king from a windy political opportunist. He would have agreed with one of the paradoxes in Shaw's *Revolutionist's Handbook*: "If the lesser mind could measure the greater as a footrule can measure a pyramid, there would be finality in universal suffrage." But since it could not, for Yeats as for Shaw, "the problem remains unsolved." [86] It was not a problem, however, with which Yeats was directly concerned, partly because he realized the whole matter was outside his true domain, partly because he was so pessimistic about the efficacy of any practical measure to curb representative government in a country so thoroughly committed to it. The extreme alternatives of revolution, and even of eugenics,[87] as ways to a more desirable world did occasionally occur to him, but in general he avoided anything beyond abstract reflection on the subject, for there was really nothing to be done. The twentieth century had, after all, arrived.

We are left, finally, with the question of what effect Yeats's loss of hope for aristocratic government in his own time had on his idea of the nonpolitical functions of the aristocracy. Was it to change their private as well as their public activities, and how would the loss of power affect their whole way of life? Yeats's thoughts on this subject at several points in his life are illuminating. From his first encounters with Lady Gregory in 1896, he saw the Anglo-Irish aristocracy in its most favorable light. At Coole, he could truly say, the force of tradition and inherited greatness had produced not only a good writer but a great patron of the arts. Yet Lady Gregory was in reality no more typical of the Ascendancy as it actually existed in twentieth-century Ireland than Yeats was of the Sligo land-owner. The Irish aristocracy had, as a matter of fact, been declining steadily ever since the eighteenth century. Standish O'Grady, one of the most important of the influences on Yeats in the formative period of the 1890s, exposed this decline in brutal words: "As I write, this Protestant Anglo-Irish aristocracy which, once owned all Ireland from the centre to the sea, is rotting from the land in the most dismal farce-tragedy of all time, without one brave deed, without one brave word." [88]

As early as 1923, in the first of the "Meditations in Time of Civil War," some doubts concerning the vitality of the privileged classes already occur to Yeats, even though in the thoughts of the first stanza he tries to reassure himself and reiterate the old values:

> Surely among a rich man's flowering lawns,
> Amid the rustle of his planted hills,
> Life overflows without ambitious pains;
> And rains down life until the basin spills,
> And mounts more dizzy high the more it rains
> As though to choose whatever shape it wills
> And never stoop to a mechanical
> Or servile shape, at others' beck and call.

But in the very next stanza such assurances already seem

> Mere dreams, mere dreams! Yet Homer had not sung
> Had he not found it certain beyond dreams
> That out of life's own self-delight had sprung
> The abounding glittering jet; though now it seems
> As if some marvellous empty sea-shell flung
> Out of the obscure dark of the rich streams,
> And not a fountain, were the symbol which
> Shadows the inherited glory of the rich.[89]

The two symbols in this poem, the sea-shell and the fountain, represent two views of the aristocracy. The fountain with its eternal vitality, its perpetually self-renewing abundance, mirrors Yeats's earlier, optimistic hopes for the class. But the sea-shell, though it is precious and beautiful, is empty and dead. It has only the shape and form of the life which it once contained.

Its life, its force are now of the past, and the shell is nothing
but an empty reminder of these things, a museum piece ejected
by the stream of life and cut off from the source of vitality. This
view of the modern aristocracy gradually begins to prevail in
Yeats's later poetry.

It was ironic that the inevitable decay of the aristocratic
tradition should be accelerated rather than delayed by some of
the aristocrats themselves. Yeats gives us a picture of this
perverse tragedy in the poem "In Memory of Eva Gore-Booth
and Con Markiewicz"; the title itself suggests that the elegy
has become the appropriate poetic form for the subject. But
in the poem, Yeats seems to elegize not the sisters but the life
which they lived in their youth, and which he feels they have
helped to destroy. Though both women are in fact dead, the
poem describes their "lonely years" in the present tense, while
the passages about Lissadell suggest either the past ("recall /
That table and the talk of youth") or—like the first sentence,
which has no verb—a timeless present. The point of the poem—
the decay of all aristocratic value when it becomes involved
in the world of mere opinion and common politics—is made by
a kind of before-and-after picture of the Gore-Booth sisters and
their beautiful Sligo house, Lissadell:

> The light of evening, Lissadell,
> Great windows open to the south,
> Two girls in silk kimonos, both
> Beautiful, one a gazelle.
> But a raving autumn shears
> Blossom from the summer's wreath;
> The older is condemned to death,
> Pardoned, drags out lonely years
> Conspiring among the ignorant.
> I know not what the younger dreams—
> Some vague Utopia—and she seems,
> When withered old and skeleton-gaunt,
> An image of such politics.
> Many a time I think to seek
> One or the other out and speak
> Of that old Georgian mansion, mix
> Pictures of the mind, recall
> That table and the talk of youth,
> Two girls in silk kimonos, both
> Beautiful, one a gazelle.[90]

Even Coole was not to last, as we see in "Coole Park and Ballylee, 1931." When Lady Gregory was dying, her great house already sold to the Land Commission, the main building pulled down, Yeats saw an image of the whole culture in her aged and fragile figure: "Sound of a stick upon the floor, a sound / From somebody that toils from chair to chair." [91] And with Coole almost gone, Yeats looks about him and sees "all that great glory spent," the glory of the house itself and the glory of what it represented displaced by a kind of aimless urban nomadism:

> A spot whereon the founders lived and died
> Seemed once more dear than life; ancestral trees,
> Or gardens rich in memory glorified
> Marriages, alliances and families,
> And every bride's ambition satisfied.
> Where fashion or mere fantasy decrees
> We shift about—all that great glory spent—
> Like some poor Arab tribesman and his tent.[92]

Yeats speaks of himself and others like him in the past tense: "We were the last romantics, chose for theme / Traditional sanctity and loveliness." But now, he realizes, that "fashion's changed, that high-horse riderless," the hopeful dawn turned melancholy dusk, and even the swan—once the symbol of Coole's eternal youth—now "drifts upon a darkening flood." Nor was Coole the only Galway estate to disappear in the past few decades: "When I was thirty years old three great Galway demesnes, within a half hour and two hours walk of each other, lay about Coole House, Tullyra Castle and Roxborough House. They were so old they seemed unchanging; now all have been divided among small farmers, their great ancient trees cut down." [93]

In one of the last poems, "The Statesman's Holiday," Yeats sums up this gradual disappearance of the aristocracy in the simplified terms of villain-and-hero melodrama:

> I lived among great houses,
> Riches drove out rank,
> Base drove out the better blood,
> And mind and body shrank.[94]

But a more interesting and subtle treatment of the problem is found in the play *Purgatory* (1939), which deals with the de struction of the aristocracy in allegorical fashion. The Old Man of the play comes back to the house in which he had murdered his own father fifty years before and asks, as he looks at the ruin it has become, "Where are the jokes and stories of a house / Its threshold gone to patch a pig-sty?" [95] The great tree too, once full of "Green leaves, ripe leaves, leaves thick as butter" [96] is now a naked skeleton. Like the other great houses of Ireland, this one had produced its share of heroes in times past:

> Great people lived and died in this house;
> Magistrates, colonels, members of Parliament,
> Captains and Governors, and long ago
> Men that had fought at Aughrim and the Boyne.[97]

But the house is dead, for the Old Man's father, a groom working on the estate, married the daughter of the family and in his half-barbaric ignorance burned the great house to the ground. His son realizes, years later, the enormity of this crime:

> to kill a house
> Where great men grew up, married, died,
> I here declare a capital offense. . . .
> There were old books and books made fine
> By eighteenth century French binding, books
> Modern and ancient, books by the ton.[98]

The civilization which is left looks back upon this arson with wild regret but can not really understand exactly what it has lost. It can only use the merchant's measure in an attempt to describe it (books "by the ton"); and all it knows of the books themselves is that their bindings were costly. Like the house in *Purgatory*, Ireland's house of aristocratic culture had also been burned to the ground; the last survivor of its great family had surrendered herself to its servant, like the Old Man's mother, like Con Markiewicz in her political slumming.

We might expect, after the example of Yeats's disillusionment with popular culture, that this loss of faith in the possibility of an aristocratic society in the Ireland of his own time would have led him into the same kind of regret and despair which he had experienced earlier. But in fact it did not do so; neither did it inspire him to make new and less ambitious plans. He understood the situation and accepted it almost, if not quite, with resignation. Despite the fact that a substantial portion of his life's work had come to nothing, something reassured him, and that something he had learned from the spiritual experience which resulted in the writing of A Vision. Much of Yeats's verse and prose had always been, in a sense, eschatological, a continual mourning over things dying or fading. The early poetry is filled with waning love and tired lovers, and the subject and mood are echoed in Yeats's later poems on the subject of old age, on the death of "romantic Ireland," and of our own civilization. But one of the most important thematic differences between the early poetry and the late is that Yeats gradually comes to see all endings as simultaneous with fresh beginnings, the death of the old instantly followed by the birth of the new. In poems like the "Two Songs from a Play," for example, there is a triumphant, joyous cry of rebirth blending with the mournful sound of death.

Such a theory of history, cyclical and perpetually self-renewing, Yeats had found confirmed in his reading of Nietzsche and later reiterated by the "instructors" of A Vision. It provided a kind of consolation for the desolate prospect of Ireland's immediate future. The aristocracy was dying if not dead, it was true, but surely in this very fact lay the hope that the spring of its rebirth would come soon. "As for the rest," said Yeats, "we wait till the world changes and its reflection changes in our mirror and an hieratical society returns, power descending from the few to the many, from the subtle to the gross, not because some man's policy has decreed it but because what is so overwhelming cannot be restrained. A new beginning, a new turn of the wheel." [99]

Only when we understand this new hope, the confidence that time will in the end restore the lost world, can we understand the last stanza of "In Memory of Eva Gore-Booth and Con Markiewicz":

> The innocent and the beautiful
> Have no enemy but time;
> Arise and bid me strike a match
> And strike another till time catch;
> Should the conflagration climb,
> Run till all the sages know.

We the great gazebo built,
They convicted us of guilt;
Bid me strike a match and blow.[100]

The great gazebo, to which the household of the aristocrat retired to spend the long, leisurely summer days, is an embodi-
ment and summing up of the ease, the grandeur, the fruitfulness
of a way of life now no longer to be found. The gazebo is at
last deserted, after the successful attacks of those who saw in
it only a mark of money and of social privilege, who did not
understand the sanctity of the seclusion which it offered to those
capable of enjoying it. Like the sea-shell it still exists, but before
it can be restored to life it must first be destroyed. Only when
the match catches, only when time itself is consumed, can the
gazebo and the culture which created it arise once more from
the ashes.

Notes

1. "The Curse of Cromwell," *Variorum*, p. 580.
2. Yeats, *Plays and Controversies* (London, 1923), p. 215.
3. Yeats, *The Trembling of the Veil*, p. 172.
4. Yeats, "John Eglinton," *United Irishman* (Nov. 9, 1901). Quoted in Richard Ellmann, *Yeats: The Man and the Masks* (New York, 1948), p. 130.
5. Edmund Wilson, *Axel's Castle* (New York, 1931), p. 266.
6. Yeats, "John Eglinton," as in n. 4, above.
7. Yeats, *On the Boiler* (Dublin, [1939]), p. 30.
8. Yeats, *The King's Threshold*, p. 22.
9. Yeats, "First Principles," *Samhain*, No. 4 (Dublin, 1904), p. 22.
10. Eglinton, *Bards and Saints*, p. 9.
11. See Joseph Hone, W. B. *Yeats, 1865–1939* (New York, 1943), p. 233. A fuller discussion of Yeats's debt to Castiglione may be found in the first part of Arnold Stein's "Yeats: A Study in Recklessness," *Sewanee Review*, 57 (1949), 603–26.
12. Baldesar Castiglione, *The Book of the Courtier*, trans. Leonard E. Opdycke (New York, 1929), pp. 34–35.
13. *Ibid.*, p. 37.
14. Yeats, *Last Poems and Two Plays*, p. 32.
15. Yeats, *Essays*, p. 390.
16. *Ibid.*, p. 316.
17. Castiglione, pp. 258–59.
18. *Ibid.*, p. 87.
19. "The People," *Variorum*, pp. 351–52.
20. Yeats, *On the Boiler*, p. 23.
21. *The Letters of Ezra Pound*, ed. D. D. Paige (New York, 1950), p. 4.

22. *Ibid.*, p. 102.

23. *Ibid.*, p. 172 n.

24. *Ibid.*, p. 181.

25. *Ibid.*, p. 221.

26. Ezra Pound, "The Renaissance," *The Literary Essays of Ezra Pound*, ed. T. S. Eliot (Norfolk, Conn., 1954), p. 221.

27. *Variorum*, p. 398.

28. Yeats, *Estrangement*, p. 26.

29. Yeats, "The Theatre, the Pulpit, and the Newspapers," *The Hour-Glass. Cathleen Ni Houlihan. The Golden Helmet. The Irish Dramatic Movement.* (Stratford-on-Avon, 1908), p. 124.

30. "On Those that Hated 'The Playboy of the Western World,' 1907," *Variorum*, p. 294.

31. Yeats, *Estrangement*, p. 29.

32. Yeats, *Collected Plays* (New York, 1953), p. 12. Note that this line is not in the original 1892 version.

33. Yeats, *The Countess Kathleen and Various Legends and Lyrics* (London, 1892), p. 59.

34. *Ibid.*, p. 44.

35. Yeats, *Samhain*, No. 1 (Dublin, 1901), p. 9.

36. *Variorum*, p. 289.

37. Yeats, *Estrangement*, pp. [1]–2.

38. "Under Ben Bulben," *Variorum*, p. 639.

39. Yeats, *On the Boiler*, p. 11.

40. From an unpublished letter to Lord Dunsany dated Dec. 22, 1919 (52 B 0636 in the Berg Collection of the New York Public Library).

41. Yeats, *Essays*, p. 310.

42. *Variorum*, p. 347.

43. Yeats, Introduction to *The Words upon the Window Pane* (Dublin, 1934), p. 9.

44. Yeats, *Dramatis Personae* (Dublin, 1935), p. 86.

45. Yeats, *The Countess Kathleen*, p. 73.

46. Yeats, Preface to Gregory, *Gods and Fighting Men*, p. xi.

47. Yeats, *Dramatis Personae*, p. 13.

48. Yeats, *Essays*, p. 339.

49. *Variorum*, p. 328. This is, of course, not the focus of interest in the poem.

50. *Ibid.*, p. 340.

51. Yeats, *Essays*, p. 313.

52. Yeats, *Samhain*, No. 4 (Dublin, 1904), p. 23.

53. Yeats, "Mr. Yeats' Opening Speech at the Debate of February 4th, at the Abbey Theatre," *The Arrow*, No. 3, no page number.

54. "Coole Park and Ballylee," *Variorum*, p. 491.

55. Yeats, *On the Boiler*, p. 17. It is interesting that by 1939, when *On the Boiler* was published, Yeats no longer lumped together the "commercial class" into one unit but rather saw it as presenting a kind of internal hierarchy of its own.

56. *Variorum*, pp. 323–28.

57. *Ibid.*, pp. 403–406.

58. Hone, p. 368.

59. *The Senate Speeches of W. B. Yeats*, ed. Donald R. Pearce (Bloomington, Ind., 1960), p. 99. For a much fuller analysis of Yeats's quarrel

with the Catholic position on divorce and censorship than is possible here, see Donald T. Torchiana's "W. B. Yeats, Jonathan Swift, and Liberty," *Modern Philology*, LXI (1963), 26–39.

60. "Blood and the Moon," *Variorum*, pp. 480–81.

61. "The Seven Sages," *Variorum*, p. 486.

62. Yeats, Introduction to *The Words upon the Window Pane*, p. 18.

63. See *The Words upon the Window Pane*, pp. 39–40 and Yeats's *Pages from a Diary Written in Nineteen Hundred and Thirty* (Dublin, 1944), pp. 4–5 for references to this essay. Swift's thesis is actually more complex than Yeats suggests, since he deals with the abuses of *various* kinds of tyranny, despite the fact that he concentrates on the tyrannical possibilities of democratic government, i.e., the potential tyranny of "the many" when their voice is all-powerful. Swift believed in a balance of power among the various classes in a society, Yeats in the retention of that power by the "higher" classes. Nevertheless, it is easy to understand what appealed to Yeats in the essay. Swift says of the "commoner" in politics, for example, "He is listed in a party where he neither knows the temper, nor designs, nor perhaps the person, of his leader; but whose opinions he follows and maintains with a zeal and faith as violent as a young scholar does those of a philosopher whose sect he is taught to profess. He has neither opinions, nor thoughts, nor actions, nor talk, that he can call his own, but all conveyed to him by his leader, as wind is through an organ. The nourishment he receives has been not only chewed, but digested, before it comes into his mouth. Thus instructed, he follows the party, right or wrong, through all his sentiments, and acquires a courage and stiffness of opinion not at all congenial with him." [*A Discourse of the Contests and Dissensions Between the Nobles and the Commons in Athens and Rome*, Temple Scott edition, Vol. I (London, 1911), 268–69.]

64. John Eglinton, *Some Essays and Passages*, ed. W. B. Yeats (Dundrum, 1905), p. 16.

65. Yeats, *Four Years*, pp. 46–47.

66. Ganconagh (pseud. W. B. Yeats), *John Sherman and Dhoya* (London, 1891), p. 13. See also Yeats's "Village Ghosts," in *The Celtic Twilight* (London, 1893), p. 29.

67. Yeats, *Where There Is Nothing* (London, 1903), p. 96.

68. *Ibid.*, p. 120.

69. *Variorum*, p. 371.

70. *Ibid.*, p. 260.

71. *Ibid.*, p. 287.

72. Yeats, *Last Poems and Two Plays*, p. 32.

73. Yeats, Preface to Gregory, *Gods and Fighting Men*, pp. xxii–xxiii.

74. Yeats, *Essays*, p. 204.

75. *Ibid.*, p. 274.

76. Yeats, "Coole Park, 1929," *Variorum*, p. 488.

77. *Variorum*, p. 490.

78. Yeats, *Estrangement*, p. 15.

79. For an interesting general study of this subject, see Eric Bentley, *A Century of Hero-Worship*. Bentley does not deal with Yeats in any detail.

80. Yeats, *Estrangement*, p. 33.

81. Yeats, Introduction to *The Words upon the Window Pane*, pp.

10–11. The similarity between this passage and the quotation from Swift in n. 63, above, is striking.

82. Yeats, *The King of the Great Clock Tower* (Dublin, 1934), p. 36.

83. *The Letters of W. B. Yeats*, pp. 811–12.

84. Yeats, *On the Boiler*, p. 11.

85. *Ibid.*, p. 10.

86. Bernard Shaw, *Man and Superman. A Comedy and a Philosophy* (London, 1952), p. 212.

87. See *On the Boiler*, pp. 19 and 27.

88. Standish O'Grady, *Selected Essays and Passages* (Dublin, Cork, and Belfast, n.d.), p. 180. L. C. Knights attacks Yeats for failing to face this problem in his essay "Poetry and Social Criticism: The Work of W. B. Yeats," *Explorations* (London, 1946), pp. 170–85. That Yeats eventually does deal with the problem I have tried to show below.

89. *Variorum*, pp. 417–18.

90. *Ibid.*, p. 475. For a persuasive discussion of the difference in literary quality between the elegaic and celebratory treatment of the aristocratic world in such poems, see Graham Martin, "Fine Manners, Liberal Speech: A Note on the Public Poetry of W. B. Yeats," *Essays in Criticism* II (1961), 40–59.

91. "Coole Park and Ballylee, 1931," *Variorum*, p. 491.

92. *Ibid.*

93. Yeats, *Dramatis Personae*, p. [1]. "The pattern was much the same everywhere: compulsory purchase of outlying property; woods cut down and sold to pay for children's education; ever-diminishing resources; and finally the end of the slow siege." (T. R. Henn, "W. B. Yeats and the Irish Background," *Yale Review* XLII [1953], 358.)

94. *Variorum*, p. 626. The refrain of this poem, "Tall dames go walking in grass-green Avalon," perpetually recalls the world which has been lost.

95. Yeats, *Last Poems and Two Plays*, p. 48.

96. *Ibid.*

97. *Ibid.*, p. 51.

98. *Ibid.*, pp. 51–52. It is perfectly true, as F. A. C. Wilson insists in *W. B. Yeats and Tradition* (New York, 1958), p. 155, that such an interpretation of *Purgatory* leaves much of the play untouched. I am merely concerned here to suggest its relevance to the subject under discussion.

99. Yeats, *Pages from a Diary Written in Nineteen Hundred and Thirty*, p. 55. The clearest statement of this idea in the poems themselves is found in "The Gyres."

100. *Variorum*, p. 476. Two lines, subsequently deleted, from a manuscript version of the last stanza seem to confirm the idea that Yeats is talking about cyclical rebirth: "For widow Nature still / Has those cradles left to fill." The passage is quoted in Jon Stallworthy's *Between the Lines: Yeats's Poetry in the Making* (Oxford, 1963), p. 171.

4 · The Public Hero

"Despising
For you the city, thus I turn my back.
There is a world elsewhere."
CORIOLANUS, TO THE PEOPLE OF ROME

THE MEN and women of Yeats's plays and poems are generally raised above the level of common humanity only by totally severing their connections with that level. For this reason his work is an important illustration of the modern idea that a hero can achieve greatness in isolation by renouncing the world and its institutions, the mass of mankind and its needs. This significant revaluation of the conservative Victorian concept of the socially useful hero is obvious in the very private vocations of some of Yeats's heroic men. They are artists, aristocrats, or visionaries and generally think of "the people," as did Yeats himself, with either indifference or contempt. It is therefore particularly puzzling that the public hero—the patriot, warrior, or statesman who *is* useful to society—should make any appearance at all in these works; and yet he does appear, and with great frequency too. How can we account for the fact that Yeats's scorn for "the people" did not apparently extend to the heroes who might presumably be taken to embody their ideals?

Obviously the public hero is in the public eye; he makes headlines; he gets things done. His actions are social actions of national, or even international, significance. His "greatness" is a matter of universal knowledge, since it springs from the deeds and actions which the media of mass information can record and bring before its tremendous audience. The public heroes of any society are the men whose accomplishments that society values or identifies with certain laudable qualities of character. They are distinct from the mere celebrities whose reputations are more momentary and less serious. They are famous because, in the eyes of their society, they merit fame. In Yeats's Ireland, the public hero was in addition often an outlaw, since his leadership and his courage were frequently demonstrated in the movement for Irish independence. He was a patriot, working for the good of his countrymen, devoted to a cause greater than himself. The public man leads a public life, and his actions are connected with certain larger and impersonal issues, opinions, and political points of view. Since Yeats frequently attacked the kind of narrow mind which moved about only in the small rooms of faction and political controversy, it is no wonder that he felt a considerable distrust of the public man. Such "heroes" were always in danger of adopting the thoughts and vocabulary of the masses to the point where they were no longer distinguishable from them. In that case, Yeats felt, the public hero lost his heroism and became merely the public.

In his early years, Yeats sometimes pointed to two potential public heroes who seemed to demonstrate that the total rejection of the world of public affairs has its own justification: Axel and Fergus. The hero of Villiers de l'Isle-Adam's play *Axel* [1] shuts himself off from the duties of the world with his beloved and contemptuously suggests that mere living could be done for them by their servants.[2] Yeats was fond of citing this famous statement as an example of giving the world its due. But even more pertinent is the figure of Fergus, one of the kings of Irish myth, who abandons his royal responsibilities and the necessities of an active heroic life to become a wanderer and a dreamer. As he says to the Druid in Yeats's poem "Fergus and the Druid," he seeks to "learn the dreaming wisdom that is yours," and to be "no more a king." [3]

These characters, however, did not represent Yeats's final attitude toward the phenomenon of the public hero or man of action. He was concerned with politics and the question of leadership during most of his life, though sometimes unwillingly, and he felt that good governments begin with the accession to power of great men. As a result, Yeats's attitude toward the public hero becomes exceedingly difficult to establish, particularly since he frequently changes his mind and contradicts himself in the course of his long career. Nevertheless, through all of this, there is an abiding appreciation of at least one kind of public man, the one who comes closest to resembling the other heroes in Yeats's pantheon.

Yeats often emphasized the essential similarity which existed among the various kinds of heroic activity. He was especially delighted by the story that some of the men who fought at the Post Office in 1916 "had the Irish legendary hero Cuchulainn so much in their minds." [4] Here was a modern heroic event which accepted as its model the Irish heroic past that Yeats had been trying so steadily to recreate for his own generation. In *The Death of Cuchulain* he reiterates this connection:

> What stood in the Post Office
> With Pearse and Connolly?
> What comes out of the mountain
> Where men first shed their blood,
> Who thought Cuchulain till it seemed
> He stood where they had stood? [5]

And in one of his speeches to the Irish Senate, Yeats again insists upon the relationship:

Already the traditional imagination in these old books has had a powerful effect upon the life, and I may say upon the politics, of Ireland. People forget that the twenties, forties and fifties of the last century was the forming period of Irish nationality, and that the work was begun by O'Donovan, Petrie and men steeped in this old literature.[6]

Yeats's later poems constantly suggest the similarities among the various heroic types. In "Easter, 1916," [7] for example, the public hero is shown as dedicated, like the visionary, to a higher purpose, and detached, like the aristocrat, from the common bourgeois world. He has "resigned his part / In the casual comedy," so that "a terrible beauty is born," a beauty which is not very different from the vision of the saint. In other poems, Yeats took to juxtaposing the different kinds of heroism, as for instance in the "Three Songs to the One Burden" and in "Long-legged Fly." The form of these poems—repetitive stanzas with a nearly identical refrain—suggests not only that the great men whom they celebrate are similar, but further that they are of equal significance and value. In "Long-legged Fly," [8] Caesar the warrior-king, Michaelangelo the artist, Helen of Troy, the heroine of myth, all merit the same attention and are identified through the refrain which isolates the creative act in all of them. The three heroic archetypes are thus made equally valuable varieties of uncommon experience:

> Like a long-legged fly upon the stream
> His mind moves upon silence.

Like "Long-legged Fly," "Three Songs to the One Burden" [9] is also a conjunction of heroic types. Here the three are Mannion the Roaring Tinker, who represents both the peasantry and the figures of Irish myth, since he is descended from Manannán Mac Lir; Henry Middleton, the country gentleman or aristocrat who scorns the modern world; and the modern Irish patriot. The cryptic "one burden" ("From mountain to mountain ride the fierce horsemen.") which occurs after every stanza in these poems, without variation, is probably intended to recall the heroes of Irish mythology to the reader's mind. They are immortal, at any rate, in the minds of their modern counterparts. As a result of the juxtaposition and the refrain, there is a kind of approximation to or echo of the older ideal society when all the heroes were one, not leading the fragmented and specialized lives which the twentieth century has imposed on them.

In both of these poems, the public hero is treated with the same kind of respect which the other kinds of heroism deserve. But we must remember that we have here a rather unusual idea of the popular hero, one which emphasizes his freedom from the crowd rather than his dependence on it. Yeats differentiates such a man from the kind of "hero" who is inspired by the crowd alone:

> Here in Ireland we have come to think of self-sacrifice, when worthy of public honour, as the act of some man at the moment when he is least himself, most completely the crowd. The heroic act, as it descends through tradition, is an act done because a man is himself, because, being himself, he can ask nothing of other men but room amid remembered tragedies; a sacrifice of himself to himself, almost, so little may he bargain, of the moment to the moment. [10]

This typically Yeatsian view of the public hero helps to explain his constant appearance in his works, since ideally he had the same independence of spirit and personal pride as did Yeats's other great men, no matter how different he seemed on the surface.

To a certain extent, Yeats's unorthodox view of the public hero is influenced by the unique situation of the Irish nationalist and patriot before independence was achieved. In Yeats's early years, Ireland, since it was not yet self-governing, had not been forced to adopt the complicated machinery of a modern bureaucratic government. Her own great men were in the tradition of the older epic heroes. Many of the names revered in Ireland—Emmet, Fitzgerald, Wolfe Tone—were rebels against the established and existing state; and since these rebels often fought hopelessly, single-handed or with a few friends against an enormous and relatively efficient organization, their heroism seemed all the more underscored. Robert Emmet's insurrection, for example, was based, according to the historian O'Hegarty, "on the principle that too extensive and too organized an organization was a mistake; that the mass of the people would join an insurrection if it once got going, and that a nucleus of determined men in any one place was sufficient to determine the event." [11] Ireland had a tradition of such heroic action, action which seemed to give the individual deed and the individual hero a greater share of the glory than the impersonal and massive efforts of modern warfare can possibly provide. The whole method of Irish insurrection isolated the exceptional individual. Each attempt at revolt, whether anything was actually accomplished or not, created another hallowed name.

The 1916 Easter Rebellion was no exception. There also a handful of men fought hopelessly against the massive retaliation of highly-trained and well-equipped British soldiers. It was precisely this fact that determined the outcome of the event and converted a relatively innocent insurrection into an Irish heroic martyrdom. Shaw wittily explains the episode in one of the prefaces to *John Bull's Other Island*:

> At Easter 1916 a handful of Irishmen seized the Dublin Post Office and proclaimed an Irish Republic, with one of their number, a schoolmaster named Pearse, as President. If all

Ireland had risen at this gesture it would have been a serious matter for England, then up to her neck in the war against the Central Empires. But there was no response: the gesture was a complete failure. All that was necessary was to blockade the Post Office until its microcosmic republic was starved out and made ridiculous. What actually happened would be incredible if there were not so many living witnesses of it. From a battery planted at Trinity College (the Irish equivalent of Oxford University), and from a warship in the River Liffey, a bombardment was poured on the center of the city. . . . It would not be true to say that not one stone was left upon another; for the marksmanship was so bad that the Post Office itself was left standing amid a waste of rubbish heaps. . . . Having thus worked up a harebrained romantic adventure into a heroic episode in the struggle for Irish freedom, the victorious artillerists proceeded to kill their prisoners of war in a drawn-out string of executions. Those who were executed became not only national heroes, but the martyrs whose blood was the seed of the present Irish Free State.[12]

Many years before, the "schoolmaster named Pearse" had commented with pleasure on precisely this quality of hero-worship in the Irish character. One of the most consistent and important aspects of an Irishman's personality, he says, "is his capacity for worshipping his heroes. . . . But there can be no doubt that hero-worship, in its highest form, is a soul-lifting and an ennobling thing. . . . And what is true of hero-worship in general is true, in an especial manner, of the hero-worship of the Gael." [13] Whether such a generalization is actually true, Yeats sometimes took the opposite view, and in his poetry he attacked the Irish people for their fickleness, their readiness to forget the great Irish patriots so easily once they were dead. In the poem "To a Shade," [14] for example, he addresses the dead Parnell and tells him that the people "are at their old tricks yet," that in refusing the Hugh Lane pictures they are repeating the pattern of ingratitude of which Parnell was the victim during his own life:

> A man
> Of your own passionate serving kind who had brought
> In his full hands what, had they only known,
> Had given their children's children loftier thought,
> Sweeter emotion, working in their veins
> Like gentle blood, has been driven from the place,

And insult heaped upon him for his pains,
And for his open-handedness, disgrace;
Your enemy, an old foul mouth, had set
The pack upon him.

"September 1913" [15] is Yeats's most vitriolic attack on the way in which the modern Irishman so easily forgets the heroic deeds of the patriots and public men of past and present. The poem identifies these great men with John O'Leary and the romantic Ireland of the past. In complete contrast, the modern Irishman, in his concentration on religion and business, has managed to forget such men completely. "Being come to sense," he need only

> fumble in a greasy till
> And add the halfpence to the pence
> And prayer to shivering prayer,

until, as Yeats says, he has "dried the marrow from the bone." The national heroes, on the other hand, had neither time to pray nor time to save. And the glory of their imprudent lives, now forgotten, prompts Yeats to ask in despair whether it was

> For this that all that blood was shed,
> For this Edward Fitzgerald died,
> And Robert Emmet and Wolfe Tone,
> All that delirium of the brave?
> Romantic Ireland's dead and gone,
> It's with O'Leary in the grave.

As "September 1913" shows, when Yeats celebrated public heroism, he was not interested in what had actually been accomplished from a military or political point of view. (Emmet, for example, accomplished nothing.) Rather, Yeats valued heroic action which demonstrated the virtues of courage, prodigality, and recklessness in contrast to the timid, secure, and uninspired world of the small shopkeeper. The phrase "all that delirium of the brave" is carefully chosen, but it is intended to mock the sanity of the coward rather than the delirium of the hero. The same ironic suggestion is made in the line "Come let us mock at the great" in "Nineteen Hundred and Nineteen." [16] In that poem Yeats suggests that the whole political arena, the world most affected by mass opinions and prejudices, can only

destroy the essential solitude and strength of the public hero
who chooses or is forced to deal with it:

> A man in his own secret meditation
> Is lost amid the labyrinth that he has made
> In art or politics;
> Some Platonist affirms that in the station
> Where we should cast off body and trade
> The ancient habit sticks,
> And that if our works could
> But vanish with our breath
> That were a lucky death,
> For triumph can but mar our solitude.

Yeats's public hero is never ambitious, or at least he is
never ambitious for power in government. Swift's previously discussed *Discourse* on Athenian and Roman politics, which Yeats
admired so greatly, approvingly quotes Plato on the subject of
the ambitious public man, and the passage can be used to sum
up Yeats's distrust as well:

> This was so well known in Greece, that an eagerness after em-
> ployments in the state was looked upon by wise men as the
> worst title a man could set up; and made Plato say: "That if
> all men were as good as they ought to be, the quarrel in a
> commonwealth would be, not, as it is now, who *should* be
> ministers of state, but who should *not* be so." [17]

"The Leaders of the Crowd" [18] is Yeats's satiric picture of
the kind of public hero who has permitted himself to become
enmeshed in political affairs. Unlike his uncorrupted heroic
counterpart, such a man has no solitude, cares only about the
response of the people and his own popularity, and despises the
thoughtfulness which is part of the life of the ideal man, even
if he is in the public eye:

> How can they know
> Truth flourishes where the student's lamp has shone,
> And there alone, that have no solitude?
> So the crowd come they care not what may come.
> They have loud music, hope every day renewed
> And heartier loves; that lamp is from the tomb.

Unlike such men, the ideal leader is a potential visionary; he
does not scorn the student's lamp, even if it is "from the

tomb." Yeats points to this ideal in the question he asks about
Leda: "Did she put on his knowledge with his power?"

Finally, in the poem "Beautiful Lofty Things," [19] Yeats
isolates five people involved at some time in their lives with the
public. In each he sees and admires the quality of aloofness,
the way in which each has deliberately cut himself off from
the public with which he is temporarily or even permanently
involved. These people are the modern Olympians, capable of
maintaining their almost godlike detachment and independence
of spirit in the midst of the most sordid ordinary circumstances:

> Beautiful lofty things: O'Leary's noble head;
> My father upon the Abbey stage, before him a
>   raging crowd:
> 'This Land of Saints,' and then as the applause died out,
> 'Of plaster Saints'; his beautiful mischievous head
>   thrown back.
> Standish O'Grady supporting himself between the tables
> Speaking to a drunken audience high nonsensical words;
> Augusta Gregory seated at her great ormolu table,
> Her eightieth winter approaching: 'Yesterday he
>   threatened my life.
> I told him that nightly from six to seven I sat
>   at this table,
> The blinds drawn up'; Maud Gonne at Howth station
>   waiting a train,
> Pallas Athene in that straight back and arrogant head:
> All the Olympians; a thing never known again.

The public hero and the visionary have one more thing
in common: they experience at moments a kind of ecstasy, a
piercing instant of joy which is similar to the fulfillment of
religious belief. The public hero, however, being more a man of
the world, experiences this more rarely, and in fact comes much
closer than any other kind of person in Yeats's work to fulfilling the demands of what Shaw called the modern "credible
hero." In discussing his *Caesar and Cleopatra*, Shaw made some
interesting comments on the way in which the whole realistic
movement in literature had modified the old romantic conception of the hero, to which Yeats, in general, still clung:

> The old demand for the incredible, the impossible, the super-
> human, which was supplied by bombast, inflation, and the piling

of crimes on catastrophes and fictitious raptures on artificial agonies, has fallen off; and the demand now is for heroes in whom we can recognise our own humanity, and who, instead of walking, talking, eating, drinking, sleeping, making love and fighting single combats in a monotonous ecstasy of continuous heroism, are heroic in the true human fashion: that is, touching the summits only at rare moments, and finding the proper level of all occasions, condescending with humour and good sense to the prosaic ones, as well as rising to the noble ones, instead of ridiculously persisting in rising to them all on the principle that a hero must always soar, in season and out of season.[20]

Yeats's public hero is certainly more credible than some of his heroic counterparts because he touches "the summits" at rarer moments, because he is more recognizably human. Nevertheless, Yeats does not deny him his moments, since they are what he lives for.

There is, then, an essential paradox in this conception of public leadership, a paradox which may perhaps be clarified by referring to an interesting distinction which Auden has made in *The Enchafèd Flood* between the "classical hero" (roughly identifiable with the public man) and the "romantic hero" (whom Auden calls here the "dream Ishmael-Don Quixote"):

The heroes of classical and Renaissance literature . . . are recognisable as heroic through the nature of their relations to other men, i.e., of their social acts. The hero is the one who conquers and rules others, or who teaches others. If he suffers a tragic fall, it is a social fall. . . . But our dream Ishmael-Don Quixote is quite alone. He is plainly not a conqueror. He is related to knowledge, i.e., he is the sole guardian of the imagination and the reason, the two human forms of knowledge, but he does not teach anyone else.[21]

Auden is playing with the familiar contrast between the doer and the thinker, the public personality and the private one, the man of action and the man of imagination. It is a distinction which most of us would ordinarily accept. The significant variation which Yeats plays on this theme, however, is the identification rather than the separation of the two. For him, the *true* public hero lives a private life as well; his actions are manifestations of an internal compulsion rather than an external necessity. He is not defined merely by his "social acts," and his

fall is not exclusively a "social fall." Rather, he is the classical
and the dream hero combined. Those who are true only to their
public function are in effect impostors, only "the leaders of
the crowd." For Yeats the true purpose of nationalism is to
create independent spirits first, a country only second. This
point is also well made by John Eglinton in one of the essays
which Yeats included in his 1905 collection. Eglinton says that
"the real nation is where its soul is, and the soul of a nation is
the men in it who have attained unto themselves. Wherever
a man has found himself, the purpose of nationality is fulfilled in him." [22] Yeats would surely have agreed with such a
statement. The hero who fulfills himself in fulfilling a national
purpose is described in some of his works as reaching a state
of "joy," "gaiety," or "exultation." The use of the word "joy"
in both his prose and verse is always special and important. And
it is precisely the perpetual insistence of the "tragic joy" of the
heroic man which would make Yeats, as a theorist, the despair
of most political philosophers and military thinkers.

The essence of the matter is that Yeats worships not victory,
but defeat. It is only in defeat that the man of action shows
his true spirit and greatness. Joy and exultation are of course
possible to the ordinary man under conditions of victory, but
they are possible only to the heroic man in defeat. In 1929
Yeats wrote to Sturge Moore that Spengler had

> confirmed a conception I have had for many years, a conception
> that has freed me from British liberalism and all its dreams.
> The one heroic sanction is that of the last battle of the Norse
> Gods, of a gay struggle without hope. Long ago I used to
> puzzle Maud Gonne by always avowing ultimate defeat as a
> test. Our literary movement would be worthless but for its
> defeat.[23]

The modern public hero whom Yeats praises is characterized
first by the fact that his struggle has been unsuccessful. Often
he is defeated by the people themselves. Parnell and the 1916
rebels, Emmet and Wolfe Tone, Oedipus and Fitzgerald and
Roger Casement and Hamlet and Lear—what did these "public
men" have in common? Their heroic and "joyous" acceptance
of defeat, according to Yeats. " 'Bitter and gay,' that is the
heroic mood," he writes to Dorothy Wellesley in 1935. "When

there is despair, public or private, when settled order seems lost, people look for strength within or without." [24] And in another letter written to her in the same year, he says, "To me the supreme aim is an act of faith and reason to make one rejoice in the midst of tragedy." [25] It is in the public realm that such tragedies most often occur, and of course it is precisely in this realm where, in the minds of most people, defeat is to be avoided at all costs. Yeats's insistence that the essence of heroism is suggested by the name of a character—"Doom-eager"—in an Anglo-Saxon poem [26] makes clear in very economical form the sharp division between his own vision of the public hero and the common conception of such a man.

The dichotomy between these two views is the basis of "Lapis Lazuli." [27] The poem has, in effect, four sets of characters: the "hysterical women," the artists, the tragic heroes, and the Chinamen of the last stanza. We begin with a debate between the women and the artists as to the true reaction to a public situation or crisis. The women insist that in a time of stress something "drastic" must be done, for if no action is taken,

> Aeroplane and Zeppelin will come out,
> Pitch like King Billy bomb-balls in
> Until the town lies beaten flat.

But their side of the debate ends here. The rest of the poem is an elaborated answer to the false argument of the women, and here the three other "characters" of the poem—tragic hero, artist, and Chinaman—join forces. Their reaction to a crisis is neither despair nor public action but rather "Gaiety transfiguring all that dread." The word "gay" connects the four last stanzas of the poem and establishes the proper heroic reaction to chaos. Though Hamlet and Lear foresee their tragic end, though Callimachus' exquisite work will perish, though the Chinamen watch their civilization crumble, they do not give way to hysteria, they do not insist on practical measures, they feel no despair. They are heroic because they fashion out of external tragedy a purely personal consummation: "Heaven blazing into the head." And their ideal is clearly endorsed by the poem; the women are never heard from again after the first stanza; their hysteria is silenced and the debate ends. The public crisis becomes the occasion for a private triumph, for "gaiety" after all is the description of a personal and individual feeling. The important emphasis in the summary lines of the poem ("All things fall and are built again, / And those that build them again are gay.") is on the last rather than the first statement. The actual building and destroying of civilizations belongs to the world of facts, but the joy of creation and, for Yeats, of destruction, is private rather than public. The criticial situation acts only as a test of the inner resources of the "public hero."

Although it is possible to say at least this much by way of generalization, it is also valuable to examine Yeats's view of the hero as public man in a more closely chronological fashion. It is predictable that during such a long career he will change his mind not once but several times on this as well as related subjects. Nevertheless, one can also find a certain order in these shifting views. If we look at Yeats's ideas on the public leader in four fairly distinct periods, the important variations in the basic conception are greatly clarified. Attaching precise dates to these four "periods" is, however, a more difficult matter. The first stage, one of growing interest in and exploitation of the theme of the popular hero, extends roughly from 1889–1903. This was followed by a time of reaction, in which Yeats's distrust of all the things which went into the creation of a public hero grew. This period extended to 1916, at which time there was a kind of reversal. From 1916 to 1928, Yeats's early interest in and high evaluation of the public hero returned in a new form. Finally, in the last ten years or so of his life, there was a more complex kind of withdrawal which to some extent echoes the earlier one, but which will have to be explained at greater length. All these dates are, of course, arbitrary, but if we take them only as approximations, they can help us to understand the shifts in Yeats's thought.

Yeats's early involvement with the cause of Irish nationalism has already been traced at length in Chapter 2 and provides us with some of the necessary background for the early years. It is important to remember, however, that from the first there was sharp disagreement between Yeats and most of the political

writers on the subject of what constituted the heroic national
ideal. If Yeats had at all times been true only to his own ideal,
the problem would be less complicated. But as a matter of fact
this was not quite the case. In the last years of the nineteenth
century Yeats was led away from the doctrines of aestheticism
into a kind of uneasy compromise with the notion of literature
as propaganda. Although there are several causes which one can
suggest for this, it seems likely that the least questionable one
is Yeats's devotion to Maud Gonne, whom he met in 1889.
Where Yeats wavered, Maud was firm. She had decided to
dedicate her life to the cause of Irish independence; everything else, literature included, was to be subservient to this first
necessity. Hone reports an interesting exchange between her and
Yeats which crystallizes, though in somewhat exaggerated form,
the opposition between them. In response to Yeats's insistence
that what Ireland needed most was books, she replied "Who
has ever read these dusty volumes? What we need is surely
action, not literature." [28] The reason the disagreement seems
exaggerated here is that Maud Gonne believed that ideally
literature leads to action, that it is useful as a political tool. A
remark in her autobiography, A Servant of the Queen, is
illuminating. She explains her acceptance of the role of Cathleen
by saying, "I did it because it was only on that condition that
Willie Yeats would give us the right of producing his play, and
I felt that play would have great importance for the National
movement." [29]

Yeats, of course, did not agree in principle with the suggestion that the true purpose of literature is propagandistic.
Nevertheless, in the period under discussion, he crossed as far
into the realm of propaganda as he was ever to do, particularly
in the plays The Countess Kathleen and Cathleen Ni Houlihan,
and in a very few poems like "How Ferencz Renyi Kept Silent"
and "Mourn—and Then Onward," neither of which he included
in later editions of his collected poems. It is not surprising that
these works were written during the time when he was under the
influence of John O'Leary and Maud Gonne, in the years when
he joined forces with a number of nationalistic organizations,
became president of the Wolfe Tone Memorial Association,[30]
and accompanied Maud on various political tours. It is, how-

ever, no exaggeration to say that he was never comfortable in
this role. Politics brought him close to Maud, they were one
way of remaining near her, yet he constantly begged her to
marry him and give up her place in that world. Had Maud
agreed, his separation from the whole domain of political
activity would surely have come sooner. Nevertheless, there is
no denying that at the time such activity meant a great deal
to him personally; that it had some influence on his work;
and, more particularly for our purposes, that it inspired him to
celebrate a certain kind of public hero in a semi-propagandistic
way.

The two poems mentioned above are good examples, despite (or perhaps because of) their very evident lack of literary
quality. "How Ferencz Renyi Kept Silent"[31] is, in a way, a
poem of Irish nationalism, since Renyi and the whole 1848
Hungarian Revolution in which he was involved was regarded
by the Irish as a counterpart to their own movement for independence.[32] Yeats makes the connection clear in the first
lines:

> We, too, have seen our bravest and our best
> To prisons go, and mossy ruin rest
> Where homes once whitened vale and mountain crest;
> Therefore, O nation of the bleeding breast,
> Libations, from the Hungary of the West.

The propagandistic phrase-making of these lines is not to be
ignored: "our bravest and our best," "nation of the bleeding
breast," and the reference to Ireland as the "Hungary of the
West" could easily be used in the rhetoric of persuasion. Most
interesting, however, is the type of heroic personality found in
Renyi. His patriotism is not to be compromised; he "kept silent"
while his mother, sister and sweetheart were all shot to death
rather than reveal the rebel hiding place and so hurt the cause
of the revolt. Renyi is that very unusual phenomenon in Yeats's
works, a hero more devoted to an external cause than to himself.

"Mourn—and Then Onward"[33] was written in 1891 as an
elegy on the death of Parnell. Yeats must have thought of this
as journalism, since it appeared only in two newspapers and
was never reprinted in any of his own collections. Nevertheless,
unlike "Renyi," it emphasizes certain qualities of this "public

hero" which make him more akin to the heroic personality of the later poetry. Yeats, for example, emphasizes Parnell's isolation in the lines "The man is gone who from his lonely station / Has moulded the hard years," as well as in the reference to him as the leader who was "derided, hated." Nevertheless, the propagandistic tone is still there, particularly in the "inspirational" last lines:

> Mourn—and then onward, there is no returning
> He guides ye from the tomb;
> His memory now is a tall pillar, burning
> Before us in the gloom!

It is a mark of Yeats's earliest attempts to deal with the public personality to suggest that the hero's primary usefulness is to inspire direct patriotic action. And yet, the most interesting thing about these two poems about patriots, for all their inspirational phrase-making, is that they are elegies. From the very first, Yeats's emphasis is on the heroically defeated, and almost every poem which he wrote in praise of some public personality was elegiac. Even when he speaks of those leaders still alive—as in the late "Parnell's Funeral"—it is only to compare them unfavorably with the heroic dead. This elegiac mode suggests a certain detachment, even in his most "patriotic" verse, from the chaos of current political life.

The two plays The Countess Kathleen and Cathleen Ni Houlihan pose more difficult problems. Although both deal with a central personality who ignores his private preoccupations and devotes himself to a public cause, there is some difficulty in determining how propagandistic these plays really are. Certainly the latter play is the closest that Yeats ever came to writing something which actually led to revolutionary action. There is some question, however, of just how aware he was of this at the time he wrote it. An acquaintance records a revealing remark by Yeats on this subject: he reflected many years later to the playwright Philip Barry that "Cathleen Ni Houlihan was propaganda, but I was not conscious of it at the time." [34] And much later, in the poem "The Man and the Echo," Yeats asked in near despair, "Did that play of mine send out / Certain men the English shot?" [35]

There is no doubt, however, that certain lines in the play do have clear political relevance. When Cathleen Ni Houlihan is asked what set her wandering, she answers "Too many strangers in the house." And to the question "What was it put the trouble on you?" her reply is, "My land that was taken from me." [36] Cathleen, who represents Ireland, insists also on the total devotion which is demanded of each person who fights for her cause: "If anyone would give me help he must give me himself, he must give me all." [37] The propaganda value of such lines is obvious. Her aim is to free Ireland from British rule, or as she puts it in not very subtle form, "the hope of putting the strangers out of my house." [38] That the audience had no difficulty in understanding the meaning of these remarks is made clear by Lady Gregory: "Of course the patriotic bits were applauded." [39] And it is equally clear that Yeats to some extent accepted his position as polemicist. Hone records that when he attempted to quiet the rioting audience of *The Playboy of the Western World*, he did not hesitate to shout from the stage "The author of *Cathleen Ni Houlihan* addresses you." [40]

The time soon came, however, when Yeats began to feel that politics and literature simply could not mix, that the whole province of public debate and controversy would only have a damaging effect on the true artist. A number of events impelled him to make this revaluation, perhaps the most important among them Maud Gonne's marriage in 1903 to John MacBride. Since, in addition, MacBride lived in Paris at the time, the marriage in effect closed a chapter of Yeats's life with relative finality. The uneasy compromise between literature and political activity which Maud had inspired need no longer be sustained. Yet her marriage was by no means the sole cause of Yeats's growing distrust and final rejection of the union between literature and politics. It merely made it possible for him to respond to certain instincts which had always been a part of him. The demands of a politically oriented audience must be destructive to the ultimate ends of art, Yeats felt, a fact which seemed to be demonstrated often enough during the first few years of the Irish National Theatre. The trouble began as early as 1899, on the occasion of the first production of *The Countess Kathleen*. Yeats's enemy F. Hugh O'Donnell wrote a

pamphlet attacking the play, in which he suggested that
Kathleen's behavior presented a degrading picture of Irish
womanhood.[41] This pamphlet came to the attention of Cardinal
Logue who in turn suggested that Catholics should not see
the play. Some of the controversy inspired by these moves is
recorded in the last chapter of Joyce's *Portrait of the Artist as
a Young Man*, when Stephen recalls the shouts which greeted
the play on its opening night: "A libel on Ireland!" "No Irish
woman ever did it!" [42]

The controversy made it perfectly clear that what an
Irish audience insisted upon in its "heroic personalities" was
a kind of moral tidiness which seemed to Yeats quite beside
the point. It was a difficult job, as director of the Abbey Theatre,
for him to maintain his own standards against the flood of
patriotic and nationalistic but artistically second-rate literature
which was presented for possible production. The crisis was
reached in the riots over Synge's *Playboy* in 1907. The issue
was precisely the same as that of *The Countess Kathleen* eight
years before, since the objections to the play were primarily on
"moral" grounds. The Dublin audiences would not accept
Synge's vision of the heroic personality any more easily than
they had accepted Yeats's. Certainly this direct failure of the
audience and their demand for what seemed to Yeats a vulgar
kind of quality in the literary personalities they accepted as
praiseworthy only served to confirm his final divorce of literature
and politics. What, after all, could one do for people who rioted
over the propriety of using the word "shifts" on the stage?

Between 1903 and 1916, then, Yeats did not write anything
resembling the earlier patriotic pieces. There were, instead, the
bitter attacks on the public discussed in the previous chapter:
"On Those That Hated 'The Playboy of the Western World,'
1907" "To a Wealthy Man. . . ," and "September 1913." The
only poem which celebrates a national hero is the previously discussed "To a Shade" (1913) [43] which is addressed to Parnell;
not to Parnell the accepted public hero of Ireland, however, but
to the man who was himself scorned by the people. The movement away from the identification of the hero and his public
world is made clear in this and in the other poems of the

same period. The people abuse and disown him as they abused the heroes of the plays of Yeats and Synge. His monument is neglected; he is "safer in the tomb." For the people, the hero has become the enemy.

In view of such a negative evaluation of the political world of modern Ireland, and with the additional knowledge that Yeats's contempt for the people remained with him for the rest of his life, it is truly surprising that he wrote more poetry in praise of what we have defined as the public hero in the period after 1916 than he did in the earlier part of his life. What were the causes of this second and even more remarkable about-face? The time between 1916 and 1928 is the period of the poems on Robert Gregory, a war hero; of the various poems on the Easter Rising; of *The Dreaming of the Bones*, which, Yeats wrote to Lady Gregory, "is strong, too strong, politically." [44] Nearly half of the poems in the two major collections, *Michael Robartes and the Dancer* (1921) and *The Tower* (1928), have a significant connection with the world of contemporary politics. This fact prompts us to ask two questions: What brought Yeats back after his disillusionment to the celebration of public events and public heroes? How do these poems differ from the work of the earliest period?

The question of causes can not be answered simply, since Yeats's renewed interest in some of the national movements which were affecting Ireland was the result of the combination of several unrelated events. The first and possibly most important of these was the Easter Rebellion itself. As the poem "Easter, 1916" suggests, everything was "changed, changed utterly" by this event. The heroic gesture of the rebels, the seizure of the Post Office, and the martyrdom of those involved can best be called a rediscovery of Ireland's heroic potential. Yeats was amazed to find his country no longer a stage for "casual comedy," but rather one in which true human dignity could find its proper place in something like the dimension of classical tragedy. That is why the speaker in the poem shows such amazement in the lines "All changed, changed utterly: / A terrible beauty is born." O'Hegarty suggests that the rest of Ireland felt the same sense of discovery:

The tale was told gradually, and gradually Ireland . . . found Irish heroism to admire, and started back towards her heroic past. Ninety-eight had come to seem a very long time ago, and Forty-eight and Sixty-seven seemed like anti-climaxes, cherished by a small minority but regarded somewhat shamefacedly by the majority. But they, and 1916, were all of the same metal.[45]

Like all true heroes, the "Sixteen Dead Men" of the Easter Rising seemed to transcend the ordinary terms of right and wrong, practical and impractical action. It is perhaps this fact which Yeats found most congenial. Always at a loss in arguments concerning practical politics, he was happy to praise a deed which went beyond the realm of the practical, which bypassed the whole complex machinery of modern warfare and politics. The two poems "Sixteen Dead Men" and "The Rose Tree" make this point:

> O but we talked at large before
> The sixteen men were shot,
> But who can talk of give and take,
> What should be and what not
> While those dead men are loitering there
> To stir the boiling pot? [46]

The Easter Rebellion, however, was only one event in a chaotic world situation which could simply no longer be ignored. It was perhaps possible to forget war and politics before 1914, but in the holocaust of the World War (which was followed in Ireland by five years of civil war), one had at any rate to come to some terms with the external catastrophes. Good men, like Lady Gregory's son Robert, were killed in action; women were left to die in the streets; there was fighting in Dublin and elsewhere. It was, in short, becoming increasingly difficult for Yeats to maintain his isolation from political realities, to ignore the fact that "mere anarchy is loosed upon the world." The "Meditations in Time of Civil War," for example, were written as a kind of examination of the values of the contemplative life when it is surrounded by a world of intense activity. To this period also belongs the bitter "Nineteen Hundred and Nineteen."

Finally, we may suggest two more reasons for the shift in subject matter, the first Yeats's appointment to the Senate in

1922, the second his growing preoccupation with the subject of old age. Yeats was of course aware of the irony of the mocker of politics transformed into a senator and a "sixty-year old smiling public man." But certainly the experience forced him to take the world from which he had previously resigned more seriously. This was, after all, also the world of men like the minister Kevin O'Higgins, a heroic man in public life capable of making the ultimate sacrifice for a cause. In the short poem "Death" [47] written on the occasion of O'Higgins' assassination,[48] he is recognized as the classic type of the hero facing his end "in his pride," utterly scornful of mere "supersession of breath."

It is also possible to argue that Yeats's renewed interest in the public hero was awakened by his increasing concern with old age. To Yeats the old man, the contemplative life no longer seemed so clearly superior to the active life, perhaps because now there was only one choice left open to him. In some of Yeats's later poems, there is an almost nostalgic praise of activity for its own sake which seems to be inspired by the fact that a truly active life is becoming less and less possible for him. We can see this in the last section of "The Tower" as well as in the fifth of the "Meditations in Time of Civil War":

> An affable Irregular,
> A heavily-built Falstaffian man,
> Comes cracking jokes in civil war
> As though to die by gunshot were
> The finest play under the sun.
>
> . . . .
> I count those feathered balls of soot
> The moor-hen guides upon the stream
> To silence the envy in my thought.[49]

In all of these poems, however, there is no longer an emphasis on the public man as at one with the public and with the society which he supports. Rather, Yeats here creates the paradoxical image of the "private public man" previously discussed. The inner lives of the heroes of this period in Yeats's work are always more important than the outer events in which they happen to be involved. The "smiling public man" in "Among School Children," for example, is really neither smiling nor public when we find out more about him. That is only his external pose. The important thing about O'Higgins is not that he was killed, but rather how he faced his death. The thoughts of the heroes of "Easter, 1916" are completely unknown to the narrator of that poem. In all of these poems, there is an essential disparity between the account which a newspaper might give of the important public event and the account which only the private mind of the hero can give. In "An Irish Airman Foresees His Death" [50] we can see this paradox most clearly. The abstract anonymity of the title is in ironic contrast to the poem itself, which records the thoughts of a highly particularized person who seems anything but the "unknown soldier" of the title. He represents, in fact, nothing but himself, as the poem makes clear: "Those that I fight I do not hate, / Those that I guard I do not love." The alienation which these lines suggest leads one to ask what then has driven this airman into the war, what has made him a "public hero." The answer is provided by the poem:

> Nor law, nor duty bade me fight,
> Nor public men, nor cheering crowds,
> A lonely impulse of delight
> Drove to this tumult in the clouds.

In Yeats's later poetry, it is always the "lonely impulse" which inspires the hero to heroism, no matter how public the physical circumstances which surround him.

In the last ten years of Yeats's life, this emphasis on the privacy of the ideal public experience is rendered even more sharply. After 1928, when his period as Senator ended, Yeats in effect retired from public life. During his last ten years, he spent much time out of Ireland, in part for reasons of health. This fact, together with the relative degree of stability which the Irish nation reached in these years, increased the distance from which Yeats examined political and national issues and personalities. This distance created a sense of detachment in the political poetry of the last ten years which is very different from the tone of passionate involvement which finally comes through in an earlier poem like "Easter, 1916."

We may ask how the sense of detachment which seems to pervade these poems is actually created. The most important factor is probably the choice of the past as subject. It is significant that the public hero of the poems of the thirties is *still* Parnell, even though he had been dead for nearly half a century. In such poems as "Parnell's Funeral," "Come Gather Round Me, Parnellites," and "Parnell," the hero represents the past, not the present; and he functions as a measure of present "public" greatness. In the second section of "Parnell's Funeral" [51] the comparison is actually made. The modern public men, the leaders of the established state—De Valéra, Cosgrave, and O'Duffy—are tried by the standards established by Parnell and found wanting, "Their school a crowd, his master solitude." We see once more, in this summary line, the important qualification which Yeats insisted on for his public leaders. The modern heroes of Ireland know nothing about solitude; they have not, metaphorically, "eaten Parnell's heart." For this reason they are not genuinely heroic, but rather only examples of the "loose-lipped demagogue" who is indistinguishable from the crowd to which he appeals. Precisely the same comparison is made in "The Three Monuments," where the older public heroes are Nelson, O'Connell and Parnell.[52]

This use of the past in the political poems of the last period may be said to give a quality comparable to Wordsworth's "emotion recollected in tranquillity." Indeed, the phrase would apply well to these poems. There is a more measured sense of evaluation, of rational argument, and of resignation here, and all these qualities of course lead away entirely from the province of propaganda. Even in such rare attempts to write poetry for a specific political movement as the "Three Songs to the Same Tune," which were originally written for the United Ireland party,[53] we can detect the same sense of detachment. There were, as a matter of fact, two versions of this poem, the second attempting to eliminate what Yeats called the "rhetorical vehemence" of the first.[54] Finally, in "The Municipal Gallery Revisited," [55] we have a classic instance of the phenomenon of public heroism examined at a distance, both temporal and emotional. Casement, Griffith, and O'Higgins are all there, but transformed first by the distance of many years and second by the distance from the immediate event which art creates. Yeats examines not them but their portraits in the Municipal Gallery and suddenly realizes that this is not " 'The dead Ireland of my youth, but an Ireland / The poets have imagined, terrible and gay.' " Even the gallery itself is visited not for the first time but "revisited."

Detachment and distance, then, characterize Yeats's last poems on political and national subjects. We might be tempted to say that this is a kind of reversal akin to the earlier rejection of politically inspired heroism in the realm of action. But once again the matter is more difficult. In his last years Yeats was pulled at once both towards and away from the celebration of the public hero. The juxtaposition of the active and the contemplative, passive life in his poetry ended in a praise of activity closely connected, at least, with the life of the heroic warrior. Thus there is a suggestion, for example, in "Under Ben Bulben" that war completes man's vision, that violence itself creates heroic opportunity:

> You that Mitchel's prayer have heard,
> 'Send war in our time, O Lord!'
> Know that when all words are said
> And a man is fighting mad,
> Something drops from eyes long blind,
> He completes his partial mind.[56]

Or, in the uncompromising words of On the Boiler: "If human violence is not embodied in our institutions the young will not give them their affection, nor the young and old their loyalty. . . . Desire some just war, that big house and hovel, college and public house, civil servant . . . and international bridge-playing woman, may know that they belong to one nation." [57]

This praise of the active, passionate life rather than the passive, contemplative one led Yeats to make some surprising omissions from his well-known anthology, The Oxford Book of Modern Verse. Reviewers attacked the exclusion of the "War Poets," such as Wilfred Owen. Yeats justified his decision by saying that "passive suffering is not a theme for poetry." [58] This idea is echoed in another of his introductions: "Only where the mind partakes of a pure activity can art or life attain swiftness, volume, unity." [59] For this reason, there is, despite all the things he can find to say against it, a continuing interest in the public world even in Yeats's most bitter disillusionment with it. It is an interest, however, which the practical politician would call hopelessly romantic and anachronistic. For Yeats in fact valued the kind of hero who no longer really had a place in the intricacies of the modern bureaucratic state. When he reflects after half a century on the earliest discussions with O'Leary and his circle, Yeats recollects "we discussed perpetually the character of public men; we never asked were they able and well-informed but what would they sacrifice?" [60]

The truth of the matter is that Yeats's public heroes were qualified only for practical failure, however "heroic" or "tragic" that might be. With success they did not know how to cope, particularly in the very different world which success had brought to the Irish nationalists: "For triumph can but mar our solitude." The whole realm of practical politics did not appeal to him. Hearing a speech of De Valéra's he could only say contemptuously, "A living argument rather than a living man." [61] Yeats would have agreed with a similarly disillusioned character in Conrad's *Nostromo*: "There was something inherent in the necessities of successful action which carried with it the moral degradation of the idea." [62]

The whole matter is very well summed up in the words of the historian Mansergh, who sees the split between the poet and politics as inevitable in Ireland after the romantic ideal had ceased to be useful:

> That background of romantic idealism which inspired the Celtic Renaissance and clothed with heroic glamour a well-nigh forgotten past, fostered an outlook on the future far removed from the realities of political and social life in the modern world. . . . The simplicity of a single idea, national independence, appealed to the imaginative poets: the complexity of modern government arouses only their protest.[63]

Yeats's ideal public hero, the hero of "the last romantics," had become a displaced enchanter in a world of facts, deprived at last of his power, his usefulness, and his moral sanction.

Notes

1. Yeats wrote a preface to H. P. R. Finberg's translation of *Axel*.
2. Jean Marie Matthias Philippe Auguste Count de Villiers de l'Isle-Adam, *Axel*, trans. H. P. R. Finberg (London, 1925), p. 284. In the

scene where Sara and Axel contemplate suicide, the following dialogue is also pertinent:

SARA: Perhaps it would be nobler to think of the common good.
AXEL: All things devour each other: such is the price paid for the common good. [p. 288]

3. *Variorum*, p. 103.
4. Yeats's letter to William Rothenstein, reprinted in William Rothenstein, *Since Fifty; Men and Memories, 1922–1938* (London, [1939]), p. 308.
5. Yeats, *Last Poems and Two Plays*, p. 47.
6. *The Senate Speeches of W. B. Yeats*, pp. 75–76.
7. *Variorum*, pp. 391–94.
8. *Ibid.*, pp. 617–18.
9. *Ibid.*, pp. 605–608.
10. Yeats, *Wheels and Butterflies* (London, 1934), p. 75.
11. O'Hegarty, *A History of Ireland under the Union*, p. 7.
12. Bernard Shaw, *John Bull's Other Island with How He Lied to Her Husband and Major Barbara* (London, 1931), p. 65.
13. Pearse, *Three Lectures on Gaelic Topics*, p. 54.
14. *Variorum*, pp. 292–93.
15. *Ibid.*, pp. 289–90.
16. *Ibid.*, pp. 428–33.
17. Jonathan Swift, *A Discourse of the Contests and Dissensions*, p. 259.
18. *Variorum*, p. 398.
19. *Ibid.*, pp. 577–78.
20. Quoted in Raymond Mander and Joe Mitchenson, *Theatrical Companion to Shaw: A Pictorial Record of the First Performances of the Plays of George Bernard Shaw* (London, 1954), p. 63. It would be tempting to invent a complete intellectual opposition between Yeats and Shaw here, one which postulated that Shaw's heroes were realists and Yeats's idealists. But although Shaw used the word "realist" to refer to the highest class of men in *The Quintessence of Ibsenism* as well as in his plays, the term itself is misleading. His "realists" are often not very different from visionaries, particularly in view of the careful distinction which Shaw made between the imaginative realist who has *seen through* his illusions, and the philistine practical man who never had any to begin with. Shaw's "realists," like Yeats's heroes, are often close to saints: St. Joan, Major Barbara, the "young saint" Father Keegan of *John Bull's Other Island.* Even Don Juan is on his way to Heaven! The two writers had more in common than is at first evident.
21. Auden, *The Enchafèd Flood*, p. 106.
22. Eglinton, *Some Essays and Passages*, ed. Yeats, p. 7.
23. *W. B. Yeats and T. Sturge Moore: Their Correspondence 1901–1937*, p. 159.
24. *Letters on Poetry from W. B. Yeats to Dorothy Wellesley* (New York, 1940), p. 8.
25. *Ibid.*, p. 13.
26. Yeats, *Essays*, p. 499.
27. *Variorum*, pp. 565–67.
28. Joseph Hone, *W. B. Yeats 1865–1939* (New York, 1943), p. 102.

29. Maud Gonne MacBride, A *Servant of the Queen* (Dublin, 1950), p. 169.
30. Hone, p. 152.
31. *Variorum*, pp. 709–15.
32. O'Hegarty, pp. 641–49.
33. *Variorum*, pp. 737–38.
34. Patrick McCartan, "William Butler Yeats—the Fenian," *Ireland-American Review*, I, 417.
35. *Variorum*, p. 632.
36. Yeats, *Cathleen Ni Hoolihan* (London, 1902), p. 17.
37. *Ibid.*, p. 22.
38. *Ibid.*, p. 23.
39. *Lady Gregory's Journals 1916–1930*, ed. Lennox Robinson (New York, 1947), p. 57.
40. Hone, p. 231.
41. *Ibid.*, p. 169.
42. James Joyce, A *Portrait of the Artist as a Young Man* (New York, 1916), p. 266.
43. *Variorum*, pp. 292–93.
44. Hone, p. 324.
45. O'Hegarty, pp. 709–10.
46. "Sixteen Dead Men," *Variorum*, p. 395.
47. *Variorum*, p. 476.
48. See Hone, p. 408.
49. *Variorum*, pp. 423–24.
50. *Ibid.*, p. 328.
51. *Ibid.*, pp. 541–43.
52. A. Norman Jeffares, W. B. *Yeats Man and Poet* (London, 1949), p. 240.
53. Hone, p. 467
54. *Variorum*, p. 543 n.
55. *Ibid.*, pp. 601–604.
56. *Ibid.*, p. 638.
57. Yeats, *On the Boiler*, p. 30.
58. Yeats, Introduction to *The Oxford Book of Modern Verse* (Oxford, 1936), p. xxxiv.
59. Yeats, Introduction to Hone and Rossi, *Bishop Berkeley*, p. xxvii.
60. Yeats, *The Words upon the Window Pane*, p. 2.
61. Hone, p. 345.
62. Joseph Conrad, *Nostromo* (New York, 1951), p. 582.
63. Nicholas Mansergh, *Ireland in the Age of Reform and Revolution*, p. 231.

5 · The Visionary

> Wherefore if a man makes right use of such means of remembrance, and ever approaches to the full vision of the perfect mysteries, he and he alone becomes truly perfect. Standing aside from the busy doings of mankind, and drawing nigh to the divine, he is rebuked by the multitude as being out of his wits, for they know not that he is possessed by a deity.
>
> PLATO

"ALL OUR ART," Yeats wrote to his father in 1913, "is but the putting our faith and the evidence of our faith into words or forms and our faith is in ecstasy." [1] This last chapter will try to clarify the meaning of this important statement by describing the final type in Yeats's heroic triumvirate, the visionary, the man whose "faith is in ecstasy." By "vision" Yeats tells us that he meant "the intense realization of a state of ecstatic emotion symbolized in a definite imagined region." [2] From the simplest point of view, then, the visionary hero is the man capable of such a state of ecstasy. Any attempt to characterize him with great precision will inevitably be difficult, since the visionary in his ecstatic state loses "himself" in gaining another world outside the realm of character and personality. The problem is thus different from any we have encountered in the previous discussions, for we shall be more interested in the act of vision and the world which vision reveals than in the actual seer.

This does not mean that there are fewer visionaries in Yeats's poetic and dramatic works than there are aristocrats or public heroes. If anything, there are more. But here more than anywhere else we must keep firmly in mind that all of Yeats's heroes were more important for their noble qualities of mind and spirit than for the accidental "facts" of their lives and personalities. When we say that the Yeatsian visionary is anyone who seeks or has found the experience of "Heaven blazing into the head," as "Lapis Lazuli" describes it, it should become clear that the category includes many of his characters. In the plays, for example, there is the Cuchulain of *At the Hawk's Well*, Forgael, the hero of *The Shadowy Waters*, Mary in *The Land of Heart's Desire*, the main characters in both *The Hour-Glass* and *The Unicorn from the Stars*, The Hebrew and The Greek in *The Resurrection*, and a number of others. In the poems we find among others the hero of *The Wanderings of Oisin*, Sheba in the Solomon and Sheba poems, Crazy Jane, Ribh, and Mohini Chatterjee. The important point to remember, however, is that many of Yeats's visionaries have practically no "personality" at all. They are the speakers, often unnamed, of some of the finest poems: "The Gyres," "Byzantium," "The Cold Heaven," "The Double Vision of Michael Robartes." The last named poem is a case in point, for though Michael Robartes is a distinct character in several of Yeats's works, in this visionary poem his personality is of no importance whatever. The only thing that matters is what he has seen. The same is true of Ribh, the speaker of the important "Supernatural Songs." We shall be interested, then, in all of these poems and plays, primarily in the visionary experience itself. With the exception of Crazy Jane, the visionaries are deliberately *transparent* characters who call little attention to themselves.

It is simpler to describe what the visionary is not than what he is. He does not, for example, know the ordinary comforts of home and family, and when his supernatural quest ends in disappointment, he is sometimes ridiculed for his useless sacrifice:

> He might have lived at his ease,
> An old dog's head at his knees,
> Among his children and friends.[3]

When he is successful, the visionary is capable of direct contact with a supernatural world of spirit, a contact not mediated by church or priest. Although such ecstatic vision is temporary and unpredictable, when it comes it makes of the seer a potential prophet: he has "mummy truths to tell / Whereat the living mock."[4] But those truths are often as obscure as were the Delphic oracles, for the visionary often cannot translate his ecstatic perceptions into rational terms. He can only describe what he has seen, and sometimes he speaks cryptically, in a foreign tongue:

> A passion-driven exultant man sings out
> Sentences that he has never thought.[5]

It is apparent that "the living mock" what they cannot understand; but then the *communication* of his private vision, although desirable, is not the duty of the Yeatsian visionary. "What matter that you understood no word!" Ribh says contemptuously:

> Doubtless I spoke or sang what I had heard
> In broken sentences.[6]

It has been suggested at the beginning of this study that Yeats's whole conception of heroism is essentially nostalgic and anachronistic. The epic warrior, the aristocrat, the ruler who has little but contempt for those he rules—all these heroic types seem to have little connection with the realities of contemporary life, with the technical impersonality of modern warfare, with the ideal of social justice, with government by democratic consent. Yet we recognize these heroic prototypes as figures from the not so distant past, and we are familiar enough with various forms of conservative thought that continue to idealize them. Yeats's peculiar celebration of the visionary hero, however, is likely to be less familiar (and therefore more incomprehensible) because such a man is not a figure from the immediate past; he seems to go back to a much more primitive, even archaic, form of religious belief. He is religious only in the broadest sense of the word; he is not identifiable with, say, the saint of Christian belief, and still less with the faithful disciple of any organized religion. To think of him in such familiar terms might make Yeats's religious beliefs more palatable to some readers, but it does so at the price of truth.

Yeats's visionary hero is closer to the figure of the shaman in archaic society than to any of the "respectable" religious types with which we are likely to be acquainted. The shaman, as Mircea Eliade defines him, "specializes in a trance during which his soul is believed to leave his body and ascend to the sky or descend to the underworld." [7] He is the seer, the prophet capable of direct perception of supernatural phenomena in moments of ecstatic transport. This form of religious belief, Eliade finds, is "fundamental in the human condition, and hence known to the whole of archaic humanity." [8] It seems likely that it is the oldest form of religious belief which *delegates* religious experience and authority to another person. It is thought to replace the very earliest religious faith, that in which all men feel capable of conversing directly with a Supreme Being. The shaman's celestial ascent is "a survival, profoundly modified and sometimes degenerated, of this archaic religious ideology centered on faith in a celestial Supreme Being and belief in concrete communications between heaven and earth." [9]

One might say, then, that the visionary or the shaman or seer is the first heroic specialist a civilization is likely to produce. He is very clearly separated from the mass of mankind; he performs a narrowly limited but essential task in a society; he is the custodian of man's delegated ecstatic powers. In addition, he is also usually a poet, *the* poet of his society; his task is to communicate his ecstatic vision, and he does this in elevated, rhythmic utterance. As N. K. Chadwick explains:

> Everywhere, then, on the periphery of the great Eurasian continent, the peninsulas and outer islands, the steppes and tundras, which have preserved in written form or oral tradition the mantic habit and the traditions associated with it, we find the art of poetry in the closest association with the trance of the seer. We may go further, and say that it is the medium by which the seer links his fellow-men with the spirit world.[10]

The very word "inspiration" associates the roles of poet and shaman-prophet.

Of course there is no equivalent to such a figure in modern civilization. If we use the word of someone in our own society, we use it metaphorically. That Yeats chose to idealize a form of heroism remarkably like that of shamanistic belief suggests that his religious preoccupations are ultimate regressions to a long-since abandoned religious form. Of course, Yeats was not entirely alone in this anachronistic religious ideal. There had been and continued to be a line of poets and religious thinkers, usually ignored or contemplated with distrust by their contemporaries, who might be said to form a tradition with which he associated himself. Yeats's interest in some of the particular forms of this tradition will be more fully discussed below. It is important to understand, however, that his most important commitment was to the basic idea of ecstatic experience itself —and to the association of that experience with poetry—rather than to any individual writer or group who may have had a similar commitment.

There is one important and revealing difference between the archaic shaman and Yeats's modern visionary: his place in society. It has already been suggested that the shaman plays an important role in the community, that he achieves his religious preeminence because he takes upon himself a demanding task which the ordinary man values but cannot duplicate. As a result, the shaman in archaic culture has the "highest claim to the reverence of his society"; he is "the leading intellectual and artistic influence" [11] in the primitive world. "This small mystical elite not only directs the community's religious life but, as it were, guards its 'soul!'" [12] In the modern world, by contrast, the visionary has no fixed place of honor; his task is not recognized as of the slightest value to the community. Even the religious establishment distrusts him, since he is not willing to submit his purely private ecstatic experience to the possible censorship of a necessarily conservative church. In Yeats's eyes, however, this isolation is heroic, since it is society's blindness which denies the latter-day shaman his vital role in the community.

In one sense, this last and most important of Yeats's heroic conceptions never changes. The seer's faith is always in the existence of a supernatural world, his only goal to establish some kind of contact with it. But something does change in the course of Yeats's career, his ideas on *how* and *what* the visionary sees. This chapter will therefore concentrate on the significant shifts in Yeats's conception of the means to vision and the supernatural world which vision reveals, as it is recorded in the plays and poems of different periods.

In attempting to clarify this problem, two great difficulties present themselves to us almost immediately, one of vocabulary, the other of belief. The first of these is no less acute for the visionary himself than for those who try to understand his experience at one remove. Our vocabulary may be adequate to describe the familiar natural world, but it is almost bound to seem seriously inadequate when it is used to describe the supernatural world of vision. Even the poetic method of metaphorical description is no more than a moderately satisfactory means of approximation to a true picture of supernatural phenomena and ecstatic experience. Yeats himself uses a variety of metaphors: the rose, the dance, the city of Byzantium, the well, white birds, the moon, even "a gold-fish swimming in a bowl," but he is always aware that this is only "a discourse in figurative speech . . . on the soul's journey." [13]

The problem of finding an adequate spiritual vocabulary for the poetry of vision is made even more difficult by the fact that Yeats, like many writers of the nineteenth and twentieth centuries, did not limit himself to the accepted, conventional body of metaphors of any orthodox faith. Or rather, to be more accurate, he exploited without very much system almost every kind of spiritual vocabulary which could conceivably have been familiar to his readers: Irish and Greek myth, Christianity, Buddhism, theosophy, spiritualism, philosophical idealism, and the systems of the Romantic poets. One might almost say that he appropriated these "consecrated vocabularies" in the most eclectic possible fashion, without regard to anything but the internal consistency of his own work. With such a variety of sources, it is absurd to claim for Yeats a positive loyalty to any one system of supernatural belief. He was not a philosopher or theologian, and his poetry does not spring from a single, unified, and coherent external source, for Yeats accepted none of the decorums of language in any of the visionary writings with which he was familiar. Rather he reversed, revised, and combined these sources to fit his own needs.

The second and more difficult problem is one of belief. We may disagree with Yeats's social and political ideas, with his concept of aristocracy or of public heroism, but we could hardly deny that such ideas are within the realm of rational argument. The supernatural is another story. As R. P. Blackmur put it, "The supernatural is simply not part of our mental furniture, and when we meet it in our reading we say: Here is debris to be swept away." [14] Yeats's interest in spiritualism and theosophy prompts W. H. Auden to ask indignantly, "How *could* Yeats, with his great aesthetic appreciation of aristocracy, ancestral houses, ceremonious tradition, take up something so essentially lower-middle class—or should I say Southern Californian—so ineluctably associated with suburban villas and clearly unattractive faces?" [15] It is tempting to answer such snobbish scepticism by citing one of Yeats's favorite writers, William Blake: "Those who cannot defend the truth shall defend an error that enthusiasm and life may not cease." [16] But Auden's objection is really more important than that, since it represents an attitude which some of Yeats's greatest admirers share.

To understand why Yeats did associate himself with such a variety of unpopular and unfashionable beliefs, we must first understand the nature of his quarrel with the influential thinkers of his youth and early manhood, and for this there is no better place to begin than with his oft-quoted explanation in *Four Years*:

> I was unlike others of my generation in one thing only. I am very religious, and deprived by Huxley and Tyndall, whom I detested, of the simple-minded religion of my childhood, I had made a new religion, almost an infallible church, out of poetic tradition: a fardel of stories, and of personages, and of emotions, a bundle of images and of masks passed on from generation to generation by poets & painters with some help from philosophers and theologians. I wished for a world where I could discover this tradition perpetually.[17]

When we see Yeats's "new religion" as in part a reaction to writers like T. H. Huxley and John Tyndall, Bertrand Russell, G. E. Moore and others like them, the impulse which created the visionary hero in a predominantly sceptical age becomes easier to understand.

The writings of T. H. Huxley deprived Yeats of his Christian faith by their rigorously scientific investigation of the authenticity of the sacred texts.[18] Huxley was of course working in the tradition of men like Strauss, Renan, Feuerbach, Hennell, and Butler. As Yeats was later to say about Péguy, "His Christianity is of course for us impossible—how take all simply when the very authority of texts is in question?" [19] But the attitude of mind behind the Higher Criticism was perhaps even more important than its specific targets. The method of both Huxley

and Tyndall in their philosophical writings is simply the method
of science, with its constant demand for evidence. Huxley says
of the existence of a spiritual world, for instance:

> I think it may be as well to repeat . . . that *a priori* notions,
> about the possibility, or the impossibility, of the existence of
> a world of spirits, such as that presupposed by genuine
> Christianity, have no influence on my mind. The question for
> me is purely one of evidence: is the evidence adequate to
> bear out the theory, or is it not? In my judgment it is not
> only inadequate, but quite absurdly insufficient. And on that
> ground, I should feel compelled to reject the theory; even if
> there were no positive grounds for adopting a totally different
> conception of the Cosmos.[20]

And this constant demand for evidence, the sceptical investigation of the Gospels, of the records of Christian miracles, and of
all forms of spiritual faith in search of "a rational ground of
belief which the writers of the Gospels . . . would regard . . .
as a kind of blasphemy" [21] could, Huxley claims, only lead the
unprejudiced observer to an honest Agnosticism. The enemy of
all "superstition," according to both Huxley and Tyndall, is
Science. "The aim and effort of science," Tyndall writes, "is to
explain the unknown in terms of the known," while the super-
stitious man will explain "the unknown in terms of the more
unknown." [22] And Huxley sees the conflict as a broad opposition
between the two forces:

> The extant forms of Supernaturalism have deep roots in human
> nature, and will undoubtedly die hard; but, in these latter
> days, they have to cope with an enemy whose full strength
> is only just beginning to be put out, and whose forces, gather-
> ing strength year by year, are hemming them round on every
> side. This enemy is Science, in the acceptation of systematised
> natural knowledge, which, during the last two centuries, has
> extended those methods of investigation, the worth of which
> is confirmed by daily appeal to Nature, to every region in
> which the Supernatural has hitherto been recognised.[23]

Christianity was not the only target of the "rational investi-
gator," however. Both philosophical idealism and various less
respectable forms of supernatural belief found themselves under
attack as well. Yeats might have been just as unhappy about the
attacks on spiritualism, for example Tyndall's "Science and

the Spirits," which concludes that "the drugged soul is beyond the reach of reason," [24] or Huxley's citation of an advertisement from a spiritualist journal as ironic evidence of the noble ideals of the spiritualist quest:

> To WEALTHY SPIRITUALISTS.—A Lady Medium of tried power wishes to meet with an elderly gentleman who would be willing to give her a comfortable home and maintenance in Exchange for her Spiritualistic services, as her guides consider her health is too delicate for public sittings: London preferred. —Address "Mary," Office of *Light*.[25]

This scientific attitude, the sceptical demand for proof, was also evident in more strictly philosophical discussion, in the attacks on various forms of Idealism. Huxley writes of the probable material basis of all man's "higher faculties": "Even those manifestations of intellect, of feeling, and of will, which we rightly name the higher faculties, are . . . known only as transitory changes in the relative positions of parts of the body. Speech, gesture, and every other form of human action are, in the long run, resolvable into muscular contraction, and muscular contraction is but a transitory change in the relative positions of the parts of a muscle." [26] Or, in Tyndall's even more positive words:

> I hardly imagine there exists a profound scientific thinker, who has reflected upon the subject, unwilling to admit the extreme probability of the hypothesis, that for every fact of consciousness, whether in the domain of sense, of thought, or of emotion, a certain definite molecular condition is set up in the brain; who does not hold this relation of physics to consciousness to be invariable, so that, given the state of the brain, the corresponding thought or feeling might be inferred; or given the thought or feeling, the corresponding state of the brain might be inferred.[27]

And what Huxley and Tyndall were doing from a scientific point of view, G. E. Moore and Bertrand Russell were corroborating from a more strictly philosophical one. Moore's "Refutation of Idealism," which Yeats called "the manifesto of modern realism," [28] attacks the Idealist's easy faith that "Reality is spiritual" with ironic logic by demonstrating that "*what is experienced*" is not "identical with *the experience of it*," [29] that the object of perception exists outside the mind of the perceiver. And in the chapter on Idealism in *The Problems of Philosophy*, Russell (who, Yeats angrily wrote Sturge Moore, "puts me into a state of incoherence") [30] attacked Berkeley's philosophy by suggesting the implausibility of "confusing the thing apprehended with the act of apprehension." [31]

Against these influential scientists and philosophers and others like them, Yeats strove to retain and even to promulgate two basically religious convictions:

1. That a supernatural world of spirit exists.
2. That man is potentially capable of perceiving it.

"Had he been a Catholic of Dante's time he would have been well content with Mary and the angels," [32] Yeats writes of Blake. But the sentence applies with even greater force to himself, for he lived in an age in which the beliefs of "Dante's time" were under even more strenuous attack, in which it seemed unthinkable that any intelligent man could retain his faith in a religion which had been "proven nonsense" by the most scientific means. His reaction to this dilemma, the need of a "very religious" man in an increasingly sceptical world, was what he called his "new religion," his "infallible church, out of poetic tradition." But unlike Blake's "new religion," that of Yeats was scarcely new at all; it was a "fardel of stories," a "bundle of images," but it was one of the most eclectic, disorganized, and undogmatic collections of "religious" tales ever put together. For Yeats's reaction to the scepticism of his generation was a desperate attempt to put together every possible bit of evidence to the contrary, every single fact or notion or idea which might be used to argue for the two religious convictions: the existence of a supernatural world, and man's potential ability to reach it. He was neither scientist, philosopher, nor theologian, yet in searching for "proof" that man's highest instincts are not merely a set of "muscular contractions," he trespassed freely into their domains, and then added to it the testimony of literature and myth. The result is a strange mélange indeed, but it is one which we must understand if we are to make sense of this most important of the Yeatsian heroes, the visionary.

Despite his frequent uneasy scepticism, Yeats had few doubts about the existence of a supernatural world as the realm of ultimate truth. In the essay on "Magic" in *Ideas of Good and Evil*, he stated the major premises of his "religion" with great succinctness:

> I believe in three doctrines . . .
> (1) That the borders of our minds are ever shifting, and that many minds can flow into one another, as it were, and create or reveal a single mind, a single energy.
> (2) That the borders of our memories are as shifting, and that our memories are a part of one great memory, the memory of Nature herself.
> (3) That this great mind and great memory can be evoked by symbols.[33]

This "great mind" and "great memory," which a more orthodox thinker might have called God, was the spiritual ultimate which Yeats felt had been denied by the modern materialistic thinkers. The symbols by which this hidden world was evoked could be the symbols of art as well as of religion, or they could be the symbolic figures of myth, which represented, for Yeats, a kind of halfway point between art and religion. "You must have a myth. No one can live without a myth," he says, because by myth man can represent "the gulf, which separates the one and the many, or, if you like, God and man." [34] In suggesting that the chief function of art was to evoke this spiritual world, Yeats felt himself to be challenging the accepted aesthetic of his time. But he was early convinced that the future would reject the limited, traditional Victorian ideal of art as a "criticism of life" or *magister vitae:* "I believe that all men will more and more reject the opinion that poetry is 'a criticism of life,' and be more and more convinced that it is a revelation of a hidden life, and that they may even come to think 'painting, poetry, and music' 'the only means of conversing with eternity left to man on earth.' " [35]

That "conversing with eternity" was still possible for men Yeats tried to show in several of his plays, three of which are in effect designed to be "replies to the sceptics." They are *The Hour-Glass, The Words upon the Window Pane,* and *The Resurrection,* produced respectively in 1903, 1930, and 1934. In each one, a materialistic, sceptical character is confronted with unquestionable proof of the reality of a spiritual world. *The Hour-Glass*, although it is one of Yeats's crudest plays, is interesting as a commentary on the idea of the neglect and final abandonment of spiritual truth in the modern world. A so-called "Wise Man" has been a teacher all his life, preaching that every spiritual world, Christian or not, is a hoax, and that the only reality is in what we can see and touch. Having managed to convince the world and himself of the truth of this idea, he is completely unprepared for the Angel who suddenly appears to announce that he is doomed to spend eternity in hell unless he can find one human being who still believes in a spiritual world. He finds to his horror that, partially through his own efforts, such people no longer exist in the world around him; and he is saved only because of his repentance and confession of faith: "I understand it all now. One sinks in on God; we do not see the truth; God sees the truth in us." [36]

The Words upon the Window Pane, although it deals with another realm of supernatural experience, that of spiritualism, follows a similar pattern. John Corbet, a sceptical Cambridge student who is writing a dissertation on Swift, is taken to a medium, a Mrs. Henderson, who evokes the spirit of Swift and speaks in his voice. The demonstration of her powers can be interpreted, and indeed is so interpreted by Corbet, as mere charlatanism by a brilliant actress who is highly informed about Swift's life. He stays behind to compliment her on her scholarship and to discuss his theories with her. But she sends him away because she understands nothing he is saying. Finally her sincerity is revealed to us after all her "customers" have left. In the final scene, on an empty stage, the trance comes over her once more, and she begins to speak in Swift's voice. The fact that this play is written with all the devices of the realistic theater suggests that it was aimed specifically at the sceptical audience of "naturalists."

The Resurrection, like *The Hour-Glass*, makes use of Christian supernaturalism. The sceptical character here is The Hebrew, convinced (until he is proven wrong by the Resurrection itself) that Christ was a very great man but no more than human. All three of these plays, then, teach the same lesson, although with varying degrees of subtlety; all are designed to demonstrate the truth of the first principle of visionary experience: that the spiritual world exists, and that the sceptical argument of the materialist is untenable.

The second premise of visionary experience, that man is capable of establishing some kind of contact with the supernatural world, does not necessarily follow from the first. Yet Yeats believed in it almost as firmly. We might call this elevated view of man romantic rather than classic, since the belief in man's capacity to achieve vision was one of the few things which all of the great English romantic poets (with the occasional exception of Byron) had in common. Yeats was reacting here against more "classical" Victorian poets like Arnold and Tennyson who emphasized both the practical uselessness of visionary experience and man's presumption in claiming it to be within his province. Like the romantics, Yeats felt impelled to establish and describe the possible link between man and a transcendent world of spirit. Unlike Arnold and Tennyson, he did not emphasize the idea of a break, a failure of connection, between the two. Such a view of man is essentially heroic, since it is based on the notion of almost unlimited human potential.

Yeats held to this belief during all of his adult life. As early as 1885, he and his fellow students of the Hermetic Society "differed from ordinary students of philosophy or religion through our belief that truth cannot be discovered but may be revealed, and that if a man do not lose faith, and if he go through certain preparations, revelation will find him at the fitting moment." [37] All men, not just some, are potentially capable of spiritual experience: "That we may believe that all men possess the supernatural faculties I would restore to the philosopher his mythology." [38] Furthermore, the belief in man's spiritual potential is of special importance to the artist, because "in the end the creative energy of men depends upon their believing that they have, within themselves, something immortal and imperishable." [39]

We can see, then, that Yeats's interest in visionary experience and his praise of the search for a spiritual world as the most important of the heroic modes was crucial and consistent. It has been suggested that in following this spiritual quest, Yeats made use of many different traditional vocabularies and beliefs. If we are to understand the role of the visionary in Yeats's poems and plays, we must first have some idea of how these traditional forms of spiritual experience are used in the poems and plays and what relationship they have to Yeats's own ideas. Broadly speaking, these sources might be said to come under four different headings: philosophical, religious, scientific, and literary.

The philosophical problem is of course not easily separated from the more strictly religious one. What is at issue here in its broadest terms is the metaphysical question of the nature of ultimate reality. Yeats needed ammunition to fight the materialists, and his search for proof of the existence of a spiritual world which was at least as "real" as the philosopher's tables and chairs forced him to come to terms with some of the possible though not inevitable concomitants of Idealist thought: the belief in man's soul, the superiority of human imagination and reason to the things which they perceive. Yeats read a great deal of philosophy in the years after the publication of the first edition of *A Vision*. Between 1924 and the end of his life he read Plato and Plotinus, Berkeley, Schopenhauer, Kant, Hegel, Croce, Gentile, Bergson, Wyndham Lewis, and many others, always searching for evidence to be used against the materialists and sceptics, against anyone who denied the existence of a world of spirit. *His* Berkeley, he says, is the man who wrote " 'things only exist in being perceived,' and I can only call that perception God's when I add Blake's 'God only acts or is in existing beings or men.' " [40] And it is clear that Berkeley's purpose accords fundamentally with Yeats's own, when he writes in *The Principles of Human Knowledge* that he addresses himself "to those who are tainted with Scepticism, or want a demonstration of the existence and immateriality of God, or the natural immortality of the Soul," [41] in order to tell them "that all the choir of heaven and furniture of the earth, in a word all those bodies which compose the mighty frame of the world, have not any subsistence without a mind; that their *being* is to be perceived or known." [42] But there were other Idealists, writing before and after Berkeley, who had come to the same conclusion by different means. Henry More, the seventeenth century English Platonist, whom Yeats had read "all summer" [43] in 1914, went so far as to use various spiritualist phenomena—"speakings, knockings, opening of doors when they were fast shut, sudden lights in the midst of a room floating in the aire"—as "an undeniable Argument, that there be such things as *Spirits* or *Incorporeal Substances* in the world." [44] And in Plotinus's idea of "The Proficient," Yeats found a parallel to his own ideal of the ecstatic visionary: "Many times it has happened: lifted out of the body into myself; becoming external to all other things and self-encentred; beholding a marvellous beauty; then, more than ever, assured of community with the loftiest order; enacting the noblest life, acquiring identity with the divine." [45]

But there were also modern philosophers, post-Moore and post-Russell, who offered valuable testimony. The Italian Giovanni Gentile, for example, confirmed the immortality of the soul in what Yeats called his "dry difficult beautiful book" [46] *The Mind as Pure Act:* "The affirmation of the immortality of the soul is immanent in the affirmation of the soul. For this affirmation is the 'I' affirming itself, and it is the simplest, most elementary, and therefore the indispensable act of thinking." [47] And Wyndham Lewis whose "most humble and admiring disciple" [48] Yeats calls himself, praises Berkeley's as "one of the best of all possible philosophic worlds." [49] Yeats's most concentrated effort to deal with the philosophical aspects of the problem can be found in the correspondence with his friend Sturge Moore between 1925 and 1928.[50] It is perfectly obvious throughout this long exchange of letters on the subject of "Idealism" that Moore's is the true philosophical mind in the debate, that Yeats is forever confusing and misquoting authorities, arguing about first principles with the aid of rumor and prejudice, and constantly being carried away by his desire to demonstrate his "necessary beliefs" at any cost. Moore on the other hand answers patiently, logically, and with great clarity. The whole correspondence suggests above all the desperation of Yeats's search for spiritual authority. It is true that in the twenties and thirties he read philosophy voraciously, but his reading was neither dispassionate nor clear-sighted. And he says more than once that he does not feel himself to be "at my ease in recent philosophy." [51] For he was essentially uncomfortable with the whole process of logical deduction and carefully reasoned statement. What he wanted was a faith which needed less subtle demonstration because it was so obviously true. In that search he turned from philosophy to religion, and it is here that his eclecticism is most in evidence, for his interest led him to ancient Ireland, to Christianity, to the mystics, to Buddhism and Hinduism, and to occult religion. It is, of course, neither possible nor necessary for us to trace fully Yeats's use of all of these spiritual disciplines, but a few words concerning his interest in each, and the relationship of each to his own ideas of visionary experience, will be helpful here.

The realm of spirit which Yeats used most frequently in his works is that of Irish myth, which has already been discussed in detail in Chapter 2. The supernatural world of Tir-na-n-Og, like that of Greek mythology, was close enough to human experience and the ordinary life of man to make it particularly useful for a poet who was trying to emphasize the relationship between the two. "In Ireland," Yeats wrote, "this world and the other are not widely sundered; sometimes, indeed, it seems almost as if our earthly chattels were no more than the shadows of things beyond." [52] In Irish mythology, the hero becomes godlike as the gods become human. As O'Grady puts it in his *Early Bardic Literature*, the hero "would pass into the world of the supernatural," [53] and as the "hero was exalted into a god, so in turn a god sank into a hero." [54]

The particular advantages of the use of Irish supernatural subject matter for a poet like Yeats were considerable. His objection to more formalized religion was essentially that the paraphernalia of priesthood, churches, and moral codes only led away from the true center of religion, from the spiritual experience itself. The fairy world of the Irish myths, on the other hand, was an unburdened realm of the imagination. Created by poets, revived by poets, it had a kind of purity and freedom from dogma which liberated rather than restrained man's imaginative spirit.

Yeats's use of Christian materials is a considerably more complicated problem. There are of course many poems and plays which seem to stress the inadequacy of orthodox Christianity: Crazy Jane argues with the Bishop and gets the last word; "Ribh Considers Christian Love Insufficient"; "Ribh Denounces

Patrick"; in the late poem "Church and State," the Church is identified with "the mob that howls at the door"; the poems "Veronica's Napkin" and "A Stick of Incense" come close to blasphemy. In the early poems and plays, Yeats often opposes two transcendental worlds: those of Christianity and Irish myth. The Priest of "The Priest and the Fairy," [55] for example, says that the souls of the fairies "are lost, they are lost, each one." Father Hart, in *The Land of Heart's Desire*, identifies the fairies with devils:

> they are the children of the fiend,
> And they have power until the end of time,
> When God shall fight with them a great pitched battle
> And hack them into pieces.[56]

In the same play, the fairy child shrieks when she sees the crucifix and demands that it be taken away; and in *Where There Is Nothing*, Paul's visions are contrasted with Father Jerome's cautious advice. Yet in all of these works, Christianity is opposed to the *true* way and comes close to playing the villain's part.

Nevertheless, in many significant works Yeats treats Christian belief and story with respect. The Countess Kathleen is really a Christian religious heroine, and her reward is the traditional Christian salvation. *The Hour-Glass*, discussed previously, uses the framework of Christianity, and *The Resurrection* is a highly orthodox play. The poem on "The Mother of God" is serious and moving, and in "Sailing to Byzantium" the speaker addresses the "sages standing in God's holy fire" with reverence. How then can we explain this seemingly inconsistent attitude?

The answer is in part that Yeats objected to the Church, not to the religion. The institutional aspect of Christianity, the "rules" and the clergy, were for him the unacceptable aspect of a powerful spiritual discipline. The original inspiration which preceded the formalized code of Christian belief had disappeared, Yeats felt, and in its place was the narrow-minded and intolerant clergy which had destroyed Parnell, which concerned itself with making rules about good and bad plays, with the moral rather than with the spiritual life. This was the world of the petty merchants who added "prayer to shivering prayer" in order to buy their way into Heaven, who had nothing but contempt for true visionaries like Crazy Jane and Tom the Lunatic. Yet Yeats's objection to institutional Christianity is only half the story, for as we shall see presently, he had a more fundamental quarrel with Christian belief, especially in his later years. It was possible, he felt, for a religion to be *too* transcendental, too anxious to devalue and debase the quality of this world in order to establish the absolute value of the world of spirit.

One can also argue that Yeats was not an orthodox Christian because he was concerned solely with the mystical experience itself and ignored the more formal and less private aspects of religion, such as dogma, creeds, liturgy, and worship. Yet "mysticism" does not quite define Yeats's belief either, although he shares with the mystic the belief in the two important premises of spiritual experience discussed above. As Evelyn Underhill suggests in her *Mysticism*, "Of all those forms of life and thought with which humanity has fed its craving for truth, mysticism alone postulates, and in the persons of its great initiates proves, not only the existence of the Absolute, but also this link: this possibility first of knowing, finally of attaining it." [57] From such a point of view, Yeats was certainly a mystic, even though he might have quarreled with the idea of man's "attaining" to, rather than simply experiencing, the Absolute. Another thing which appealed to Yeats about mysticism was its relative freedom from ethical argument, especially since he believed that Christianity had been corrupted by an overemphasis on morality. In a letter to his father, written in 1918, he objects to the idea of Bunyan as a mystic and suggests that "it is not possible to make a definition of mysticism to include him." Bunyan is more "pietist" than mystic. The true mystic "does not give his reasons." [58]

Yet there are also significant differences between Yeats's beliefs and those of the mystic. As he writes to Ethel Mannin in 1938, "Am I a mystic?—no, I am a practical man. I have seen the raising of Lazarus and the loaves and fishes and have made the usual measurements, plummet line, spirit-level and have taken the temperature by pure mathematic." [59] What Yeats probably means by this ironically cryptic statement is that the mystic is too willing to accept supernatural phenomena on faith alone, while our own age demands a kind of scientific certainty because of the nagging scepticism which affects even the most willing believers. The mystic's faith—though enviable—is not tested by doubt, it is too easy. And beyond this, Yeats departs from mysticism in yet another way. Like Bergson, like Nietzsche, he is as much interested in the movement which leads downward into life as upward away from it:

> I am content to live it all again
> And yet again, if it be life to pitch
> Into the frog-spawn of a blind man's ditch,
> A blind man battering blind men.[60]

For Yeats, as for Heraclitus (whom he admired), life is a chaos, a world in constant motion, a flux, and man's spiritual search is not a desire to escape into stillness and serene contemplation. The only absolute realm is itself in constant motion, or at least seems so to the human observer. Any *more* transcendent reality than that is inevitably beyond man's reach.

The mystical and contemplative elements of Eastern religions attracted Yeats greatly, particularly after he met a Brahmin named Mohini Chatterjee through the Hermetic Society in 1885. In 1912 he was introduced to Tagore, whose *Gitanjali* he edited the next year. Twenty years later, Yeats met Shri Purohit Swami, "an Indian saint," [61] and wrote introductions to two of his works: *An Indian Monk, His Life and Adventures* and the translation of his master's *The Holy Mountain*, the story of a pilgrimage and religious initiation. In 1935 he was collaborating with the Swami on a translation of *The Ten Principal Upanishads*, and in 1936 he wrote another introduction for his friend's translation of *The Aphorisms of Yoga*.

Despite this continuing interest, however, there is relatively little direct reference to any specifically Indian religious themes or subjects in Yeats's work. There are, of course, a few early poems such as "Kanva on Himself" (excluded from the Definitive Edition) and the various Indian poems in *Crossways*. But the important poems on this subject, "Mohini Chatterjee" and "Meru," were published in 1930 and 1934, respectively. It seems clear, from these two poems, that what attracted Yeats was the idea of the eternal return, the cyclical view of history which

stressed the recurrence of life in perpetual reincarnation. It is
interesting that about the Buddhist Nirvana, the release from
the cycles, he says little. Thus in "Mohini Chatterjee," the de-
vout man consoles himself by saying,

> I have been a king,
> I have been a slave,
> Nor is there anything,
> Fool, rascal, knave,
> That I have not been.[62]

The acceptance of such a cyclical pattern may itself abolish the
tyranny of Time for the initiate:

> Birth is heaped on birth
> That such cannonade
> May thunder time away.[63]

"Meru" makes the same point:

> Hermits upon Mount Meru or Everest
> . . . know
> That day brings round the night, that before dawn
> His glory and his monuments are gone.[64]

In the end, nevertheless, there were things which Yeats
found unsatisfactory in both Buddhism and Hinduism as well.
He said that his friend Tagore wrote "too much about God.
. . . My mind resents the vagueness of all such references." [65]
When asked for a "message to India," Yeats said, "Let 100,000
men of one side meet the other. That is my message to India,
insistence on the antinomy . . . . Conflict, more conflict." [66]
The goal of Buddhism (at least before Mahāyāna Buddhism)
after all, was Nirvana, the release from the cycles. Yeats's instincts led him too much in the other direction, as he realized as
early as 1906 in a letter to Florence Farr: "I have myself by the
by begun eastern meditations—of your sort, but with the object
of trying to lay hands upon some dynamic and substantialising
force as distinguished from the eastern quiescent and super-
sensualising state of the soul—a movement downwards upon
life, not upwards out of life." [67] Once again an orthodox spiritual
discipline had proved unsatisfactory.

Certainly the most difficult relationship of all to unravel is
that between Yeats and the interrelated systems of the occult:

magic, spiritualism, and theosophy. It is here that the patience of many modern readers, no matter how much they may admire Yeats as a writer, often ends. A thorough study of this phase of Yeats's thought would be out of all proportion to its importance for our particular purposes and would lead us far afield. There are, however, certain general facts which should be briefly recorded. First of all, Yeats was interested in various theosophical and spiritualist organizations during practically all of his adult life. In 1886 he organized the Dublin Hermetic Society and went to meetings of the Dublin Theosophic Lodge. The next year he began to attend sessions of Mme Blavatsky's London Lodge of the Theosophical Society, the Esoteric Section of which he joined in 1888. In 1890 he joined MacGregor Mathers' Order of the Golden Dawn and resigned from the Theosophical Society. A few years later he was busily planning an Irish mystical order. Although during the period of his greatest involvement with the Irish National Theatre there was some abatement in his interest, the period after 1911 saw a renewal or the earlier fascination. And with his marriage in 1917 to George Hyde-Lees, herself interested in these movements, Yeats felt at last that revelation had come to him, particularly when the "messages of the unknown instructors" came through the lips of his wife. These were to become the foundation of A Vision, on which he worked on and off for the next twenty years. It is therefore simply not possible to ignore completely this important aspect of Yeats's spiritual quest, particularly in view of such strong statements as this one in a letter to John O'Leary written in 1892: "Now as to Magic. It is surely absurd to hold me 'weak' or otherwise because I chose to persist in a study which I decided deliberately four or five years ago to make next to my poetry the most important pursuit of my life." [68] In this pursuit, Yeats read much in the literature of spiritualism, magic, and theosophy.

For our purposes, it will be sufficient to attempt provisional answers to two important questions: What appealed to Yeats in this kind of spiritual experience? How convinced was he of the truth of its findings? The answer to the first question is relatively simple, and is connected with Yeats's interest in mysticism. The belief that ultimate spiritual truth can be communicated directly to the living, or indirectly by way of a medium, and that certain facts of a world beyond the grave are thus revealed to the limited understanding of those still chained to the earth would obviously be very attractive to a man who was interested not merely in the existence of a world of spirit but in the ways by which human beings could establish some sort of contact with it. Both spiritualism and theosophy, despite their different methods, promised the man of faith such contact. Each had "mummy truths to tell" to its initiates. Furthermore, Yeats felt, occult religion differs from most religions in that its concentration is generally metaphysical rather than ethical, and that it seldom descends to the level of everyday morality.

The occult was useful also because it seemed to provide a kind of answer to the sceptical scientist. Even Huxley was forced to admit:

> that the spiritualists . . . do not venture to outrage right reason so boldly as the ecclesiastics. They do not sneer at 'evidence'; nor repudiate the requirement of legal proofs. In fact, there can be no doubt that the spiritualists produce far better evidence for their manifestations than can be shown either for the miraculous death of Arius, or for the Invention of the Cross.[69]

Several of the theosophists writing around the turn of the century seemed very distinctly aware of the threat of science. Mme Blavatsky, for example, sums up the times with sarcasm: "And, withal, to reject a *scientific hypothesis*, however absurd, is to commit the one unpardonable sin! We risk it." [70] For to the theosophist and the spiritualist, there is no doubt of the truth of psychic phenomena: "Their fundamental and only unimpeachable truth," writes Mme Blavatsky, "namely, that phenomena occur through mediums controlled by invisible forces and intelligences—no one, except a blind materialist of the Huxley 'big-toe' school, will or *can* deny." [71]

It is through his interest in the occult, as a matter of fact, that Yeats is led to the most unusual of the attempts to meet the challenge of a sceptical scientific demand for evidence of a spiritual universe. For the literature of the occult in his time was itself undergoing an interesting change which reflects the prevalence of scientific thought. The end of the nineteenth century saw the publication of the first specifically scientific efforts to study occult phenomena. The *Journal* of the English Society for Psychical Research, for example, published the results of the attempt "to make investigations in the despised region of occultism, in order to discover by rigorous scientific method the truths underlying these strange facts." [72] The work of the scientists associated with this new enterprise interested Yeats very much, for here at last he seemed to find proof of the existence of a spiritual world in the form of a direct answer to the challenge of the Huxleys and the Tyndalls, using their methods and apparently defeating them at their own game. The writings of men like Osty, Richet, J. W. Dunne, Myers, and Ochorowicz were familiar to Yeats. In fact, he frequently recommended them to those who treated the occult with contempt. What characterizes these works, in all cases, is the relatively dispassionate, often even sceptical attempt to investigate the "truths" of spiritualism and other occult phenomena with the tools of the scientist rather than those of the man of faith. Ochorowicz writes, for example, that "the experimental method, after having founded positive psychology, is itself introducing us into the domain of the miraculous." [73] And Osty, some thirty years later, can already say: "Just as astrology, alchemy, the notions of Hermetic forces, and miraculous cures, have become astronomy, chemistry, physics, and medical science, so human supernormality has become a chapter in human biology." [74] In this way, the "dead" religion of the past might yet become as respectable and unquestionable a part of human knowledge as the most rigorously demonstrable facts of science itself. F. W. H. Myers looks to the future and imagines the "new religion":

> Bacon foresaw the gradual victory of observation and experiment—the triumph of actual analysed fact—in every department of human study;—in every department save one. The realm of "Divine things" he left to Authority and Faith. I here urge that that great exemption need be no longer made. I claim that there now exists an incipient method of getting at this Divine knowledge also, with the same certainty, the same calm assurance, with which we make our steady progress in the knowledge of terrene things. The authority of creeds and Churches will thus be replaced by the authority of observation and experiment. The impulse of faith will resolve itself into a

reasoned and resolute imagination, bent upon raising even
higher than now the highest ideals of man.[75]

The work of these scientists seemed to Yeats, in his hunger for
certainty, of incalculable value; for it took account of the
scientific and philosophical objections to the idea of a "spiritual
universe," and yet proved its contentions by the scientific
method. "Forty years ago," Yeats wrote to Sturge Moore, "the
Society for Psychical Research succeeded in transferring mental
images (numbers, geometrical forms, simple drawings) between
two people (1) in the same room, (2) in different rooms, (3) in
different towns. From that moment all philosophy based upon
the isolation of the individual mind became obsolete." [76]

The question of Yeats's feelings about the truth of occult
phenomena is, however, one which he himself might have had
trouble answering. Because of the derision with which the
matter was treated by some of his friends and family, he is
almost always on the defensive when challenged with the
"absurdity" of his belief. But his anxiety to believe made him
more than charitable to the spiritualists and theosophists, and
he certainly did not investigate "the evidence" with anything
resembling scientific detachment. His faith in the existence of a
supernatural world, however, was not really rewarded until the
experience with his wife's automatic writing. At that moment,
no doubt, he was almost completely unsceptical, though perhaps another kind of person would have had serious doubts. But
during the rest of his life, and even as the automatic writing and
speech went on, it seems that Yeats's interest was predominantly
exploratory, and that he almost always retained at least a
modicum of scepticism about the "facts" of seances, revelations,
and other such experiences. One of the things he admired most
about Mme Blavatksy, as a matter of fact, was her ironic detachment, which contrasted so curiously with the hungry will to
believe in some of her disciples.[77]

Yeats's sources of spiritual authority were not, however,
limited to the philosophical, the religious and the scientific.
There was also an important literary tradition involved, and
Yeats, like others of his generation, speculated on the possibility
of treating poetry as a kind of substitute spiritual voice. There
is and had always been, he felt, a poetry of vision or revelation

which could disclose a supernatural world for man's contemplation as easily as the more organized religions. If we have been following Yeats through his positions on the various orthodox religions and spiritual disciplines, such a proposition will seem almost inevitable, for the poet is free to make use of his private insight without moralizing or submitting the products of his imagination to orthodox censorship. In fact, the poet is presumably even more capable of the direct perception of transcendent truth than the spiritualist, since the inspired poet needs no middleman. For this reason Yeats can say, "I believe that the elaborate technique of the arts, seeming to create out of itself a superhuman life, has taught more men to die than oratory or the Prayer-Book." [78] The poet was the visionary, scribe, and priest of his private religion. The final source of Yeats's ideas of visionary experience, then, is in poetry itself, and more particularly in the English romantic poets, with whom he felt a strong affinity. Blake, Shelley, Keats, Coleridge, and Wordsworth were the poets to whom he felt closest. All of them were visionaries: "Keats the type of vision," [79] says Yeats, is one of the two "types" of poet.

Each of these five romantic poets was concerned like Yeats with the visionary experience, and each, again like Yeats, had to invent a consecrated vocabulary to deal with spiritual experience, a vocabulary which was not familiar to or accepted by most of his readers. Their solutions to this problem varied, of course. Keats, in a sense the most conservative, made extensive use of Greek mythology; Shelley invented a language of ordinary words with extraordinary, but internally consistent, meanings; Wordsworth experimented with the heightening of ordinary phenomena; Coleridge made use of a kind of surrealist dream technique; Blake—the poet who interested Yeats most— created an entire mythology of personage and story unfamiliar to his readers. Yeats was extremely interested in all of these experiments. He and his friend Ellis collaborated on a three-volume edition of Blake which included a full "explanation" of Blakean mythology. In addition he wrote several essays on both Blake and Shelley, and what he says of the former could apply almost as well to himself. Blake "was a symbolist who had to invent his symbols. . . . He was a man crying out for a mythology, and trying to make one because he could not find one to his hand." [80]

Yeats did not object to the inevitable obscurity of such a private spiritual language or mythology. Even of Coleridge he says "he seems to have some kind of illumination which was, as always, only in part communicable." [81] The "as always" of this statement suggests Yeats's awareness of its applicability to himself. The only crime, in his eyes, is that of distrusting and consequently over-rationalizing the vision one is granted. This was the flaw in the poetry of Wordsworth, who destroyed the integrity of his visionary experiences by indulging in the same kind of moralizing that Yeats so disliked in the Church:

> He strikes me as always destroying his poetic experience, which was of course of incomparable value, by his reflective power. His intellect was commonplace, and unfortunately he has been taught to respect nothing else. He thinks of his poetical experience not as incomparable in itself but as an engine that may be yoked to his intellect. He is full of a sort of utilitarianism and that is perhaps the reason why in later life he is continually looking back upon a lost vision, a lost happiness.[82]

Nevertheless, despite Yeats's affinity with the romantic poets, it cannot be said that he made great use of the special vocabulary or mythology which any one of them had created. The very fact that they had invented them encouraged him in a similar attempt. There are, of course, occasional similarities: the vision of eternity in "The Cold Heaven" and Shelley's "Mont Blanc"; the familiar romantic usage of the "One" and the "Many" in "A Meditation in Time of Civil War"; or the echoes of the sexual metaphor used in poems like Shelley's *Epipsychidion*. In general, however, Yeats did not choose to use Blake's private mythology, Shelley's specialized vocabulary, or even Wordsworth's transcendent Nature in his own poetry. Yet the example of the romantic poets was extremely important for him. Their poetry, like his own, seemed to him to have important connections with an anti-materialist philosophy: "The romantic movement seems related to the idealist philosophy, the naturalistic movement, Stendhal's mirror dawdling down a lane, to Locke's mechanical philosophy . . . through their whole substance." [83] The real problem was that the "romantic movement, with its turbulent heroism, its self-assertion, is over, superseded by a new naturalism that leaves man helpless before the contents of his own mind." [84]

It was the goal of Yeats's work to re-establish this romantic, heroic, idealistic movement and to usurp the "new naturalism" with its view of man's limited potentiality for spiritual achievement. In order to do this, Yeats made use of every possible kind of spiritual orthodoxy available to him. As we have seen, each of these disciplines left something to be desired. None expressed fully the spiritual world which he sought to evoke in his own work. Yeats's answer to this problem, however, was not to create a new, private system, like Blake's. Rather he chose the method of complete eclecticism. For the purposes of his poetry, all spiritual languages were one. That is why, when we discuss the idea of the visionary in Yeats's poetry and drama, we find ourselves speaking at some time or other in so many different vocabularies, Idealist, Christian, Buddhist, occult, metapsychic, poetic, and mythological. All description of a supernatural world was at best metaphorical in any case. It therefore seemed legitimate to make use of the whole immense store of metaphors, some more, some less familiar to his audience, which religious thinkers of the past had invented.

When one considers only the individual poem or the individual play, the complete heterodoxy of Yeats's spiritual language is not always evident, since he is usually careful to preserve the internal consistency of his individual works. But if we take his writings as a whole, the variety of his spiritual vocabularies and "religious" authorities is astonishing. One can get a sense of this total lack of orthodoxy by reading his introduction to Hone and Rossi's book on Berkeley, where he is concerned with all kinds of "evidence" and "testimony" for a world of spirit. In the course of this fifteen-page essay, Yeats uses—in no particular order—the following "authorities": his sister Lolly, Berkeley, Blake, Vasiliev, J. W. Dunne, McTaggart, Plotinus, the Archangel Michael, Kant, Hegel, Shelley, Osty, "some Indian Buddhists," a medium named Mrs. Crandon, Zarathustra, Coleridge, "a Sligo countryman," "one of the oracles of Delphi," Swedenborg, "a Zen monk," "a Cabbalist," and "God." In a way, then, Yeats's poetry is very strongly traditional; the great variety of the traditions which he uses, however, is likely to confuse the only partially prepared reader. For Yeats, as for Blake, "all religions are one," for all affirm the existence of a realm of ultimate spiritual truth and all seek to explain the nature of this realm to the earthbound mentality in metaphor or myth.

We might, of course, simplify the entire problem by saying that the result of Yeats's search for spiritual authority is found in *A Vision*. Such a position is untenable, however. We know that shortly after Yeats's marriage in 1917, his wife amazed him by successfully attempting automatic writing. During the next few years, he and his wife filled many copybooks with the answers to Yeats's metaphysical questions, coming, he was convinced, from the "unknown instructors" speaking through the medium of his wife. But as he himself confesses, many of the "answers" were thoroughly incomprehensible It was only after a long and agonizing process of sifting and arranging the material, and no doubt interpreting it rather fully too, that *A Vision* was born. The final version was published a full twenty years after the automatic writing began. In that time Yeats had read much philosophy and history—Spengler, Vico, Henry Adams, Berkeley, Hegel, and Kant among others—and much of the fruit of his reading and thought is included in *A Vision*.

Any reader of the book will see immediately that far from being a coherent, original, and comprehensive philosophical or religious work, it is actually a conglomeration of many different "spiritual vocabularies," and that supernatural elements from Christianity and Greek and Irish mythology, from the mystical writers and the romantic poets, appear in *A Vision* along with material which had never formed a part of any previous orthodoxy. Furthermore, it is a mistake to assume that all of Yeats's poetry on the subject of visionary experience is directly connected with the material in *A Vision*. It is easy enough to see the connection in poems like "The Phases of the Moon" and "Ego Dominus Tuus," or even, in more subtle form, in "The Gyres" and the Byzantium poems. There are, however, many significant works which make use of the idea of visionary experience and yet do not refer directly to the material of *A Vision*, for example: "The Cold Heaven," "Presences," "A Meditation in Time of Civil War," "Fragments," "Ribh in Ectasy," "A

Crazed Girl," "The Apparitions," and the play *The Words upon the Window Pane*. Together with "The Second Coming," "All Souls' Night," "Byzantium," and "Gratitude to the Unknown Instructors," which are somewhat more closely connected with *A Vision*, these form the part of Yeats's work most significantly concerned with the idea of visionary experience without benefit of clergy.

What do these works have in common? In each case, the poem or play describes a visionary's "communication" with a supernatural world accomplished through dream, "ecstasy," madness, or through the aid of a medium. The vision thus achieved is always of vital significance, and its validity is not questioned sceptically. The particular revelation in each of these poems is of ultimates: Ribh speaks of how Godhead is created; "Byzantium" clarifies the relationship between the natural and the supernatural life; "The Second Coming"—not a Christian poem despite its title—deals with the process of history. Most of these poems are familiar and have been much discussed. It might therefore be more useful to see something of the general pattern of these works by examining one of the less familiar poems, "The Cold Heaven":

> Suddenly I saw the cold and rook-delighting heaven
> That seemed as though ice burned and was but the more ice,
> And thereupon imagination and heart were driven
> So wild that every casual thought of that and this
> Vanished, and left but memories, that should be
>   out of season
> With the hot blood of youth, of love crossed long ago;
> And I took all the blame out of all sense and reason,
> Until I cried and trembled and rocked to and fro,
> Riddled with light. Ah! when the ghost begins to quicken,
> Confusion of the death-bed over, is it sent
> Out naked on the roads, as the books say, and stricken
> By the injustice of the skies for punishment? [85]

Even the most casual reading of this poem suggests that the "heaven" of the title has little connection with the familiar Christian conception. Perhaps the closest parallel is Shelley's "Mont Blanc," which also associates ice and eternity and suggests the ultimate destructiveness of the eternal world. The conception, however, is clearly based on a private "vision," achieved through no particularly familiar spiritual discipline, and seemingly not induced at all: "Suddenly I saw . . . ." The validity of this direct vision of the cold heaven, it should be noticed, is not questioned. Yet there is a question at the end of the poem which suggests the incompleteness of the revelation. It is interesting that the end of the poem tenuously brings us back from the private vision to more orthodox thought, for Yeats speculates whether his own vision conforms with "what the books say."

"The Cold Heaven" also illustrates how Yeats solves the problem of effectively describing something which is both private and supernatural. We can see the same method used in the vivid evocation of Byzantium, or of the beast in "The Second Coming." Yeats lavishes his finest descriptions, his most precise pictures, on material with which he cannot expect the reader to be familiar. The "cold and rook-delighting heaven / That seemed as though ice burned and was but the more ice" becomes as real as the more traditional descriptions of heaven with which we are presumably familiar. The emotion of the speaker is described with equal care. Yeats suggests the quality of the ecstatic state by ending the descriptive portion of the poem with the ambiguous, telling phrase (emphasized by its placement at the beginning of the line and before a transition), "riddled with light." This brings us to a final important point about the poem, that it concentrates less on the nature of the vision than on the heroism of the visionary, a reminder that we are still dealing with a heroic individual whose visionary power is itself more important than *what* he sees. The poem "A Crazed Girl" also illustrates this point, for it says nothing specific about the visions which the girl has, but rather emphasizes the idea that she is "A beautiful lofty thing, or a thing / Heroically lost, heroically found." [86] Whoever the "unknown instructors" were, whether heard in dreams, in waking visions, or in a seance, they spoke only to those with a special gift for going beyond the limits which other people assume to be final. Of all the ways of attaining to some kind of supernatural insight, the direct contact with a spiritual world, untrammeled by rules, dogma, and the paraphernalia of organized religion, provided the greatest freedom for man's imagination and stressed the primary importance of ecstatic experience itself.

One does not stretch words too far, then, when one calls the Yeatsian visionary hero a religious one, even though at times he is a one-man religion. As Auden says in *The Enchafèd Flood*, "The religious hero is one who is committed to anything with absolute passion, i.e., to him it is an absolute truth, his god." [87] For this reason the visionary is different in an important sense from the other heroic men in the Yeatsian gallery. Or rather, to put it more accurately, the other heroes can only approach the perfection of the visionary but never actually reach it, since they have more than themselves to contend with. The visionary has only to be true to himself since, unlike the aristocrat and the public hero, he does not work in the social or political sphere. And yet, as has been suggested in the previous chapters, all three work towards the perfect position of independence, of *self*-fulfillment, which is the true heroic state. It is only that for the visionary this is essentially simpler, since, as Yeats says, such a man admits "no duty to us, communing with God only." [88]

It would be a great mistake to assume, despite the extensive use Yeats made of traditional spiritual systems or vocabularies, that his own contribution, even in the realm of ideas, is merely that of an eclectic editor. Even a brief look at a poem like "The Magi" can show us that in using some of the concepts or personages of other religious systems, Yeats's changes are likely to be more important than the tradition invoked. In order to understand the visionary hero in these poems and plays, we will therefore have to examine the overarching ideas of the visionary goal, the means to vision, and the value of the visionary hero in Yeats's work in order to understand precisely to what use he put the material he borrowed from others.

Yeats's quarrel with the commonly accepted goal of visionary experience is important. This traditional goal is well summed up in the words of St. John of the Cross: "It is, therefore, supreme ignorance for any one to think that he can ever attain to the high estate of union with God before he casts away from him the desire of natural things." [89] As St. John suggests, the religious mind ordinarily strives to move *toward* perfection, toward a final union with God or a transcendent realm of spirit, and in an antinomic system of belief like Platonism or Christianity, this implies the logical corollary of a movement *away from* "the desire of natural things," from the mortal world itself, multitudinous, impermanent, decaying, and ultimately undesirable. It is precisely this "necessary" corollary which Yeats found impossible to accept. The central problem which his visionary heroes face, the reconciliation of the two worlds, perfect and imperfect, grows out of his refusal to accept the necessity of pursuing one at the expense of the other. Yeats's dissatisfaction with either world taken separately, his unwillingness to accept one or the other as the province of ultimate value, inspired his attempt to reconcile the two apparently opposed realms.

This restless search for an escape from the implications of an antinomic religious belief has been misunderstood by many of Yeats's readers. It is a critical commonplace, for example, that in the later poetry the powerful attraction of the mortal, physical, perishable world is seen as greater than that of the flawless spiritual one. In reality this movement—which we might call the rejection of the perfect—presents itself in Yeats's work from the very first, as we shall see, and yet never actually becomes powerful enough to "find," in Auden's words, "the mortal world enough."

In Yeats's early work, the inadequacy of an independent spiritual realm is suggested most clearly by the treatment of Irish myth. The ideal world of Tir-na-n-Og, the paradise of Irish mythology and the home of the Shee or immortal fairies, was traditionally one of permanence, gaiety, and perfect bliss, a land of eternal youth and happiness. It is therefore interesting that Yeats consistently chooses incidents and characters which reveal the inadequacy of this perfect world. His most characteristic means of suggesting this is to make the "imperfect" mortal world seem highly desirable to his immortal characters. Yeats was, for example, fond of quoting a remark which George Russell ("AE") once heard "an old religious beggar" repeating: " 'God possesses the heavens, but He covets the earth—He covets the earth.' " [90]

Yeats's immortals also "covet the earth," for there is something about the mortal world, for all its limitations and imperfections, which to the flawless spiritual one seems unattainable and therefore desirable. Again and again in the early work, we find Yeats making use of this idea, as for instance in the characteristic story of the immortal fairy who snatches a mortal away to her own world. The most familiar examples which come to mind are *The Land of Heart's Desire* and *The Wanderings of Oisin*, but there are others. In a little known short story published in 1891, *Dhoya*, the pattern of the Oisin legend is reworked. Dhoya is a mortal of great strength and passion who leads a life of self-sufficient isolation for many years until an immortal fairy falls in love with him and agrees to share his mortal existence. She explains:

> "Dhoya, I have left my world far off. My people—on the floor of the lake they are dancing and singing, and on the islands of the lake; always happy, always young, always without change. I have left them for thee, Dhoya, for they cannot love. Only the changing, and moody, and angry and weary can love. . . . I left the places where they dance, Dhoya, for thee!" [91]

Some of the stories in the 1897 collection *The Secret Rose* are based on a similar idea, that the people of the Shee, the "gentry" of the Irish immortal world, envy men their passions. In "The Book of the Great Dhoul and Hanrahan the Red," for instance, the fairy Cleena says to Hanrahan, "I love you, for you are fierce and passionate, and good and bad, and not dim and wave-like as are the people of the Shee." [92] And the poem "The Host of the Air" is a variation on the story of *The Land of Heart's Desire*; here, it is O'Driscoll's bride Bridget who is stolen by the fairies. Yeats makes clear in a note to the first edition of the collection *The Wind among the Reeds* that all of these tales merely appropriate a constant theme of Gaelic literature itself: "The old Gaelic literature is full of the appeals of the Tribes of the goddess Danu to mortals whom they would bring into their country." [93]

Later poems and plays continue to stress the same theme. "The Grey Rock," from *Responsibilities* (1914), describes the grief of Aoife when the mortal hero she loves spurns her offer

of immortality and chooses to die fighting a human battle
with his king. She asks in despair,

> Why should the faithfullest heart most love
> The bitter sweetness of false faces?
> Why must the lasting love what passes,
> Why are the gods by men betrayed? [94]

We can see the answer to her question in Yeats's poems, for it
is man's mortality, and the way in which he squanders the
precious gift of life, that gives him a kind of greatness the gods
cannot possess. The point is made clearly in a poem from the
same collection, "The Two Kings." Here Edain, asked to return
to the immortal world by her immortal husband, spurns his
offer and refuses to leave her mortal husband, the warrior
Eochaid. When the former asks, uncomprehendingly, "What
happiness / Can lovers have that know their happiness / Must
end at the dumb stone?" [95] Edain replies,

> "How should I love . . .
> Were it not that when the dawn has lit my bed
> And shown my husband sleeping there, I have sighed,
> 'Your strength and nobleness will pass away'?
> What can they know of love that do not know
> She builds her nest upon a narrow ledge
> Above a windy precipice? . . .
> Never will I believe there is any change
> Can blot out of my memory this life
> Sweetened by death, but if I could believe,
> That were a double hunger in my lips
> For what is doubly brief." [96]

The idea that human life is "sweetened by death" differentiates the Yeatsian visionary from others and is at the heart of
the paradox which is given its definite statement in the play *The
Only Jealousy of Emer* (1919). There Cuchulain, the mortal
warrior-hero, is wooed by the woman of the Shee but finally
returns with relief to "mere" humanity, and the Chorus explains,

> He that has loved the best
> May turn from a statue
> His too human breast.[97]

And in the play *The King of the Great Clock Tower* (1934),
we find the baldest answer to the question of what the im-

mortals lack, why they descend into human life: "For desecration and the lover's night." [98] In the words of one of Yeats's favorite poets, William Blake, "Eternity is in love with the productions of time." [99]

It should be clear, then, that the visionary hero's "rejection of the perfect," with its concomitant praise of the human world of passion, is not the product of Yeats's later years but begins at the beginning of his career. It is equally misleading, however, to suggest that the movement away from perfection was more powerful in Yeats's work than the movement toward it. Certainly the "mere" mortal world was hardly the ideal state either, and few writers could have been more conscious of its imperfection than Yeats. We will see presently that the visionary's celebration of the physical world in the later poetry is never at the *expense* of the spiritual one. The problem, then, is not which to choose but how to avoid the necessity of making a choice between mortal and immortal.

Yeats found two "solutions" to this vexing problem: the first a sceptical vacillation and refusal to accept the necessity of commitment, the other an actual attempt to resolve the dichotomy. Yeats must have realized that scepticism presented a poetic problem, that in hesitating to renounce either of two contradictory worlds, his poetry was in danger of itself becoming confused, uncertain, and so robbed of its essential energy. He solved this technical problem in a technical way, by inventing a series of *personae* and using them in a kind of poetic debate. These *personae* are very distinct, dramatically conceived characters who have a clear and unambivalent point of view about the desirability of a certain way of life. The best examples are the three people involved in the story of "The Three Bushes," the lover, the lady, and the chambermaid. Each has an intense and passionate conviction despite the fact that all three are the product of a highly sceptical and "unconvinced" consciousness.

The technique itself is very different from the use of named characters in Yeats's earlier poetry. In *The Wind among the Reeds*, for example, some of the poems originally appeared under such titles as "Aedh Laments the Loss of Love," "Mongan Laments the Change . . . ," "Michael Robartes Bids His Beloved Be at Peace," and "O'Sullivan the Red to Mary Lavell." In the later editions, however, all these names and characters disappear, or rather become merged into a kind of generic figure simply called "The Lover." This is very different, clearly, from the method of the later poems. It is inconceivable, for example, to imagine someone else speaking Crazy Jane's lines. Her personality is made too precise and distinct. Neither is it accurate to identify these *personae* with Yeats himself, or to assume that in the later poetry Yeats dropped the mask that separated him from his creations. Vivienne Koch, in her *W. B. Yeats: The Tragic Phase,* has suggested that it is "Yeats who is looking through the eyes of all the Lunatic Toms and Crazy Janes and Wild Old Wicked Men." [100] But it was precisely because Yeats was no longer able to see through the eyes of such passionate but limited characters that he felt obliged to invent them.

Yeats's *personae* are most frequently involved in a kind of debate, a natural medium for the sceptic. The method is simply to have more than one speaker, more than one point of view, represented in a single poem. Much of the later poetry exploits this technique by recording a dialogue between two or more characters about the relative value of physical and spiritual life: "Crazy Jane Talks with the Bishop," "Michael Robartes and the Dancer," "A Dialogue of Self and Soul," "For Anne Gregory," "Ego Dominus Tuus," and others. But if we expand the definition of "debate" a little so that it means simply the juxtaposition of opposing ideas, we can see how persistent the method actually is, for many of Yeats's poems fall into this category even though no actual verbal debate occurs: for example, "Crazy Jane and the Bishop," "Oil and Blood," the two Byzantium poems, or "Ribh Denounces Patrick." The advantages of such a method are obvious, for a desirable ambiguity can be retained without sacrificing either clarity or the energy generated by passionate conviction.

Nevertheless, the *personae* and the debate were after all only methods; they did not resolve the vacillation in Yeats's own mind, but merely exploited it. The visionaries of the later poetry go further than this by denying the necessity of an exclusive choice, by demonstrating how the soul can "attain to the high estate of union with God" *without* "casting away the desire of natural things." When one sees beyond the logically acceptable position of the inevitable conflict between one principle and its opposite, man's spiritual quest and the "desire of natural things" are seen to be simultaneous and inseparable.

Yeats might have learned this from the work of Henri Bergson, whom he read in 1927. Although Bergson is the villain of Wyndham Lewis's *Time and Western Man*, a book which Yeats admired extravagantly, his own attitude to the highly influential French philosopher was considerably more sympathetic. For though he disliked what could be made of Bergson's worship of Time by lesser minds, he was still "full of admiration and respect." [101] It was Bergson's contention that matter and mind were simultaneously created, and that the great error of philosophers since Plato had been the separation of the two and the relegation of matter to an inferior status: "The great error of the doctrines on the spirit has been the idea that by isloating the spiritual life from all the rest, by suspending it in space as high as possible above the earth, they were placing it beyond attack, as if they were not thereby simply exposing it to be taken as an effect of mirage!" [102] But body and spirit can not be separated in this way, and philosophy, if it does not want to be swept away entirely by science, must "resolve to see the life of the body just where it really is, on the road that leads to the life of the spirit." [103]

One of Yeats's richest and most interesting attempts to suggest the inseparableness of these two worlds is the well-known but often misunderstood "Among School Children." That poem begins with the problem of old age but quickly moves on to the much more general subject of how man idealizes earthly existence in order to avoid facing its unpleasant facts, such as physical decay. In the first stanza, the aged poet and the wondering children stare at each other across the great gulf of age. The experience takes the poet back suddenly to his own youth, and the gulf is temporarily annihilated. And yet the present quickly reasserts itself; he sees himself once more as only "a comfortable kind of old scarecrow." The experience makes him generalize about the absurdity of all human hopes, if they should come to this. Would any young mother think her child worth bringing into the world if she could see it "with sixty or more winters on its head?" [104]

If the poem had ended here, it would have been a bitter and totally negative picture of man's grim progress toward death. But Yeats goes on to look at some of the human "solutions" to the problem he raises. Mankind, it seems, can not bear very much reality: if the real world is ugly and hateful, man fabricates an ideal world to stand against the real and console him for its imperfections. Plato and the philosophers invented such a world, in which nature seems nothing "but a spume that plays / Upon a ghostly paradigm of things." [105] In the same way, the nuns (like the nun in the first stanza) and mothers learn to ignore the physical world of fact and worship "images," the nuns, religious abstractions and the mothers, idealized versions of their real children. All three—the nuns, the mothers, and the philosophers—are in effect shutting their eyes to the "defilement" of mortal life, to the physical inperfection and decay with which the poem begins. By idealizing the world, they mock man as he really is.

The difficult last stanza of the poem is an answer to these idealists: their perfect world is purchased at too high a price, for they bruise the body "to pleasure soul." They see selectively, not comprehensively; they are forced to censor. The truer vision is a synthesis, in which man's youth, maturity, and age are seen as one, in which none has to be rejected: for man "is" all of these things. In the same way, the images of this stanza suggest that we cannot abstract the essence of life from life itself, the dance from a particular dancer, the chestnut-tree from each of its time-bound selves, leaf, blossom, and bole. The Yeatsian visionary does not leave the actual world behind in the moment of vision. He sees *both* the tree and its form, *both* the dancer and the dance, *both* the scarecrow and the child, in one instant of time. In doing that he celebrates, rather than defames, life itself.

The most important metaphor which Yeats uses to describe the intersection of the two worlds is that of sex, a fact which might suggest that he is praising the world of flesh at the expense of the world of spirit. That is not, however, the case. Yeats pictures sexual experience as a moment of ecstasy which takes man, in a kind of transport, out of himself. It is useful to remember that before the word "ecstasy" became part of the language of the marriage manuals, it was used to describe religious experience. Yeats exploits the word in its modern ambiguity. The poem "Solomon and the Witch," [106] for example, records such an ecstasy:

> Last night, where under the wild moon
> On grassy mattress I had laid me,
> Within my arms great Solomon,
> I suddenly cried out in a strange tongue,
> Not his, not mine.

And in the poem "Ribh Denounces Patrick," [107] the metaphor is reversed and the suggestion made that eternal creation is like sexual reproduction on earth:

> Natural and supernatural with the self-same ring are wed.
> As man, as beast, as an ephemeral fly begets, Godhead
>   begets Godhead.

In Yeats's final view of the visionary, then, physical and spiritual are seen as inseparable, mutually dependent, and simultaneous. The change is recorded in the two Byzantium poems. The earlier "Sailing to Byzantium" [108] is a "debate" which emphasizes the dichotomy between physical and spiritual very sharply. "That country" and "the holy city" are set against each other, the one a world of youth, sex, and decay, the other a world of art, religion, and the changeless. The speaker in the poem does not reconcile these two but abandons one for the other: "Once out of nature I shall never take / My bodily form from any natural thing." Although the later "Byzantium" [109] superficially exploits the same contrast, the last stanza in particular shows that there is an essential difference. The perfect world of Byzantium and the changing world of "the fury and the mire of human veins" are not only connected literally by the constant movement of the dolphins but seen as mutually dependent on each other. Although it is true that the poem records the process whereby mortal becomes immortal, it is also true that this process is described in metaphors of eating and burning, and that the mortal world provides the necessary food and fuel to keep the immortal world alive. And it is significant that the final image of the poem is not only of the eternal world, but also of the world of nature which is feeding it:

> Astraddle on the dolphin's mire and blood,
> Spirit after spirit! The smithies break the flood,
> The golden smithies of the Emperor!
> Marbles of the dancing floor
> Break bitter furies of complexity,
> Those images that yet
> Fresh images beget,
> That dolphin-torn, that gong-tormented sea.

The idea of an actual world intersected at innumerable points by a spiritual one appealed to Yeats because it raised the actual world to an ultimate level, thus making its rejection unnecessary, while at the same time it created an opportunity for ecstatic visionary experience which did not leave man's world behind. In such a view, the actual physical world became sacred territory. Yeats felt that these ideas echoed Plotinus, the philosopher whom he read with such enthusiasm in 1926. Plotinus, he says,

> was the first to establish as sole source the timeless individuality, or daimon, instead of the Platonic Idea, to prefer Socrates to his thought. This timeless individuality contains archetypes of all possible existence whether of man or of brute. . . . Plotinus thought that we should not 'baulk at this limitless-ness of the intellectual; it is an infinitude having nothing to do with number or part' (Ennead V.7.1.) *yet it seems that it can at will re-enter number and part and thereby make itself apparent to our minds.* If we accept this idea, many strange or beautiful things become credible. . . . All about us there seems to start up a precise, inexplicable, teeming life, and *the earth becomes once more, not in rhetorical metaphor, but in reality, sacred.*[110]

This notion of the earth itself as sacred, along with the possibility that spiritual reality can "make itself apparent to our minds," appealed greatly to Yeats. It is no wonder, then, that Plotinus becomes the hero of some of the later poems and is usually contrasted with Plato, as in the two related poems "The Delphic Oracle upon Plotinus" and "News for the Delphic Oracle." In both, Plotinus is pictured as striving to reach the safe harbor of Platonic Love, a world of perfection, but still "buffeted by such seas" and with "salt blood" blocking his eyes.[111] As in the Byzantium poems, the sea represents the physical world of passion and blood. It is therefore significant that Plotinus reaches the shore only after a passionate struggle with the sea, while Plato and the stately "choir of Love" look on blandly from the safety of the shore.

It should be pointed out, however, that Yeats evolved this heroic visionary ideal dependent on the intersection of the spiritual and actual worlds only in the work of his last fifteen or twenty years, and that the early poetry is based for the most part on the traditional dichotomy between spiritual and physical —without, as has been pointed out, always preferring the former. Unlike the visionary hero of the later Yeats, the seer of the early poetry is forced to abandon the mortal world if he wants to reach the spiritual one. The predominant symbol of spiritual reality in these poems and plays is the island, separated from the mainland and providing a kind of absolute isolation from it. We might say that there is a gradual shift in Yeats's poetry from the *goal* of the spiritual quest to the quest itself, and that metaphorically this can be seen in the later poetry in the greater use of the images of the sea and of water—symbolizing the quest—which replace the numberless islands of the early work.

An interesting example of the early ideal of the isolated island of spiritual contemplation is Yeats's plan (mentioned first in the nineties) for a "Castle of the Heroes," to be located on an unoccupied island in Lough Key.[112] There the potential visionaries of Irish society could retire, very much like monks to a monastery, for spiritual contemplation, and there they might "establish mysteries like those of Eleusis and Samothrace." [113] The plan suggests the necessity of divorcing oneself completely from the actual world in order to find the spiritual one, and thus emphasizes the distinction between Yeats's early and late views. The same idea is suggested in *The Shadowy Waters*, when Forgael says that it is only "where the world ends" that the "mind is made unchanging," and finds "Miracle, ecstasy, the impossible hope." [114] In *Where There Is Nothing* (1902), the hero insists that "We must destroy the World; we must destroy everything that has Law and Number, for where there is nothing, there is God." [115] He has learned, he says, "that one needs a religion so wholly supernatural, that is so opposed to the order of nature that the world can never capture it." [116] The Yeats of the twenties and thirties would never have accepted such a statement. As early as 1888 he was already writing to Katharine Tynan, "I have noticed some things about my poetry I did not know before, in this process of correction, for instance, that it is almost all a flight into fairyland from the real world, and a summons to that flight." [117] But many years were to pass before the Yeatsian visionary could combine the "flight into fairyland" with the real world from which the flight began.

The change in Yeats's idea of the visionary can best be understood in terms of the traditional faculties of man: reason, imagination, and the passions. Ordinarily, we consider the former two the less "earth-bound," reason being often identified as "man's divine spark." In Yeats's early poetry, accordingly, much more stress is laid on the so-called higher faculties of reason and imagination. Through them (and particularly, as in the romatic poets, through the imagination at work in dreams and visions) man may reach the world of spirit. The reversal comes first in some of the poems in the 1920 collection, *Michael Robartes and the Dancer*. At this point it is the "passions" which become the higher faculty, and the link between them and visionary experience is clearly made in several poems: "Solomon and the Witch," "An Image from a Past Life," "Towards Break of Day." In the later poetry, this connection is retained, the only significant change being that human "passions" become interpreted in a more and more blatantly sexual way. At the same time, there is a complementary rejection of and exaggerated contempt for reason alone, as in the poem "A Prayer for Old Age":

> God guard me from those thoughts men think
> In the mind alone;
> He that sings a lasting song
> Thinks in a marrow-bone.[118]

In the *Pages from a Diary Written in Nineteen Hundred and Thirty*, Yeats sees himself "set in a drama where I struggle to exalt and overcome concrete realities perceived not with mind only but as with the roots of my hair. The passionless reasoners are pariah dogs and devour the dead symbols." [119]

We may legitimately ask why this reversal took place, why it is now man's physical and passionate life which opens the doors to the spiritual world. There is, of course, a possible biographical explanation, for the praise of physical life seems always to be connected with another theme in Yeats's later poetry, the lament for old age. In poem after poem this juxtaposition is made: "Among School Children," "The Tower," "A Prayer for Old Age," "The Wild Old Wicked Man," "Politics," and many others, including the Crazy Jane poems. "The Tower" [120] answers the question of what connection there is between old age and the praise of physical life, for here we see that age brings with it a narrowing of the possibilities of life. "Decrepit age" has made the life of passion impossible, and one must reconcile oneself and "be content with argument and deal / In abstract things." In a sense, then, the poems of old age continue a basic pattern established early in Yeats's work, that of longing for the unattainable and scorning the easily attainable. The only difference is that the terms have been reversed. In youth it was abstraction, wisdom, philosophy which one longed for, because they seemed so difficult to reach. In old age, on the other hand, the physical vigor which has been so prodigally wasted in youth seems much more desirable than the "wisdom" which has come.

Yet the neatness of such an explanation obscures a more important reason for the great emphasis on the value of the actual world among the visionaries of the late poetry. In a letter to John O'Leary written in 1892, Yeats suggests that he has made "magic"—meaning by this the cultivation of the means of discovering the spiritual world—"next to my poetry the most important pursuit of my life." [121] It is highly significant that he thus places artistic creation first, for Yeats never really changed his mind about this hierarchy. If anything, his art seemed always to become more and more demanding. And art, he came to realize, must inevitably begin with the actual physical world and cannot ever completely bypass it. During the period when Ezra Pound acted as Yeats's secretary (1913-

1916), Yeats asked him to go through his poetry and point out all the abstract words he could find.[122] The number was so startling that Yeats embarked upon an attempt to deemphasize abstraction in his work. Pound convinced him that a vague "spiritual" language was the curse of the poetry of the nineties, and that all poetry must be more strongly rooted in the actual and the physical than Yeats's had been heretofore.

Here, then, is a partial explanation of the constant insistence in the later poetry that art begins with physical reality and the actual world rather than with abstraction. To those who feel that lust and rage are not fit subjects for an old man's poetry, Yeats answers in "The Spur," [123] "What else have I to spur me into song?" And in "Vacillation," [124] the Heart gets the better of a dialogue with the Soul:

> *The Soul.* Seek out reality, leave things that seem.
> *The Heart.* What, be a singer born and lack a theme?

Despite the attractions (such as they are) of a life of pure spirit, the artist's example must be "Homer . . . and his unchristened heart," the Homer whose theme was not salvation but "original sin." Finally, in "The Circus Animals' Desertion," [125] the most uncompromising poem on this subject, Yeats speculates on the origin of all the spiritual images of the artist. Though they "grow in pure mind," their origin is not only in the actual world, but in the most grossly physical part of it. The "ladders" of artistic creation all lead up from "the foul rag-and-bone shop of the heart":

> Those masterful images because complete
> Grew in pure mind, but out of what began?
> A mound of refuse or the sweepings of a street,
> Old kettles, old bottles, and a broken can,
> Old iron, old bones, old rags, that raving slut
> Who keeps the till. Now that my ladder's gone,
> I must lie down where all the ladders start,
> In the foul rag-and-bone shop of the heart.

These, then, are two possible explanations, biographical and aesthetic, for the increased emphasis on the actual world, on man's physical and passionate nature, in the later poetry of Yeats. For all that emphasis, however, it cannot be repeated too often that Yeats's celebration of the physical world in the poetry of the last years is never at the expense of the visionary goal, is never proof that the mortal world taken independently is enough. Though it is the place "where all the ladders start," it is not where they end. Only the *means* to vision had undergone an important transformation. As a result of the shift from the "higher" faculties to the "lower," true vision now seemed possible in ecstatic transcendence through, rather than apart from, the physical world. This idea of the intersection of physical and spiritual experience seemed to open a new world of visionary possibility and to resolve the self-destructive antagonism of flesh and spirit in poems like "Sailing to Byzantium."

The apparent dichotomy of mortal and immortal, then, is seen finally as potential harmony, for man "thinks in a marrow-bone" and "perceives" with "the roots of his hair." Yet at the same time, we realize with Yeats that even this is in a sense a false resolution. For though the visionary may be able to combine physical life with spiritual truth, though it is true that such experience is within man's scope, the ultimate fruition is still denied to the Yeatsian seer: his "vision" does not last. We get a sense of this when Sheba, in describing her visionary experience to Solomon, suddenly realizes that it has been nothing but a momentary release from a humdrum existence: " 'Yet the world stays.' " [126] And here is the basic problem with all of Yeats's visionaries, that, in spite of a momentary fruition, "the world stays," and the ordinary conditions of life are reestablished. The very metaphor of sexual union obviously emphasizes the transience of the experience, but even in poems which do not describe "ecstasy" in strictly sexual terms, the visionary state is at best a few moments snatched from the immense flow of time, as the poem "Vacillation" suggests:

> While on the shop and street I gazed
> My body of a sudden blazed;
> And twenty minutes more or less
> It seemed so great my happiness,
> That I was blessèd and could bless.[127]

Although time and eternity may occasionally intersect, Yeats's visionary is always ultimately frustrated by the reassertion of the laws of time. Even in the early "Song of Wandering

Aengus" (1897), the vision of the "glimmering girl" almost instantly fades "through the brightening air," and Aengus spends the rest of his life in a fruitless search to recapture the lost vision. The frustration of the devoted visionary in the play *At the Hawk's Well* is even more complete, for here Cuchulain's search for spiritual reality is frustrated by the guardian hawks who cast a spell over him whenever the water—which represents the immortal here—rushes into the well.[128] Yeats's visionary, then, like all his other heroic men, is not a success but a failure, and it is only through the transcendence of that failure and the despair which it might bring that he becomes truly heroic.

The philosophic implications of this frustrated search for ultimate truth were described in Yeats's *A Vision*. In that book, he formulated a theory of history based upon a notion of human existence as a series of endlessly repetitive cycles. "Immortality," for man at least, was simply the necessity of rebirth after rebirth in age after age. Yeats's system is, of course, a variation of the familiar idea which Mircea Eliade has called the "myth of the eternal return," but it is essential to stress that it is not conceived as moving toward a clear terminal point and thus creating the sense of direction and meaning. Rather, existence seems to repeat itself eternally, life following upon life, civilization upon civilization, the second coming following the first, and no doubt, the third following that, and so on. What hope does such a system offer man in his search for apocalypse, for a spiritual world no longer subject to the frustrating exclusive reassertion of time?

The escape from the "wheel" of existence is stressed unduly by some interpreters of Yeats, particularly by Ellmann in his *Yeats: The Man and the Masks*.[129] It is true, as Ellmann says, that Yeats postulates an eventual release in something which he calls the "thirteenth cycle." Yet this scarcely makes his system a very optimistic one, since the knowledge of this ultimate reality is denied to man and "has kept the secret." [130] Unfortunately, "the day is far off when the two halves of man can define each its own unity . . . and so escape out of the Wheel." [131] As Yeats says in his essay on *Prometheus Unbound*, "Divinity moves outside our antinomies, it may be our lot to worship in terror." [132]

It is clear, then, that Yeats offers no easy faith to his visionaries, nor to any of his heroes. But is is also clear that his last poems emphasize the supreme necessity of conquering the despair which such a gloomy view of the universe might generate. Yeats devoted much thought to the final problem of how the hero, caught in a cyclical pattern of existence which could only minimize the meaning of his achievement, is to react to the knowledge that his own heroic actions, of whatever kind, have little meaning and no permanence in the endless repetition of human events. Despair itself is destructive and makes any sort of heroic achievement impossible. Under no circumstances must the hero give way to it. Rather, his own reaction must be one of love, but a love "which does not desire to change its object," a love which is "a form of the eternal contemplation of what is." [133] Perversely, the Yeatsian hero looks on the inevitable destruction of what is valuable and beautiful in life as in some way right and good though he despises death for taking it away. Such joyous acceptance brings with it "an energy so noble, so powerful, that we laugh aloud and mock, in the terror or the sweetness of our exaltation, at death and oblivion." [134] To an inevitably tragic situation, the hero perpetually sings a song of innocence rather than of weary wisdom and disillusionment.

The false "resolution" of the antithesis between mortal and immortal thus leads ultimately to an exaltation of man himself, for its pessimistic message is a test of heroic resiliency. If ultimate reality—or God—is unattainable except in rare and irregular moments of ecstatic communion, the "joyous" hero himself becomes of supreme importance, for his acceptance of the situation is at least self-generated and self-sustained. In a sense, then, Yeats's variations on the visionary quest lead him closer and closer to a position which we might call consecrated humanism, the elevation of humanity to near-Godlike status, for man's ultimate and inevitable defeat makes his refusal to surrender and his occasional triumph all the more meaningful and offers the consolation that

> Whatever flames upon the night
> Man's own resinous heart has fed.

Notes

1. *The Letters of W. B. Yeats,* p. 583.
2. *Ibid.*
3. *At the Hawk's Well,* in *The Collected Plays of W. B. Yeats* (New York, 1953), p. 143.
4. "All Souls' Night," *Variorum,* p. 474.
5. "Supernatural Songs: VIII," *Variorum,* p. 560.
6. "Supernatural Songs: III," *Variorum,* p. 557.
7. Mircea Eliade, *Shamanism: Archaic Techniques of Ecstasy,* trans. Willard R. Trask (New York, 1964), p. 5.
8. *Ibid.,* p. 504.
9. *Ibid.,* p. 505.
10. N. Kershaw Chadwick, *Poetry and Prophecy* (Cambridge, Eng., 1942), p. 27.
11. *Ibid.,* p. 57.
12. Eliade, p. 8.
13. "All Souls' Night," *Variorum,* p. 472.
14. R. P. Blackmur, "The Later Poetry of W. B. Yeats," in *The Permanence of Yeats,* ed. James Hall and Martin Steinman (New York, 1950), p. 43.
15. W. H. Auden, in *The Permanence of Yeats,* p. 345.
16. Quoted in Joseph Hone, *W. B. Yeats 1865–1939,* p. 97.
17. Yeats, *Four Years,* p. 4.
18. See, for example, the essay "The Keepers of the Herd of Swine," in his *Science and Christian Tradition.*
19. *W. B. Yeats and T. Sturge Moore: Their Correspondence 1901–1937,* p. 26.
20. T. H. Huxley, *Science and Christian Tradition,* in *Collected Essays* (New York, 1894), V, xvi.
21. *Ibid.,* p. 191.
22. John Tyndall, *Fragments of Science* (New York, [1880]), pp. 611–12.
23. Huxley, *Science and Christian Tradition,* p. 32.
24. Tyndall, *Fragments of Science,* p. 342.
25. Huxley, *Science and Christian Tradition,* pp. 339–40, n. 1.
26. T. H. Huxley, *Method and Results,* in *Collected Essays* (New York, 1894), I, 133–34.
27. John Tyndall, *Essays on the Use and Limit of the Imagination in Science* (London, 1870), p. 62.
28. In his Introduction to Hone and Rossi, *Bishop Berkeley,* p. xxiv, n. 1.
29. G. E. Moore, "The Refutation of Idealism," *Philosophical Studies* (Paterson, N. J., 1959), p. 19.
30. *W. B. Yeats and T. Sturge Moore,* p. 69.
31. Bertrand Russell, *The Problems of Philosophy* (New York, 1959), p. 42.
32. Yeats, *Essays* (New York, 1924), p. 140.
33. *Ibid.,* p. 33.
34. In a conversation with John Sparrow recorded in William Rothen-

stein, *Since Fifty. Men and Memories. 1922–1938* (New York, 1940), III, 242.

35. Yeats, "John Eglinton and Spiritual Art," in *Literary Ideals in Ireland*, ed. John Eglinton (London, 1899), p. 36.

36. Yeats, *The Hour-Glass, Cathleen Ni Houlihan, The Pot of Broth* (London, 1904), p. 31.

37. Yeats, *A Vision* (London, 1925), p. x.

38. *Ibid.*, p. 252.

39. Yeats, *Samhain*, No. 4 (Dublin, 1904), p. 17.

40. *W. B. Yeats and T. Sturge Moore*, p. 80.

41. George Berkeley, *Essay, Principles, Dialogues with Selections from Other Writings*, ed. Mary W. Calkins (New York, 1929), p. 102.

42. *Ibid.*, p. 127.

43. *The Letters of W. B. Yeats*, p. 588.

44. *Philosophical Writings of Henry More*, ed. Flora Isabel MacKinnon (New York, 1925), pp. 105–106.

45. Plotinus, *The Enneads*, trans. Stephen MacKenna, revised B. S. Page (London, 1956), p. 357.

46. *The Letters of W. B. Yeats*, p. 782.

47. Giovanni Gentile, *The Theory of Mind As Pure Act*, trans. H. Wildon Carr (London, 1922), p. 141.

48. *The Letters of W. B. Yeats*, p. 734.

49. D. B. Wyndham Lewis, *Time and Western Man* (Boston, 1957), p. 463.

50. Published separately in 1953. See n. 9, above.

51. *W. B. Yeats and T. Sturge Moore*, p. 83.

52. Yeats, *The Celtic Twilight* (London, 1893), p. 165.

53. Standish O'Grady, *Early Bardic Literature, Ireland*, p. 78.

54. *Ibid.*, p. 84.

55. Yeats, *The Wanderings of Oisin*, p. 120.

56. Yeats, *The Land of Heart's Desire* (London, 1894), p. 15.

57. Evelyn Underhill, *Mysticism: A Study in the Nature and Development of Man's Spiritual Consciousness* (New York, 1955), p. 23.

58. *The Letters of W. B. Yeats*, p. 650.

59. *Ibid.*, p. 921.

60. "A Dialogue of Self and Soul," *Variorum*, p. 479.

61. *The Letters of W. B. Yeats*, p. 794.

62. *Variorum*, pp. 495–96.

63. *Ibid.*, p. 496.

64. *Ibid.*, p. 563.

65. Hone, p. 491.

66. *Ibid.*

67. *The Letters of W. B. Yeats*, p. 469.

68. *Some Letters from W. B. Yeats to John O'Leary and His Sister*, p. 14. For a fuller discussion of Yeats's interest in theosophy and magic, see Morton I. Seiden's *William Butler Yeats: The Poet as Mythmaker 1865–1939* (East Lansing, Mich., 1962), pp. 33–48, as well as Virginia Moore's *The Unicorn: William Butler Yeats's Search for Reality* (New York, 1954).

69. Huxley, *Science and Christian Tradition*, p. 342.

70. H. P. Blavatsky, *The Secret Doctrine* (Point Loma, Cal., 1909), II, 655.

71. H. P. Blavatsky, *The Key to Theosophy* (Point Loma, Cal., 1923), p. 31.

72. Charles Richet, *Thirty Years of Psychical Phenomena*, trans. Stanley De Brath (New York, 1923), p. 33.

73. J. Ochorowicz, *Mental Suggestion* (New York, 1891), p. 9.

74. Eugene Osty, *Supernormal Faculties in Man: An Experimental Study*, trans. Stanley De Brath (London, 1923), p. 8.

75. F. W. H. Myers, *Human Personality and Its Survival of Bodily Death*, ed. L. H. Myers (London, 1907), p. 341.

76. *W. B. Yeats and T. Sturge Moore*, pp. 85–86.

77. See, for example, the letter to John O'Leary of May 7, 1889 in *The Letters of W. B. Yeats*, pp. 124–26.

78. Yeats, *Essays*, p. 291.

79. *The Letters of W. B. Yeats*, p. 583. A much more complete discussion of the similarity between the idea of vision in Yeats and in romantic poetry may be found in Frank Kermode's *Romantic Image* (London, 1957).

80. Yeats, *Essays*, p. 140.

81. Yeats, *Pages from a Diary Written in Nineteen Hundred and Thirty* (Dublin, 1944), p. 12.

82. *The Letters of W. B. Yeats*, p. 590.

83. Yeats, Introduction to Hone and Rossi, *Bishop Berkeley*, p. xxiii.

84. *Ibid.*

85. *Variorum*, p. 316.

86. *Ibid.*, p. 578.

87. Auden, *The Enchafèd Flood*, p. 97.

88. Yeats, *Four Years*, p. 69.

89. St. John of the Cross, *The Ascent of Mount Carmel*, trans. David Lewis (London, 1906), p. 22.

90. Yeats, *The Trembling of the Veil*, p. 130.

91. Yeats, *John Sherman and Dhoya*, p. 183.

92. Yeats, *The Secret Rose* (London, 1897), pp. 138–39.

93. Yeats, *The Wind among the Reeds* (London, 1899), pp. 84–85.

94. *Variorum*, p. 275.

95. *Ibid.*, p. 284.

96. *Ibid.*, p. 285.

97. Yeats, *Two Plays for Dancers* (Churchtown, Dundrum, 1919), p. 38.

98. Yeats, *The King of the Great Clock Tower* (Dublin, 1934), p. 11. For a full analysis of this theme in *The King of the Great Clock Tower*, see F. A. C. Wilson, *W. B. Yeats and Tradition*, pp. 53–94.

99. "The Marriage of Heaven and Hell," *Poetry and Prose of William Blake*, ed. Geoffrey Keynes (London, 1946), p. 183.

100. Vivienne Koch, *W. B. Yeats: The Tragic Phase* (Baltimore, 1951), p. 26. On the relationship between Yeats's use of such *personae* and his other "poetic voices," see Thomas Parkinson, *W. B. Yeats, The Later Poetry* (Berkeley and Los Angeles, 1964), pp. 42–57.

101. *The Letters of W. B. Yeats*, p. 782.

102. Henri Bergson, *Creative Evolution*, trans. Arthur Mitchell (New York, 1911), p. 268.

103. *Ibid.*, p. 269.

104. *Variorum*, p. 444.

105. *Ibid.*, p. 445.
106. *Ibid.*, pp. 387–89.
107. *Ibid.*, p. 556.
108. *Ibid,*. pp. 407–408.
109. *Ibid.*, pp. 497–98. See the fine analysis of the last stanza of the poem in Vendler's *Yeats's Vision and the Later Plays*, pp. 117–18.
110. Yeats, *The Words upon the Window Pane*, pp. 32–33. (Italics mine.)
111. *Variorum*, p. 530.
112. See Ellmann, *Yeats: The Man and the Masks*, pp. 121–23.
113. Yeats, *The Trembling of the Veil*, p. 136.
114. Yeats, *Poems, 1899–1905* (London, 1906), p. 19. These lines were not in the first version of *The Shadowy Waters*.
115. Yeats, *Where There Is Nothing*, p. 98.
116. *Ibid.*, p. 90.
117. *W. B. Yeats: Letters to Katharine Tynan*, p. 47.
118. *Variorum*, p. 553.
119. P. 15.
120. *Variorum*, pp. 409–16.
121. *Some Letters from W. B. Yeats to John O'Leary and His Sister*, p. 14.
122. Ellmann, p. 212.
123. *Variorum*, p. 591.
124. *Ibid.*, pp. 499–503.
125. *Ibid.*, pp. 629–30.
126. "Solomon and the Witch," *ibid.*, p. 388.
127. *Variorum*, p. 501.
128. This is confirmed by F. A. C. Wilson's analysis of the play in *Yeats's Iconography* (London, 1960): "*At the Hawk's Well* is a play of consummate spiritual disillusion, and its theme is that the search for the higher self is inevitably doomed to failure." (p. 59)
129. Pp. 281–84. See, however, the much more comprehensive treatment of the subject in Ellmann's *The Identity of Yeats*, pp. 151–64, as well as in Giorgio Melchiori's *The Whole Mystery of Art: Pattern into Poetry in the Work of W. B. Yeats* (London, 1960), pp. 185–89.
130. Yeats, *A Vision* (London, 1937), p. 302.
131. Yeats, *A Vision* (1925), p. 215.
132. Yeats, *Essays 1931 to 1936*, p. 62.
133. *Letters on Poetry from W. B. Yeats to Dorothy Wellesley*, p. 126.
134. Yeats, *Essays*, p. 399.

List of Works Cited

Auden, W. H. *The Enchafèd Flood*. London, 1951.

Bentley, Eric. *A Century of Hero-Worship*. Philadelphia and New York, 1944.

Bergson, Henri. *Creative Evolution*, trans. Arthur Mitchell. New York, 1911.

Berkeley, George. *Essay, Principles, Dialogues with Selections from Other Writings*, ed. Mary W. Calkins. New York, 1929.

Blake, William. *Poetry and Prose of William Blake*, ed. Geoffrey Keynes. London, 1946.

Blavatsky, H. P. *The Key to Theosophy*. Point Loma, Cal., 1923.

————. *The Secret Doctrine*. Point Loma, Cal., 1909. 2 vols.

Bowra, C. M. *From Virgil to Milton*. London, 1945.

————. *Heroic Poetry*. London, 1961.

Brooke, Stopford A. *The Need and Use of Getting Irish Literature into the English Tongue*. London, 1893.

Bryant, Sophie. *Celtic Ireland*. London, 1889.

Campbell, Joseph. *The Hero with a Thousand Faces*. New York, 1949.

Carlyle, Thomas. *Sartor Resartus; On Heroes and Hero Worship*. London, 1956.

Castiglione, Baldesar. *The Book of the Courtier*, trans. Leonard E. Opdycke. New York, 1929.

Chadwick, H. M. *The Heroic Age*. Cambridge, 1912.

Chadwick, N. Kershaw. *Poetry and Prophecy*. Cambridge, Eng., 1942.

Clough, Arthur Hugh. *The Poems of Arthur Hugh Clough,* ed.
    H. F. Lowry, A. L. P. Norrington, and F. L. Mulhauser.
    Oxford, 1951.
Common, Thomas. *Nietzsche as Critic, Philosopher, Poet and
    Prophet.* London, 1901. [The copy with Yeats's marginal
    notations is in the Northwestern University Library, T.R.
    193 N 67 n.]
Curtin, Jeremiah. *Myths and Folk-Lore of Ireland.* Boston,
    1890.
Daiches, David. *Poetry and the Modern World.* Chicago, 1948.
Dillon, Myles. *Early Irish Literature.* Chicago, 1948.
Duffy, Sir Charles Gavan, et al. *The Revival of Irish Literature.
    Addresses by Sir Charles Gavan Duffy, K.C.M.G., Dr.
    George Sigerson, and Dr. Douglas Hyde.* London, 1894.
Dunn, Joseph. *The Ancient Irish Epic Tale Táin Bó Cúalnge.*
    London, 1914.
Eglinton, John. *Bards and Saints.* Dublin, 1906.
————, et al. *Literary Ideals in Ireland,* London, 1899.
————. *Pebbles from a Brook.* Dublin, 1901.
————. *Some Essays and Passages,* ed. W. B. Yeats. Dun-
    drum, 1905.
Eliade, Mircea. *The Myth of the Eternal Return,* trans. Willard
    R. Trask. London, 1955.
————. *Shamanism: Archaic Techniques of Ecstasy,* trans.
    Willard R. Trask. New York, 1964.
Ellmann, Richard. *The Identity of Yeats.* New York, 1954.
————. *Yeats: The Man and the Masks.* New York, 1948.
Frye, Northrop. "Yeats and the Language of Symbolism," *Uni-
    versity of Toronto Quarterly* XVII (1947), 1–17.
Gentile, Giovanni. *The Theory of Mind As Pure Act,* trans.
    H. Wildon Carr. London, 1922.
Gregory, Lady Augusta. *Cuchulain of Muirthemne.* London,
    1902.
————. *Gods and Fighting Men.* London, 1905.
————, ed. *Ideals in Ireland.* London, 1901
————. *Journals 1916–1930,* ed. Lennox Robinson. New York,
    1947.
Gwynn, Stephen. *Today and Tomorrow in Ireland.* Dublin and
    London, 1903.

Hall, James, and Martin Steinman, eds. *The Permanence of Yeats*. New York, 1950.

Henn, T. R. *The Lonely Tower*, London, 1950.

———. "W. B. Yeats and the Irish Background," *Yale Review* XLII (1953), 351–64.

Hone, Joseph. *W. B. Yeats 1865–1939*. New York, 1943.

Hook, Sidney. *The Hero in History: A Study in Limitation and Possibility*. Boston, 1955.

Houghton, Walter E. *The Victorian Frame of Mind, 1830–1870*. New Haven, 1957.

———. "Yeats and Crazy Jane: The Hero in Old Age," *Modern Philology* XL (1942), 316–29.

Hull, Eleanor. *The Cuchullin Saga in Irish Literature*. London, 1898.

Huxley, T. H. *Method and Results*. (*Collected Essays*, Vol. I.) New York, 1894.

———. *Science and Christian Tradition*. (*Collected Essays*, Vol. V.) New York, 1894.

Hyde, Douglas. *A Literary History of Ireland*. London, 1906.

———. *The Story of Early Gaelic Literature*. London, 1895.

James, Henry. *The Princess Casamassima*. London, 1886.

———. *The Tragic Muse*. London, 1948.

Jeffares, A. Norman. *W. B. Yeats Man and Poet*. London, 1949.

St. John of the Cross. *The Ascent of Mount Carmel*, trans. David Lewis. London, 1906.

Johnson, E. D. H. *The Alien Vision of Victorian Poetry*. Princeton, 1952.

D'Arbois de Jubainville, H. *The Irish Mythological Cycle*. Dublin, 1903.

Kermode, Frank. *Romantic Image*. London, 1957.

Knights, L. C. "Poetry and Social Criticism: The Work of W. B. Yeats" in *Explorations*. London, 1946, pp. 170–85.

Koch, Vivienne. *W. B. Yeats: The Tragic Phase*. Baltimore, 1951.

Levy, G. R. *The Sword from the Rock: An Investigation into the Origins of Epic Literature and the Development of the Hero*. New York, 1954.

Lewis, C. S. *A Preface to Paradise Lost*. London, 1942.

Macaulay, Thomas Babington. "Milton," *Critical and Miscellaneous Essays*. New York, 1880, I, 9–59.

MacBride, Maud Gonne. *A Servant of the Queen*. Dublin, 1950.

Mansergh, Nicholas. *Ireland in the Age of Reform and Revolution*. London, 1940.

Martin, Graham. "Fine Manners, Liberal Speech: A Note on the Public Poetry of W. B. Yeats," *Essays in Criticism* II (1961), 40–59.

McCartan, Patrick. "William Butler Yeats—the Fenian," *Ireland-American Review* I, 417.

Meander, Raymond, and Joe Mitchenson. *Theatrical Companion to Shaw: A Pictorial Record of the First Performances of the Plays of George Bernard Shaw*. London, 1954.

Melchiori, Giorgio. *The Whole Mystery of Art: Pattern into Poetry in the Work of W. B. Yeats*. London, 1960.

Narayana Menon, V. K. *The Development of W. B. Yeats*. Edinburgh, 1942.

Moore, G. E. "The Refutation of Idealism" in *Philosophical Studies*. Paterson, New Jersey, 1959.

Moore, Virginia. *The Unicorn: William Butler Yeats's Search for Reality*. New York, 1954.

More, Henry. *Philosophical Writings of Henry More*, ed. Flora Isabel MacKinnon. New York, 1925.

Myers, F. W. H. *Human Personality and Its Survival of Bodily Death*, ed. L. H. Myers. London, 1907.

Nutt, Alfred. *Cuchulain, The Irish Achilles*. London, 1900.

Ochorowicz, J. *Mental Suggestion*. New York, 1891.

O'Faolain, Sean. *The Vanishing Hero: Studies in Novelists of the Twenties*. London, 1956.

O'Grady, Standish. *Early Bardic Literature, Ireland*. London, 1879.

————. *Selected Essays and Passages*. Dublin, Cork, and Belfast, n.d.

————. *Silva Gadelica*. London, 1892. 2 vols.

O'Hegarty, P. S. *A History of Ireland under the Union, 1801 to 1922*. London, 1952.

Osty, Eugene. *Supernormal Faculties in Man: An Experimental Study*, trans. Stanley De Brath. London, 1923.

Parkinson, Thomas. *W. B. Yeats—The Later Poetry*. Berkeley and Los Angeles, 1964.

Pearse, P. H. *Three Lectures on Gaelic Topics*. Dublin, 1898.

Plotinus. *The Enneads*, trans. Stephen MacKenna, revised B. S. Page. London, 1956.

Pound, Ezra. *The Letters of Ezra Pound*, ed. D. D. Paige. New York, 1950.

————. *The Literary Essays of Ezra Pound*, ed. T. S. Eliot. Norfolk, Connecticut, 1954.

Praz, Mario. *The Hero in Eclipse in Victorian Fiction*. Oxford, 1956.

Raglan, Lord. *The Hero: A Study in Tradition, Myth and Drama*. London, 1949.

Richet, Charles. *Thirty Years of Psychical Phenomena*, trans. Stanley De Brath. New York, 1923.

Rolleston, T. W. *The High Deeds of Finn*. London, 1910.

Rothenstein, William. *Since Fifty: Man and Memories, 1922–1938*. London, [1939].

Russell, Bertrand. *The Problems of Philosophy*. New York, 1959.

Seiden, Morton I. *William Butler Yeats: The Poet as Mythmaker 1865–1939*. East Lansing, Mich., 1962.

Shaw, Bernard. *John Bull's Other Island with How He Lied to Her Husband and Major Barbara*. Standard edition. London, 1931.

————. *Man and Superman. A Comedy and a Philosophy*. Standard edition. London, 1952.

Stallworthy, Jon. *Between the Lines: Yeats's Poetry in the Making*. Oxford, 1963.

Stein, Arnold. "Yeats: A Study in Recklessness," *Sewanee Review* 57 (1949), 603–26.

Stokes, Whitley, trans. "Cuchulainn's Death," *Revue Celtique* III (1876–78), 175–91.

————, trans. "The Second Battle of Moytura," *Revue Celtique* XII (1891), 52–111.

————, trans. "The Training Cuchulain," *Revue Celtique* XXIX (1908), 109–52.

Strachey, Lytton. *Eminent Victorians*. New York, 1918.

Suss, Irving D. "Yeatsian Drama and the Dying Hero," *South Altantic Quarterly* LIV (1955), 369–80.

Swift, Jonathan. *A Discourse of the Contests and Dissensions Between the Nobles and the Commons in Athens and Rome*. Temple Scott edition, I. London, 1911.

Synge, John M. *The Works of John M. Synge*. Dublin, 1910.

Torchiana, Donald T. "W. B. Yeats, Jonathan Swift, and Liberty," *Modern Philology* LXI (1963), 26–39.

Tyndall, John. *Essays on the Use and Limit of the Imagination in Science*. London, 1870.

————. *Fragments of Science*. New York, [1880].

Underhill, Evelyn. *Mysticism: A Study in the Nature and Development of Man's Spiritual Consciousness*. New York, 1955.

Vendler, Helen Hennessy. *Yeats's Vision and the Later Plays*. Cambridge, Mass., 1963.

Villiers de l'Isle-Adam, Count Auguste de. *Axel*, trans. H. P. R. Finberg, with a Preface by W. B. Yeats. London, 1925.

Wilde, Lady. *Ancient Legends, Mystic Charms, and Superstitions of Ireland*. Boston, 1888.

Wilson, Edmund. *Axel's Castle*. New York, 1931.

Wilson, F. A. C. *W. B. Yeats and Tradition*. New York, 1958.

————. *Yeats's Iconography*. London, 1960.

Wyndham Lewis, D. B. *Time and Western Man*. Boston, 1957.

Yeats, J. B. *Letters to His Son W. B. Yeats and Others, 1869–1922*. London, 1944.

EDITED BY W. B. YEATS

The Arrow, 1906–1909.

The First Annual Volume of Beltaine. London, 1899–1900.

The Oxford Book of Modern Verse 1892–1935. Oxford, 1936.

Samhain, 1901–1908.

Selections from the Writings of Lord Dunsany. Churchtown, Dundrum, 1912.

WORKS BY W. B. YEATS

Cathleen Ni Hoolihan. London, 1902.

The Celtic Twilight. London, 1893.

The Collected Plays of W. B. Yeats. New York, 1953.

The Countess Kathleen and Various Legends and Lyrics. London, 1892.

Dramatis Personae. Dublin, 1935.

Essays. New York, 1924.

Essays 1931 to 1936. Dublin, 1937.

Estrangement: Being Some Fifty Thoughts from a Diary Kept by William Butler Yeats in the Year Nineteen Hundred and Nine. Dublin, 1926.

Four Years. Churchtown, Dundrum, 1921.

The Hour-Glass, Cathleen Ni Houlihan, The Pot of Broth. London, 1904.

The Hour-Glass. Cathleen Ni Houlihan. The Golden Helmet. The Irish Dramatic Movement. Stratford-on-Avon, 1908.

In the Seven Woods. Dundrum, 1903.

Introduction to J. M. Hone and M. M. Rossi, *Bishop Berkeley: His Life, Writings, and Philosophy.* London, 1931.

"The Irish Dramatic Movement," *Les Prix Nobel en 1923.* Stockholm, 1924, pp. 1–11.

John Sherman and Dhoya. London, 1891. [Written under the pseudonym of Ganconagh.]

The King of the Great Clock Tower. Dublin, 1934.

The King's Threshold. Dublin, 1905.

The King's Threshold. On Baile's Strand. Deirdre. Shadowy Waters. Stratford-on-Avon, 1908.

The Land of Heart's Desire. London, 1894.

Last Poems and Two Plays. Dublin, 1939.

The Letters of W. B. Yeats, ed. Allan Wade. London, 1954.

Letters on Poetry from W. B. Yeats to Dorothy Wellesley. New York, 1940.

Letters to the New Island, ed. Horace Reynolds. Cambridge, Mass., 1934.

"Modern Irish Literature," *Irish Literature,* ed. Justin McCarthy, et al. Philadelphia, 1904.

On the Boiler. Dublin, 1939.

Pages from a Diary Written in Nineteen Hundred and Thirty. Dublin, 1944.

Plays and Controversies. London, 1923.

Poems. London, 1895.

Poems, 1899–1905. London, 1906.

Representative Irish Tales. New York, 1891.

Responsibilities. Churchtown, Dundrum, 1914.

The Secret Rose. London, 1897.

The Senate Speeches of W. B. Yeats, ed. Donald R. Pearce. Bloomington, Ind., 1960.

Seven Poems and a Fragment. Dundrum, 1922.

Some Letters from W. B. Yeats to John O'Leary and His Sister, ed. Allan Wade. New York, 1953.

The Trembling of the Veil. London, 1922.

Two Plays for Dancers. Churchtown, Dundrum, 1919.

Unpublished letters in the Berg Collection, New York Public Library.

The Variorum Edition of the Poems of W. B. Yeats, ed. Peter Allt and Russell K. Alspach. New York, 1957.

A Vision. London, 1937.

A Vision: An Explanation of Life Founded upon the Writings of Giraldus and upon Certain Doctrines Attributed to Kusta Ben Luka. London, 1925.

The Wanderings of Oisin. London, 1889.

W. B. Yeats Letters to Katharine Tynan, ed. Roger McHugh. Dublin and London, 1953.

W. B. Yeats and T. Sturge Moore: Their Correspondence 1901–1937, ed. Ursula Bridge. London, 1953.

Wheels and Butterflies. London, 1934.

Where There Is Nothing. London, 1903.

The Wind among the Reeds. London, 1899.

The Words upon the Window Pane. Dublin, 1934.

THE GOTHAM LIBRARY

Oscar Cargill, General Editor

Robert J. Clements, Associate Editor for Modern Languages

A paperback series devoted to major figures in world literature and topics of enduring importance

The Art of Paul Verlaine *by Antoine Adam (translated by Carl Morse)* $1.95

Shakespeare's Life and Art *by Peter Alexander* $1.95

Gabriela Mistral: The Poet and Her Work *by Margot Arce de Vázquez (translated by Helene Masslo Anderson)* $1.75

The Literary Reputation of Hemingway in Europe *edited by Roger Asselineau* $1.95

Borges the Labyrinth Maker *by Ana María Barrenechea (translated by Robert Lima)* $1.95

The Landscape of Nightmare: Studies in the Contemporary American Novel *by Jonathan Baumbach* $1.95

The Importance of Scrutiny *edited by Eric Bentley* $2.25

Balzac and the Human Comedy *by Philippe Bertault (English version by Richard Monges)* $2.25

Virginia Woolf *by Dorothy Brewster* $1.75

Passages from the Prose Writings of Matthew Arnold *edited by William F. Buckler* $1.95

Stendhal *by Armand Caraccio (translated by Dolores Bagley)* $2.25

O'Neill and His Plays *edited by Oscar Cargill, N. Bryllion Fagin, and William J. Fisher* $2.95

The Poetry of Michelangelo *by Robert Clements* $3.95

The Imagination of Charles Dickens *by A. O. Cockshut* $1.95

The Stanislavsky Heritage: Its Contribution to the Russian and American Theatre *by Christine Edwards* $3.50

The Modern Spanish Novel *by Sherman H. Eoff* $1.95

Dante and His Comedy *by Allan Gilbert* $1.95

Kipling and the Critics *edited by Elliot L. Gilbert* $1.95

The Three Jameses *by C. Hartley Grattan* $2.75

A Critical History of Old English Literature *by Stanley B. Greenfield* $2.25

A Short History of Literary Criticism *by Vernon Hall, Jr.* $1.95

A Thoreau Handbook *by Walter Harding* $1.95

Explorations *by L. C. Knights* $1.95

Bergson and the Stream of Consciousness Novel *by Shiv K. Kumar* $1.75

The Great Tradition *by F. R. Leavis* $1.95

Robert Penn Warren: A Collection of Critical Essays *edited by John Lewis Longley, Jr.* $2.25

Mallarmé *by Guy Michaud (translated by Marie Collins and Bertha Humez)* $1.95

F. Scott Fitzgerald: His Art and His Technique *by James E. Miller* $1.95

A Definition of Tragedy *by Oscar Mandel* $1.95

Horace *by Jacques Perret (translated by Bertha Humez)* $1.95

A History of German Literature *by Ernst Rose* $2.75

Faith from the Abyss: Herman Hesse's Way From Romanticism to Modernity *by Ernst Rose* $1.95

Baudelaire *by Marcel A. Ruff (translated by Agnes Kertesz)* $1.95

Gogol: His Life and Works *by Vsevolod Setchkarev (translated by Robert Kramer)* $2.25

D. H. Lawrence and *Sons and Lovers*: Sources and Criticism *edited by E. W. Tedlock, Jr.* $1.95

The Art of Bertolt Brecht *by Walter Weideli (English version by Daniel Russell)* $1.95

The Theater of Protest and Paradox: Developments in the Avant-Garde Drama *by George E. Wellwarth* $2.25

Art and Order: A Study of E. M. Forster *by Alan Wilde* $1.95

Critical Essays on the Theatre of Calderón *edited by Bruce W. Wardropper* $2.25

Yeats and the Heroic Ideal *by Alex Zwerdling* $1.95

If these titles are not available at your bookstore, you may order them by sending a check or money order direct to: New York University Press, 32 Washington Place, New York 3, New York. *The Press will pay postage.*